Building Multicultural Competency

Building Multicultural Competency

Development, Training, and Practice

edited by
Joseph L. White
and
Sheila J. Henderson

ROWMAN & LITTLEFIELD PUBLISHERS, INC.
Lanham • Boulder • New York • Toronto • Plymouth, UK

ROWMAN & LITTLEFIELD PUBLISHERS, INC.

Published in the United States of America
by Rowman & Littlefield Publishers, Inc.
A wholly owned subsidary of The Rowman & Littlefield Publishing Group, Inc.
4501 Forbes Boulevard, Suite 200, Lanham, Maryland 20706
www.rowmanlittlefield.com

Estover Road
Plymouth PL6 7PY
United Kingdom

British Library Cataloguing in Publication Information Available

Library of Congress Cataloging-in-Publication Data:

Building multicultural competency / [edited by] Joseph L. White and Sheila J.
Henderson.
    p. cm.
Includes bibliographical references.
ISBN-13: 978-0-7425-6420-6 (cloth : alk. paper)
ISBN-10: 0-7425-6420-7 (cloth : alk. paper)
e-ISBN-13: 978-0-7425-6338-4
e-ISBN-10: 0-7425-6338-3
1. Minorities—Mental health services. 2. Cultural psychiatry. 3. Multiculturalism. I.
White, Joseph L., 1932– II. Henderson, Sheila J., 1960–
[DNLM: 1. Counseling—education. 2. Cultural Competency. 3. Cultural Diversity.
4. Ethnic Groups—psychology. 5. Ethnopsychology—methods. 6. Minority Groups—
psychology. WM 55 P965 2008]
 RC455.4.E8.P74 2008
 362.1089—dc22   2008007146

Printed in the United States of America

⊗™ The paper used in this publication meets the minimum requirements of
American National Standard for Information Sciences—Permanence of Paper
for Printed Library Materials, ANSI/NISO Z39.48-1992.

Contents

~

The Quest for Multicultural Competence

Nima Patel

As I look back, I can see that my own lived experience, growing up as an Asian Indian female, shaped my interests and values in activism, social justice, and multiculturalism in psychology. Because I had the good fortune of dedicated mentors in college, I had a growing sense of my place in the psychology field. Like others, I chose graduate programs that had at least a minimum level of multicultural training and went with the ensuing opportunity. Now, having finished my doctoral training and licensing, I look toward progressing forward as an early career professional. The salient questions in my professional life are, Has my graduate training in multicultural competence been adequate? Did my internship and postdoctoral training compensate for gaps and help me to consolidate my theoretical, research, and clinical experiences into a strong multiculturally competent professional identity? What will be my contribution now and in the future to pushing forward a national and global multicultural vision in psychology?

This volume on promising practices[1] in multicultural competency training illustrates the result of years of brave struggle on the part of my mentors. Thanks to their strength, there is a strong platform from which my student colleagues and I can contribute. In Part I of this book, the White and Henderson multiracial/multiethnical/multicultural competency building model sets the stage now for an excellence to emerge in psychology. Each of the chapters featured in this book addresses unique dimensions of promising practices in multiculturalism. Like so many other early career psychologists, I look back and see that I have benefited from some dimensions of multicultural training and missed out on others.

My colleagues and I want our high school and undergraduate mentees, the next generation of graduate psychology students, to have it all. Together, the dimensions of multicultural competency training and organization change represented by this book would represent an unprecedented transformation in graduate psychology education. Clearly this book makes a national acknowledgment of changes that need to be done and can be done. To identify needed change is just one step toward implementing change; the hard work comes next. In Part II, the chapters by Fleming, Kirby, Grandbois, Chiwengo, Welch, and Pierce; Heppner, Neville, and Flories; Parks; Park and Manese; and Takemoto and Parham provide a meaningful and frank assessment of their progress and the obstacles faced during the implementation of a multicultural competency initiative among faculty, staff, students, trainees, and interns.

From a student's perspective, recruitment of graduate students and faculty of color indicates commitment and cannot be overemphasized. Parks, as well as Takemoto and Parham, emphasize that successful minority recruitment requires equal consideration to lived experience over and above traditional assessment metrics. My own life experiences can confirm that it has been my own minority struggle, not my test scores, that has given me the fire and commitment to continue the work of our brave pioneers. Not only do students of difference need to be recruited, but as Parks and Heppner et al. indicate, program changes are needed in order to *retain* people of difference at all levels.

Quality of leadership in the multiculturalism movement of the future is also vital. I believe this applies also to university, departmental, and program leadership. Enhanced leadership training must provide us not only with skills to lead and to innovate, but also as Fleming et al. and Heppner et al. point out, the self-efficacy to manage conflict successfully and work through the obstacles. In Part III Borrayo as well as Queener and Smith provide us with guidance on how to handle resistance that is inevitable as classes attempt new dialogue, as programs venture into new models of training, and as universities dare to implement campus-wide initiatives in building multicultural competency training. Queener and Smith discuss aversive racism at the core of institutional, cultural, and individual resistance and discuss a process model for resolution. It is my experience that we students of color are ready to take on the racial identity development and the difficult dialogues, but that faculty and staff have been reticent to respond, much less to lead us in this journey. We need leaders among us! If faculty, staff, and clinic directors are uncomfortable, inexperienced, or unwilling to discuss growth through these issues, then how are we as students going to progress with our ideas?

One cannot overlook what Cokley and also Chan emphasize in their chapters in Part III on training and mentoring when it comes to career development of students. Whether a student is moving toward an academic research career or a clinical track, practical experiences in research and in counseling are paramount to our development. Once we have the practical experiences to challenge our growth, it is the mentorship that helps us process the multicultural issues in ways that promote professional resilience and maturity. Cokley, Parks, Heppner et al., Chan, Takemoto and Parham, and Park and Manese point out that graduate training programs must assist students in developing alliances with faculty of color and also with their surrounding communities, whether it be on or off campus, as a way for students to get immersion-oriented experiences with communities of color. I particularly appreciated the commitment that these programs have demonstrated in developing a synchrony among curriculum, supervision, mentorship, and experience where the complex issues of power, class, gender, disability, religion, and sexual orientation can be discussed with faculty and mentors in terms of their complex intersections with traditional issues of race and ethnicity.

Finally, I was struck by the enduring commitment to students and alumni expressed by Takemoto and Parham, who explain that connections made in graduate school and internship determine our collective survival. Equally impressive in Part IV is Parham and Parham's illustration of how leadership can happen outside the university environment as it has in the National Multicultural Conference and Summit. It is my hope that the field of psychology innovates new models of training so that collectively we, students of difference, will find the training and institutional support to match our fire to create change in the world.

Notes

1. White and Henderson have credited Dr. Michael Stevenson with introducing the term *promising practices* in a call for manuscripts for the new journal *Journal of Diversity in Higher Education* (see www.apa.org/journals/dhe/callforpapers.html).

~

Introduction
Sheila J. Henderson

This book will be helpful to undergraduate and graduate students interested in starting their journey in multicultural competency in psychology and in learning more about the larger field of multicultural psychology. Similarly, it will be helpful to professionals in the mental health field who are interested in building their multicultural competency but did not receive adequate training in their graduate training. For mental health professionals who are in leadership positions to promote multicultural competency through teaching, administration, business consulting, research, and clinical services delivery, this book will be especially useful.

Why? The goal for this book was to articulate and substantiate in written form a multiracial/multiethnic/multicultural competency building model (M³CB) that Joseph L. White has been sharing in speeches and consulting meetings with universities, medical institutions, businesses, and mental health organizations all over the country. Those who have heard Dr. White speak were inspired and suggested many times that he put the model in writing. I joined Dr. White in this effort six years ago, and with the help of our inspiring editorial director, Arthur Pomponio, Ph.D., this book has come into being. We also benefited greatly from the talents of acquisitions editor Mary Catherine La Mar. At Rowman & Littlefield, we want to acknowledge the talents of several dedicated individuals on the editorial and production staff, Sarah Stanton, Ashlee Mills, and Elaine McGarraugh, who saw us

1

through production of the book right through to the end. Indeed, it takes a village to publish a book.

In Part I, the M³CB model is presented theoretically, against a brief snapshot of cultural trauma, racism, and other "isms" in the United States. Then in Part II,[1] pioneering graduate training institutions were invited to share the history of how they transformed their programs to provide stellar multicultural competency training for their students and trainees. In this way, one can read the theory of multicultural competency development and see how it might translate into actual practice. Part III covers specialty topics, such as (a) mentoring the next generation of ethnic minority researchers, (b) multicultural mentoring in general, (c) managing resistance in training, and (d) the dynamics of aversive racism in the resistance process. Part IV includes the history of one of the important institutions in multicultural competency development, the National Multicultural Conference and Summit. Finally, the book begins and ends with commentary from early career professionals and one student in the Foreward, Conclusion, and Afterword.

When Dr. White graduated from his doctoral program in developmental psychology at Michigan State University in the 1960s, there were few fellow Ph.D.s of color to rely on as mentors. Dr. White and the few other scholars of color emerging in the field at that time had to navigate their careers on their own, and the field of psychology was not receptive to their ideas. At that time there was no public notion of multicultural psychology, and clinicians routinely pathologized the struggles of people of color and people of gay, lesbian, bisexual, and transgender orientation. Professors and journal editors rejected graduate papers and manuscripts that focused on the strengths of multicultural peoples. The door was shut tight.

Sometimes the popular media will pick up on trends well before the field of psychology adopts a change. This was the case when *Ebony Magazine* published Dr. White's article "Toward a Black Psychology" in 1970. That article was instrumental in opening doors. No longer could black psychology and ethnic psychology be held down. Dr. White and the growing cadre of ethnic minority psychologists seized their ground and put down the roots of multicultural psychology.

Early on in his career, Dr. White began to mentor new people of color coming through high school and university who were interested in psychology. This pattern of giving started with a few mentees and grew into a way of life for Dr. White, where he has fostered the careers of hundreds of high school, college, undergraduate, graduate, and early career professionals in psychology. The mentoring tradition expanded exponentially as Dr. White's mentees took on mentees of their own, and so forth over the decades. This tradition became informally known as the Freedom Train.

Although I met Dr. White much earlier by happenstance, I came into the Freedom Train just as I was graduating from my doctoral program in counseling psychology at Stanford University, School of Education, in 2002. The tremendous good fortune of being welcomed into the Freedom Train as a European American ally and working with Dr. White has resulted in one question related to building a new paradigm in psychology—a question central to this book—*What are the changes that mental health professionals will need to make individually and collectively to lead multiculturalism in America and throughout the world?*

Notes

This section is entitled *Promising Practices* to underscore a concept that Dr. Michael Stevenson introduced in a call for manuscripts for the new journal, *Journal of Diversity in Higher Education.* Dr. Stevenson wrote, "A one-size-fits-all approach to diversity and inclusion is destined to failure. An approach, strategy, program, or policy that is successful in one context (e.g., a private undergraduate-focused liberal arts college) may not be appropriate or effective in another (e.g., a large public institution). Rather than 'best practices," the phrase 'promising practices' underscores the importance of context and the continuing need to evaluate." (See www.apa.org/journals/dhe/callfor papers.html.)

PART I

MULTIRACIAL/MULTIETHNIC/ MULTICULTURAL COMPETENCY BUILDING M³CB MODEL

CHAPTER ONE

~

Cultural Trauma

A Critical Backdrop to
Building Multicultural Competency

Sheila J. Henderson and Joseph L. White

This chapter is designed to provide a snapshot of some of the cultural trauma that has occurred in America. This short overview is followed by a look at racism today and the various forms racism takes in modern-day behavior. This discourse can apply to virtually any "ism," such as sexism, sizism, heterosexism, and ageism. Then we look at the question of responsibility in fighting racism, prejudice, and bigotry in the United States. The discussion provides a backdrop for the journey to build multicultural competency.

Snapshot of Cultural Trauma

There is no question that this country has a grim record of cultural trauma for people on American soil. The injustices date back to the discovery of the Americas and the subsequent decimation of the South, Central, and North American indigenous peoples (Zinn, 1995). In the centuries that followed, the American participation in the transatlantic slave trade contributed to an estimated 15–18 million African captives. The death toll was staggering. In the early centuries, five African people are thought to have died in the long capture and transport ordeal for every one African captive who made it to the Americas; once put to work, African slaves had life expectancies of a half-decade or so (Stenou, 2004). Slave ownership on American soil allowed for the worst in human behavior to play out against Africans, their children, and their children's children (*Voices from the days of slavery*, no date), which was institutionally encouraged by laws allowing heinous treatment of black slaves, men and women (Shahadah, 2005). Laws limiting the civil rights of African American people continued well after slavery was abolished. For an excellent account, see *Slavery by Another Name* (2008) by Douglas Blackmon.

Later in American history, oppressive socioeconomic and political policy continued with tenacity. Restrictive American immigration laws led to misery for Asian, Mexican, and South American peoples by detaining arriving immigrants for months at a time under harsh conditions and also by disallowing spouses and other family members to enter the United States to join the immigrant laborers (Chinese Exclusion Act 1882, no date; Immigration from China, 2004; Randall, no date). The Japanese internment in the early 1940s was another dark period in American history (Hirohata and Hirohata, 2003; Randall, 2001), as was the pernicious and perpetual persecution of people of gay, lesbian, bisexual, and transgender sexual orientation before and after Stonewall (Scagliotti, 1984, 1999). Just when American law and policy makers should be exercising reformed action based on lessons learned, elected executive and legislative branch officials continued to persist with oppressive policy and social injustice at the U.S. Naval Base detention center at Guantánamo Bay (Amnesty International, 2007) and by signing the Border Security Act in 2006 (Robbins, 2006). These events are but a few (international human rights injustices are not mentioned here) that rest heavily on the collective soul of America's dominant culture that influences the attitudes and beliefs of even the most progressive individuals in the white, straight dominant culture. These wounds in turn engender a profoundly deep mistrust within the collective soul of multicultural groups still feeling the effects of this devastating history of cultural trauma (Jenkins, 2001).

Cool on the Surface, Hot Below

Nonetheless, despite our legacy of collective historical trauma, our daily interactions in the early twenty-first century are notably cordial in many workplace and public community settings. Single-episode cultural awareness training seminars are now common on student campuses and on the job. People can learn just enough for arm's-length interactions across cultures. The result is our current era of political correctness, superficial tolerance, cultural and psychological separateness, and tenuous coexistence. Below the surface, however, racial profiling, culture-related violence, youth gangs, and hate crimes still occur with regularity. Organizations that monitor hate crimes such as the Southern Poverty Law Center (www.splcenter.org) report that hate groups are on the rise. However, just like a lid on a simmering pot, it is generally no longer acceptable to be a bigot publicly, sling racist labels, make homophobic comments, crack bigoted jokes, or refer fondly to prior eras of segregation, oppression, and slavery.

The recent trend against blatant racism is evidenced, for example, by the student protests of racist cartoons published in the University of California's Berkeley campus newspaper (Burress, Heredia, and Lee, 2001) and the public outcry that followed Senator Trent Lott's acknowledgment to Strom Thurmond about the "good old days" (*Senator Lott steps down as majority leader*, 2002). Other examples are the public boycott of Abercombie and Fitch t-shirts with cartoons denigrating Chinese people (Strasburg, 2002), the firing of talk show host Don Imus from CBS and MSNBC after his racists/sexist comments about African American players on the Rutgers women's basketball team (Smith, 2007), and the public aghast at the hanging of the noose and the painting of the swastika on the office doors of two professors in psychology and education at the Teacher's College in New York (Garland, 2007; Goldman, 2007). All of these incidents demonstrate selective incidents of public pushback against public bigotry and humiliation of marginalized groups.

How broadly do these examples of social activism actually extend? Actor and playwright Harvey Fierstein (2007) wrote an opinion piece for the *New York Times* observing that public outrage against prejudice and "isms" is not necessary consistent. Just at the time of the firing of Don Imus, Fierstein observed that other talk show hosts could still make jokes freely about people of plus size without reproach or use reprehensible terms against other nondominant groups if done so in the "right" spirit. Our point: Social activists have made change happen, but progress is spotty, with ups and downs. Social activism takes relentless persistence, tenacity, and perseverance over the long term.

If blatant racism is not as common, then what has taken its place? Why do we still experience racial tension? Studies show significant differences among whites and blacks in perception of discrimination and fair treatment of African American people economically, politically, and socially using both overt and covert methods of data collection (Dovidio et al., 2002; Mazzocco et al., 2006; Nosek et al., 2007). With this difference in perspective, there can be a big elephant of ethnocultural inequity and white privilege in the room when two individuals—one from the dominant culture and one not—engage in conversation. When this big elephant stands between two people, they may have difficulty seeing each other, masked at first by who they appear to represent (Eberhardt et al., 2004).

Origins of Racism

Just as in the study of other human behaviors and abnormal psychology, part of the answer to this is to look at the *origins of racism*. The explanations reviewed by prominent multicultural psychologists (Ponterotto, Utsey, and Pedersen, 2006; Sue, 2003; Sears and Henry, 2003) in the past half-decade suggested that racism might

- be learned rather than innate;
- result from holding white privilege (unearned entitlement and conferred dominance);
- be a way to cope psychoanalytically with the threat of identity loss and identity diffusion;
- be an unconscious mechanism to project unwanted and despised aspects of self onto the minority; and/or
- be similar to the psychopathology of addiction where, for the racist, there is an irresistible attachment to the worldview of racial superiority and blaming the so-called inferior minority for the effects of racism in such a way that the racist is sure to find relief from any possible anxiety that could arise from external information contradicting such beliefs.

A review of the possible origins of racism indicate that change in this respect is a complex, dynamic process highly correlated to how much an individual invests in the change process.

Racism Today

Racism has changed form from blatancy to subtlety, from overt, old-fashioned racism to a new kind of racism, sometimes termed *aversive* racism, *symbolic*, and/or *modern* racism (Sue et al., 2007). To understand the racial tension of the twenty-first century, we must ground ourselves in some basic definitions.

The definition of racism itself is complex and multivariate involving "rational and illogical" (Carter, 2007, p. 20) beliefs and attitudes and "power" (Sue, 2003). The behavioral use and abuse of power *consciously insists on* and *acts on* the supposed superiority of the dominant culture, which denigrates, dehumanizes, violates, and oppresses individuals broadly categorized by race, limits minority access to resources and opportunity, and acts in the dominant groups' self-interest politically, socially, and economically (Carter, 2007; Sue, 2003). From a definition perspective, the term *racism* and its meaning provides a keystone "ism" that can be expanded to apply to other cultural groups (e.g., genderism, sexism, sizism, heterosexism, zenophobism, monoculturalism, able-bodied-ism, etc.). The prefix for the *ism* may change, but the fundamental forces of exclusion and oppression of difference behind the *ism* stay the same.

Now we juxtapose old-fashioned racism, which often brutally targeted specific individuals of color (e.g., through lynching, burning at the stake, cross burnings on lawns, etc.) to the now more generalized *symbolic* and *aversive* racism. Sears and Henry (2005, p. 100) explained *symbolic* racism as a belief system with four themes: "The beliefs that

1. blacks no longer face much prejudice or discrimination,
2. their failure to progress results from their unwillingness to work hard enough,
3. they are demanding too much too fast, and
4. they have gotten more than they deserve."

An excellent example of symbolic racism in action was one of the two white participants in the dialogue group shown in the documentary *Color of Fear* (Wah, 2004). The white participant David insisted that he was not prejudiced or racist yet argued his *symbolically* racist beliefs with the men of color in the dialogue circle. The men in the circle engaged passionately (and painfully) until finally a fundamental change took place on an emotional level with David that paved the way for him to dare to open up to the men of color in the room on a behavioral level. The men of color expressed the hope that the experience would have a long-term impact on David's outlook and life choices.

Aversive racism tends to involve less conscious and sometimes more insidious processes. As in symbolic racism, people with aversive racism may not identify as having, and often deny having, prejudiced beliefs or negative feelings toward people of color (Dovidio et al., 2002). An aversive racist, however, will often unconsciously discriminate on a candidate selection, for example, when a denial of a candidate of color can be justified by some other minimal factor other than race (Dovidio et al., 2002). Consciously, an aversive racist is likely to be highly averse to the idea of acting against the interests of people of color.

The racial climate of today is clogged by what Derald Wing Sue and his colleagues (2007) referred to as *microaggression*. This is a behavioral phenomenon common for European-Americans in self-conscious encounters with other multicultural groups. Usually well-intended, an underexposed

European-American may fear saying something that could be interpreted as racist and thereby come across as uncomfortable, with halting or hesitant speech patterns. While an individual using this approach might intend to avoid unpleasant racial tension, Sue and his colleagues (2007) classified this awkwardness as a *microaggression*, which leaves the other person with a sense of "otherness." Paraphrasing from Sue et al. (2007), microaggressions can also be subtle but stunning behaviors, nonverbal exchanges of put-downs, insults, snubs, negative facial expressions or body language, tone, or a look that may be brief but communicate a lasting disrespectful and devaluing message to a person of color or other cultural minority. Microaggressions are most commonly perpetrated by whites against people of color, but sometimes also between ethnocultural groups who have unequal levels of social privilege and lack understanding for each other (Ponterotto, Utsey, and Pedersen, 2006). One highly stressful dimension of being victimized by microaggressions is that one is *unlikely* to receive validation for the meaning or hurtful nature of the event. When describing such an event to others, one is likely to receive invalidating comments like, "Don't be so sensitive," "ignore him," "she was probably just having a bad day," "she probably reacted because of something that had nothing to do with you." Such invalidation erodes confidence, increases stress, confuses the victim, and increases the power of the perpetrator.

Racism—Whose Problem Is It?

Most contemporary scholars in multicultural psychology have explained that racism is a problem of the dominant culture, which in this country means the white culture (Sue, 2003; Ponterotto, Utsey, Pedersen, 2006; Rothenberg, 2008). Oppression has been a cruel phenomenon of dominant cultures over world history. Europeans and European Americans have a particularly grisly historical record in this respect. Much of the responsibility for the resolution of racism—the necessary change in beliefs, attitudes, and behaviors of those in power—falls squarely on the shoulders of white Americans. European-Americans are called to challenge their mainstream beliefs, attitudes, and way of life that perpetuates white privilege and oppression of nondominant cultures. This is a primary challenge for European-Americans, as citizens and as mental health professionals.

Sue (2003) in his book, *Overcoming Our Racism*, explained that European-Americans in this country have a lot of internal work to do as they go through the process of embracing the new face of America. There is no question that American life is changing permanently. White privilege is beginning to lose its hold on daily life as the demographics of the population shifts and nondominant cultures begin to assume their place as more active participants in American society. Many European-Americans are engaging cross culturally and enjoying it immensely. Change is happening.

We want to emphasize, however, that the bar is also higher for mental health professionals of color and professionals of other multicultural difference. *All individuals* must address their biases, within and between groups. These biases can weaken alliances between people of difference. Some individuals from various multicultural groups have more privilege of higher socioeconomic status or the privilege of passing[1] as white, or fairer skinned, or heterosexual, or able-bodied, etc., when other nondominant groups may not. The critical question is: Are those individuals within those particular groups aware of their relative privilege? How do the individuals attribute their relative privilege relative to other groups without such privilege? Are they aware of their attitudes, beliefs, and biases toward other groups? Harvey Fierstein's point (2007, p. 2):

> you cannot harbor malice toward others and then cry foul when someone displays intolerance against you. Prejudice tolerated is intolerance encouraged. Rise up in righteousness when you witness the words and deeds of hate, but only if you are willing to rise up against them all, including your own.

Quite similarly, Dr. Gwendolyn Puryear Keita (2007, p. 36), now the American Psychological Association's Executive Director for Public Interest, explained in the *APA Monitor on Psychology* how she regularly questions her actions, however minor, as an ongoing commitment to "a vigilant sensitivity to others' situations; refusing to participate, either overtly or through silence, in activities or conversation where prejudice or degradation is taking place; remaining steadfast in creating and nurturing a culture of inclusion and becoming an agent of education and change." Change depends on everyone!

There is no question, however, that multicultural competent European-Americans can have an important role as allies in the multicultural movement. Notwithstanding, the role of an ally is complex with *at least* three dimensions to consider: (1) addressing one's own prejudices, biases, and racism; (2) embarking on one's own journey of recognizing "whiteness" as a racial group and experientially progressing through white racial identity development, from the *contact* stage all the way through to *autonomy* (Helms, 1990); and (3) influencing multicultural recognition, awareness, competency, and social justice within one's own white culture (Sue, 2003). Work on these three dimensions can be tremendously challenging, especially in the early stages of one's multicultural journey (Helms et al., 2003; Ridley, 2005).

Conclusion

As more and more research becomes available on the power of empathic attunement in the therapeutic process, it becomes more important for mental health professionals to understand the cultural trauma for people of diverse backgrounds. People feel the wounds of cultural trauma for generations in a way that impedes communication in cross-cultural interactions. Mental health professionals must do what it takes to cultivate cultural empathy for individuals who come from cultures affected by cultural trauma whether they themselves have been directly affected or not.

To fully resolve racism or any other "ism," mental health professionals must take the initiative to commit to the journey toward antiracism. In particular, they must be willing to reach out, risk rejection, tolerate failures, and try again with a different approach. This means being not just tolerant but enthusiastic about embracing others and their ways of being. This journey is not for the fainthearted in that it can be arduous, sometimes involving unpleasant feelings of defensiveness and guilt. Those in psychology and in other disciplines who have taken this journey toward antiracism, antihomophobia, antisizism, antisexism, and prohumanity in the fight for human rights for all nondominant cultures stand as warriors in and out of the limelight to show that multicultural competency development is real and possible.

Note

1. For research on the concept of "passing" with an invisible disability, see Mcdonald, Keys, and Balcazar (2007).

References

Amnesty International. (2007). Close Guantánamo Bay. Retrieved October 21, 2007 from web.amnesty.org/pages/guantanamobay-index-eng.

Blackmon, Douglas A. (2008). *Slavery by another name: The re-enslavement of Black Americans from the Civil War to World War II*. New York: Doubleday.

Burress, C., Heredia, C., and Lee, H. K. (2001, September 20). UC Berkeley paper's cartoon criticized for Muslim images. *San Francisco Chronicle*. Retrieved May 25, 2007 from http://sfgate.com/cgi-bin/article.cgi?f=/c/a/2001/09/20/MN227499 .DTL&hw=racist+cartoon+berkeley+daily+californian+2001&sn=001&sc=1000.

Carter, R. T. (2007). Racism and psychological and emotional injury: Recognizing and assessing race-based traumatic stress. *The Counseling Psychologist, 35*, 1, 13–105.

Chinese Exclusion Act 1882. (no date). Immigration to the United States, 1789–1930. Harvard University Library. Open collections program. Retrieved May 29, 2007 from ocp.hul.harvard.edu/immigration/themes-exclusion.html.

Dovidio, J. F., Gaertner, S. L., Kawakami, K., and Hodson, G. (2002). Why can't we just get along? Interpersonal biases and interracial distrust. *Cultural Diversity and Ethnic Minority Psychology*, 8(2), 88–102.

Eberhardt, J. L., Goff, P. A., Purdie, V. J., and Davies, P. G. (2004). Seeing black: Race, crime, and visual processing. *Journal of Personality and Social Psychology*, 87, 876–963.

Fierstein, H. (2007, April 13). Our prejudices, ourselves. *New York Times*. Retrieved July 2, 2007 from select.nytimes.com/search/restricted/article?res=F00612FA385 B0C708DDDAD0894DF404482.

Garland, S. (2007). Swastika is found at Columbia. *New York Sun*. Retrieved November 11, 2007, from www.nysun.com/article/65632.

Goldman, A. (2007). Noose incident reinvigorates NYC prof. *USA Today*. Retrieved November 11, 2007, from www.usatoday.com/news/nation/2007-10-11-72947355_x .htm.

Helms, J. E. (1990). *Black and white racial identity: Theory, research, and practice*. New York: Greenwood Press.

Helms, J. E., Malone, L. T. S., Henze, K., Satiani, A., Perry, J., and Warren, A. (2003). First annual diversity challenge: "How to survive teaching courses on race and culture." *Journal of Multicultural Development*, 31(1).

Hirohata, J., and Hirohata, P. T. (Eds.) (2003). *Nisei voices: Japanese American students of the 1930s—Then and now*. San Jose, CA: Hirohata Design. Retrieved May 29, 2007, from www.niseivoices.com/.

Immigration from China. (2004). Pacific Link: The KQED Asian Education Initiative. Retrieved October 21, 2007 from www.kqed.org/w/pacificlink/history/ange-lisland/china.html.

Jenkins, P. (2001). African Americans "a culture of hope" (Dissertation, California School of Professional Psychology, Los Angeles).

Keita, G. P. (2007). From Imus to "I must." *Monitor on Psychology*, 38(8), 36.

Mazzocco, P. J., Brock, T. C., Olson, K. R., and Banaji, M. R. (2006). The cost of being black: White Americans' perceptions and the question of reparations. *Du Bois Review: Social Science Research On Race* 3(2), 261–97.

McDonald, K., Keys, C., and Balcazar, F. (2007). Disability, race/ethnicity, and gender: Themes of cultural oppression, acts, of individual resistance. *American Journal Community Psychology* 39, 1–2.

Nosek, B. A., Smyth, F. L., Hansen, J. J., Devos, T., Lindner, N. M., Ranganath, K. A., et al. (2007). Pervasiveness and correlates of implicit attitudes and stereotypes. *European Review of Social Psychology*, 18, 36–88.

Ponterotto, J. G., Utsey, S. O., and Pedersen, P. B. (2006). *Preventing prejudice: A guide for counselors, educators, and parents* (2nd ed.). Thousand Oaks, CA: Sage Publications.

Randall, V. R. (no date). Immigration and race. Retrieved October 21, 2007, from academic.udayton.edu/race/02rights/immigration.htm.

———. (2001). Internment of Japanese Americans in concentration camps. *Race, Racism and the Law* (University of Dayton School of Law). Retrieved December 29, 2004, from academic.udayton.edu/race/02rights/intern01.htm.

Ridley, C. R. (2005). *Overcoming unintentional racism in counseling and therapy: A practitioner's guide to intentional intervention.* Thousand Oaks, CA: Sage Publications.

Robbins, T. (2006, October 26). Bush signs border fence act; Funds not found. *All Things Considered.* National Public Radio. Retrieved November 16, 2007. from www.npr.org/templates/story/story.php?storyId=6388548.

Rothenberg, P. S. (2008). *White privilege: Essential readings on the other side of racism* (3rd ed.). New York: Worth Publishers.

Scagliotti, J. (1984). *Before Stonewall.* DVD Documentary. New York: First Run Features.

———. (1999). *After Stonewall.* DVD Documentary. New York: First Run Features.

Sears, D. O., and Henry, P. J. (2003). Origins of symbolic racism. *Journal of Personality and Social Psychology, 85*(2), 259–75.

———. (2005). Over thirty years later: A contemporary look at symbolic racism. *Advances in Experimental Social Psychology, 37,* 95–150.

Senator Lott steps down as majority leader (2002, December 20). PBS Online News Hour. www.pbs.org/newshour/updates/lott_12-20-02.html.

Shahadah, O. A. (2005). *500 years later.* DVD documentary. Halaqah Media. Retrieved October 15, 2007, from www.500yearslater.com/.

Smith, R. (2007, April 12). CBS radio fires Don Imus in fallout over remarks. *All Things Considered.* National Public Radio. Retrieved July 1, 2007, from www.npr.org/templates/story/story.php?storyId=9556159.

Stenou, K. (2004). *Struggles against slavery international year to commemorate the struggle against slavery and its abolition.* UNESCO. Retrieved May 28, 2007, from unesdoc.unesco.org/images/0013/001337/133738e.pdf#page=9.

Strasburg, J. (2002, April 18). Abercrombie and Glitch: Asian Americans rip retailer for stereotypes on T-shirts. Retrieved May 25, 2007 from www.sfgate.com/cgi-bin/article.cgi?file=/c/a/2002/04/18/MN109646.DTL.

Sue, D. W. (2003). *Overcoming our racism: The journey to liberation.* San Francisco: Jossey-Bass.

Sue, D. W., Capodilupo, C. M., Torino, G. C., Bucceri, J. M., Holder, A. M. B., Nadal, K. L., and Esquilin, N. (2007). Racial microaggressions in everyday life: Implications for clinical practice. *American Psychologist, 62*(4), 271-86.

Voices from the days of slavery: Former slaves tell their stories. (no date). Library of Congress. Retrieved October 24, 2007, from http://memory.loc.gov/ammem/collections/voices/.

Wah, L. M. (2004). *Color of fear.* Berkeley, CA: Stirfry Productions.

Zinn, H. (1995). *A people's history of America.* New York: HarperCollins Publishers.

CHAPTER TWO

~

"The Browning of America"

Building a New Multicultural, Multiracial, Multiethnic Paradigm

Joseph L. White and Sheila J. Henderson

During the twenty-first century, our country will experience the "browning of America."[1] That is to say that, by the year 2050, over half the population of the United States will be people of color (Nasser, 2004). "Minorities" will be the collective majority in many states, cities, and regions of the country; this is the case already in states such as Arizona, California, New Mexico, and Texas (Guidelines on Multicultural Education, Training, Research, Practice, and Organizational Change for Psychologists, 2003). Health care research has indicated that mental health disparities between white Americans and people of color are rising, disfavoring people of color. Statistics also show that ethnic and racial minorities pursue mental health services at lower rates than white Americans (U.S. Department of Health and Human Services, 2000). One can conclude therefore that we have not yet adequately met the mental health needs of people of color. How then can we possibly expect to do so in the future without significant change?

The current mental health workforce is not adequately trained, nor is it appropriately staffed to meet the needs of this growing multicultural population. The multicultural composition of the mental health professions in the United States does not come close to matching the changing demographics around the United States (U.S. Department of Health and Human Services, 2000). This problem appears no better as we peer into the training pipeline in psychology. Although the number of people of color entering undergraduate and graduate psychology programs may be increasing, in 2004 only about 27 percent of Master's-level graduates and 20 percent of doctoral-level graduates were students of color in 2004 (American Psychological Association Commission on Ethnic Minority Recruitment, Retention and Training in Psychology Task Force Progress Report, 2007). Therefore, if the field of psychology is to address this problem, one critical step is to improve our recruiting and training practices to encourage people from diverse backgrounds into the graduate psychology pipeline, beginning at the high school level and forward.

In the meantime, many European-American mental health professionals are and will need to be involved in cross-cultural counseling. Studies have confirmed that nonminority counselors can be effective if they have had adequate multicultural competency training (Castillo et al., 2007; Constantine, 2002; Pope-Davis et al., 2002). Unfortunately most institutions, whether academic institutions or direct service clinics, are still not providing suitable multicultural competency training for their mental health students and/or staff and trainees (Constantine, 1997; Constantine and Ladany, 2001; D'Andrea et al., 2001). So we can conclude that, unless radical change takes place across the nation, many of our current and future mental health practitioners engaged in cross-cultural counseling will not be adequately trained to meet the challenge. As authors, our premise for addressing this critical situation is that a *paradigm shift* in graduate training and continuing education for mental health professionals is required to effectively serve the mental health needs of the rapidly changing U.S. population.

The browning of America refers to the increase in the number of people who are living in the United States who identify by race (African Americans, Asian Americans, Latin Americans, Native Americans, European-Americans, biracial or mixed-race Americans) or by ethnicity (Arab Americans, Armenian Americans, etc.). Multiculturalism, however, is a broader term inclusive of individuals who may identify by race *and/or* by (a) intersecting identities such as gender (men, women), religion (Jewish Americans, Muslim Americans, Hindu Americans, etc.), age (children, seniors), sexual orientation (gay, lesbian, bisexual, transgender, intersex, queer, questioning), different ability (people who suffer deafness, physical disability, mental impairment, learning difficulties, etc.), size (people who are short in stature, plus size, etc.), social class, and by (b) by different ways of life (Kibbutz, Quaker communities, and so forth).

The definition of multiculturalism has in the past been controversial, beginning perhaps with Paul Pedersen's call for *multicultural* to have a more inclusive scope with culture as the organizing frame rather than race and ethnicity only (Adams, 2002; Pedersen, 1991). Now the broad construct of multiculturalism is more accepted and reflects popular multicultural textbooks such as Sue and Sue (2008) and Lee and Ramsey (2006), in the 2005 and 2007 National Multicultural Conference and Summit programming, in the vision and mission of the new College of Education and Human Development at University of Minnesota, and in the International Multicultural Initiatives (I-MERIT) at Alliant International University.

Multicultural competency for mental health providers, as covered in detail in the Guidelines (2003) means being aware of one's "own assumptions, values and biases," "understanding the worldview of the culturally different," and "developing appropriate intervention strategies and techniques" (Ponterotto, Utsey, and Pedersen, 2006, 152–56). We are referring to a paradigm shift that will bring multiculturally competent mental health services to all peoples, which are responsive to their cultural needs associated with whatever constellation of identities they may hold.

The conundrum is that leaders of the fourth force[2] have been advocating to central psychology associations (American Psychological Association (APA), American Counseling Association, etc.) and graduate psychology training institutions since the 1930s for increased attention to multicultural issues and opportunities for people of color in psychology (see timeline at www.apa.org/pi/history/aframertimeline.pdf). Change has been slow. Landmarks of progress are Brown v Topeka Board of Education in 1954 followed by opportunities associated with the Civil Rights Act in 1964. Many critical events followed, such as the creation of the Association of Black Psychologists (ABPsi) in 1968, which spurred further positive changes in the fight for multicultural psychology. Graduate psychology training programs, however, have dragged their feet in terms of providing opportunities for and recruiting diverse students, diverse faculty, and providing adequate multicultural training.

At one point in the mid to late 1990s, Dr. Thomas Parham, then the Director of the University of California, Irvine (UCI) Student Counseling Center (now the assistant vice chancellor of Counseling and Health Services at UCI), wrote a letter to approximately one hundred fifty to two hundred U.S. graduate training programs requesting more adequate multicultural training for intern applicants. Nearly twenty years later, programs continue to offer inadequate training. Even after the APA endorsed the multicultural guidelines in 2003, most graduate programs still persisted with insufficient multicultural course offerings. In 2007, some graduate psychology programs continued to offer only one course on multicultural counseling, believing that strategy to be appropriate. Continuing education institutions continue the pattern by offering a broad spectrum of course offerings in psychology without sufficient attention to multicultural issues.

Nonetheless, real change in psychology is under way (Worthington, Soth-McNett, and Moreno, 2007). A vision of psychology leading multiculturalism comes more into view and raises one central question (Murray, 2002):

> What are the changes that mental health professionals in psychology will need to make individually and collectively to lead multiculturalism in America and thoughout the world?

Every individual in this country has a tremendous journey ahead to embrace a more diverse country. For mental health professionals, the bar is higher. According to the Guidelines on Multicultural Education, Training, Research, Practice, and Organizational Change for Psychologists (2003), approved by the APA as policy in 2002, psychologists are responsible for integrating their knowledge of traditional psychology in multicultural terms, whether or not it was taught during their graduate experience. This alone is not an easy task. Many mental health professionals have a bastion of knowledge about human behavior from the Western psychology perspective. With Master's and/or doctoral level of graduate training, hours upon hours of clinical training, and years of experience in specialty areas, mental health professionals can claim expertise in psychology. Soon, however, this expertise will apply to only half of the U.S. population—the European-American portion.

Who will have the knowledge that pertains to the diverse population of people in the United States? Diverse peoples need multiculturally relevant mental health services. When mental health professionals work closely with clients and students of diverse multicultural origins, they must work within the appropriate multiethnic and culturally centered models (Carter, 1991). These new models, which range from identity development to how DSM-IV diagnoses vary according to culture, facilitate our understanding of individuals, groups, and organizations within their differing cultural contexts. As authors, our goal is to provide our readers with a *multiculturally centered* model for how to achieve a change in levels of multicultural competency on individual, group, institutional, and societal dimensions. Our multiracial/multiethnic/multicultural competency building (M³CB) model suggests that change will occur if action is taken across four levels: (1) conceptual/theoretical/intellectual, (2) emotional through multicultural dialogue, (3) behavioral engagement, and (4) skill building. This chapter's contribution to the literature is that *our model not only suggests that this change will occur but also offers ideas on how individuals can undertake this change process.*

Our vision for mental health professionals who pursue growth through our process model is that, as they grow in their individual competency, they might encourage others toward pursuing multicultural competency. Soon, they might assume leadership in developing strategies for bringing multicultural competency to institutions. Later, those same professionals might adopt social advocacy roles that affect APA policy and state and federal initiatives. Today's frequent discussions on the globalization of psychology (Marsella, 2007) imply global dimensions in multicultural psychology, so mental health professionals might consider even larger creative initiatives that include a global scope such as working in collaboration with the United Nations (Murray, 2002) and much more. Our message here is to start with small steps, allow time to learn, dialogue, process emotionally, and build the skills, but always think big!

Is multiculturalism approaching a *tipping point*?[3] One can certainly dare to hope! Whether a European-American or a person of color, the personal journey toward a *multicultural personality*[4] awaits you, whose ripple effect is likely to change the world.

Moving Beyond: A New Paradigm for Multiculturalism

Imagine a day where a new paradigm for multiculturalism encourages *every* marginalized group to participate fully in American society. Is it difficult to conjure more than a vague image? Part of the problem is our shallow and unsatisfying cross-cultural encounters. An individual wanting more might look around for role models but find very few who can demonstrate the steps for how to initiate meaningful cross-cultural conversation, generate ongoing engagement, and share in enjoyable experience. What can be done to pursue multicultural competency and rewarding multicultural engagement?

Models of Multicultural Competency

So what does one do? In order to answer this question adequately, we offer a look at why and how people change.

Why Do People Change?

So why do people change in the first place? Pearson and Bader,[5] prominent therapists in the San Francisco Bay area in California, answer a complex answer in simple terms by explaining that people change to (a) resolve emotional discomfort (e.g., physical pain, emotional pain, cognitive dissonance); (b) avoid greater pain (e.g., more severe mental or physical health issues, problems with the law, relationship problems, loss of employment); and/or (c) to become better, more fulfilled, and/or more fully functioning. This Pearson and Bader explanation can be related to our earlier discussions in this chapter. First, overt racism has become socially and politically unacceptable. Second, the "browning of America" is occurring at exponential rates. These two trends in themselves may motivate people to change by increasing their multicultural competency to avoid interpersonal difficulties thereby becoming more politically, socially, and economically successful. Once embarking on the journey for whatever self-interest, one hopes that the journey itself becomes motivating to create more satisfying cross-cultural relationships. Perhaps those relationships in turn will lead to new levels of social justice concern for a better, more equitable world.

How Do People Change?
So if people are motivated to change, by what process will they change? Perhaps the most common change model in European-American psychology is Prochaska and DiClemente's stages of change model,[6] where an individual moves through phases of *precontemplation, contemplation, preparation, action,* and *maintenance,* perhaps most often used in health behavior research and practice. In terms of multicultural competency, one common stage model of change in cultural awareness originally developed by William Howell (1982) is widely available on the Internet and most often found in the expatriate adjustment literature (Peace Corps Information Collection and Exchange, no date). The Howell model has four levels of competence, through which an individual moves from *unconscious incompetence,* where one is literally unaware of cultural differences between individuals, to *conscious incompetence, conscious competence,* and finally to *unconscious competence* where one's culturally appropriate behavior becomes a way of being and a way of life.

Recently in a book chapter entitled "Models of multicultural competence: a critical evaluation," Mollen, Ridley, and Hill, (2003) offered a solid review of an array of additional multicultural competency change models used across disciplines. One example of those reviewed is Bennett's developmental model of intercultural sensitivity (1993) where an individual is theorized to move through six stages of change from *ethnocentrism* with three substages of *denial, defense,* and *minimization* to *ethnorelativism* with three substages of *acceptance, adoption,* and *integration.* Bennett conceptualized that an individual may start with recognition of cultural differences but is likely to defend against that recognition with psychoanalytic defenses. With exposure and skill building, this individual may grow in his/her identity development such that the ego identity function can expand and strengthen to include broader multicultural perspectives. While varying considerably in their level of psychological depth, what both the Howell and the Bennett models imply are both conscious and unconscious processes involved in the resolution of racism and other cultural biases.

An anchor among multicultural models has been Derald Wing Sue's multidimensional model for developing cultural competence (Sue and Sue, 2008). This model, groundbreaking to the field, provided a conceptual structure for cultural competence in the field of psychology. This model, well known for its cube illustration in *Counseling the Culturally Diverse* (p. 49), integrates the following three dimensions:

- Dimension I: Race- and culture-specific attributes of cultural competence—African American, Asian American, Latino American, Native American, and European American.
- Dimension II: Components of cultural competence:
  i. awareness of attitudes/beliefs,
  ii. knowledge, and
  iii. skills.
- Dimension III: Foci of cultural competence
  i. individual,
  ii. professional,
  iii. organizational, and
  iv. societal.

One cannot discuss the Sue and Sue model (2008) for developing cultural competence without mentioning the Guidelines on Multicultural Education, Training, Research, Practice, and Organizational Change for Psychologists (2003). The levels of Dimensions II and III, Components and Foci of cultural competence, of the 2008 Sue and Sue model, first offered in 2001, can be easily spotted in the conceptual structure or the Guidelines (2003). Over twenty years of collaboration among multicultural leaders in psychology culminated in success when the APA adopted these Guidelines as policy in 2002 (Arredondo and Perez, 2006). It was a celebration! The Guidelines now exist to uphold the highest multicultural standards in our profession.

Toporek and Reza (2001) developed the multicultural counseling competency assessment and planning (MCCAP) model, which builds on the Sue and Sue (2008) model for developing cultural competence. The MCCAP model adds an important dimension to the literature addressing the cognitive, behavioral, and affective dimension of the change process involved in multicultural competency development. The model also addresses the critical mode of strategic planning that any individual must engage in to orchestrate the kind of learning, cognitive and emotional processing, and behavioral engagement necessary to achieve successes along the journey of multicultural competency development. This is perhaps the first model to articulate explicitly, particularly in a visual model, the role of emotion and planning in multicultural competency development.

The Multiracial/Multiethnic/Multicultural Competency Building Model

How does our model contribute to the literature today? The White and Henderson multiracial/multiethnic/multicultural competency building (M³CB) model is designed to offer a way for *both* European-American and multicultural minority mental health professionals to progress on their journey. The scope of the M³CB model is designed to be broad enough to accommodate the standards and competencies of the Multicultural Guidelines (2003), as well as the Guidelines for Practice with Older Adults (2004) and the Guidelines for Psychotherapy With Lesbian, Gay, and Bisexual Clients (2000) endorsed by the APA in the past ten years. The M³CB model is also created to be flexible enough to expand to include guidelines long overdue but still yet to come for other disenfranchised groups, such as transgender individuals, the differently abled, plus size, socioeconomically disadvantaged, and others. As depicted in Figure 2.1, the M³CB model is a change model that builds on the best of the aforementioned models to address multicultural competency growth on four levels:

1. conceptual/theoretical/intellectual charge,
2. emotional change through multicultural dialogue,
3. behavioral change through multicultural engagement, and
4. skill building integration of the conceptual, emotional, and behavioral changes.

Both planning and action, or *planful action*, become important as one embarks upon self-study and self-initiated engagement on intellectual, emotional, and behavioral levels. In this way, a motivated mental health professional can plan and customize their own multicultural journey at every level of the M³CB, cycling back through levels to meet their own needs at critical points of change. The integration of learning will most likely happen in the skill building stage, where the conceptual, emotional, and behavioral learning comes together in new multiculturally competency skills that facilitate better services to diverse peoples. Our hope is that interested mental health professionals will first strive to progress themselves as individuals. Then as their base of skills sharpens and widen to intermediate and advanced levels,

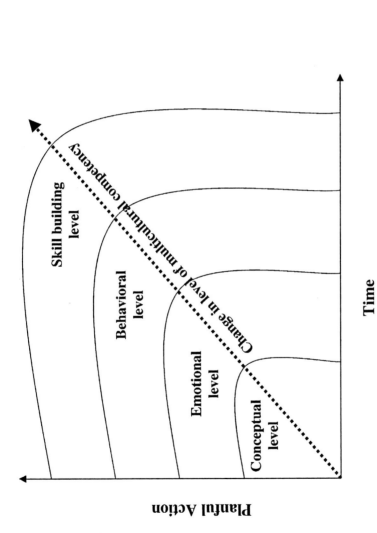

Figure 2.1. Multiracial/ Multiethnic/Multicultural Competency Building Model (M³CB)

Inspired by W. Wayne Young Jr., Ph.D., Assistant Vice President of Student Services/Student Learning, Creighton University.

we hope these same mental health professionals will lead others in the journey toward multicultural competency. As each individual is ready, the need for leadership will await them to motivate new individuals, groups, communities, organizations, and institutions toward multicultural competency. The national need is clear; the global need is inevitable.

Conceptual/Theoretical/Intellectual Change
The conceptual level has two primary objectives of understanding how to build knowledge about

- multicultural ways of life,
- within multicultural group variation by intersections, and
- key topics in the multicultural literature.

Then, under the latter category "key topics in the multicultural literature," in the first two sections, we discuss resources available in the multicultural journal literature, multicultural associations, books film, and other reference sources as a guide to navigate the plethora of multicultural material now available. In the first two sections we offer suggestions on how to build knowledge about multicultural ways of life and within-group variation by intersections.

Understanding Multicultural Ways of Life
There is a growing notion in multicultural psychology that attempting to understand individuals based solely on their category membership (such as racial category or by sexual orientation, age, social class, gender, ability, size, religion, or any other intersection) can lead to oversight of vital information (Cokley and Helm, 2007). Lynch and Hanson (2004) offered an alternative approach of getting to know various multicultural groups from a psychological, spiritual, and phenomenological perspective. Following their reasoning, one can develop an intellectual understanding of nondominant cultures in America by exploring the literature on multicultural groups as it applies to their cultural history, cultural depth and complexity, unique worldview, spiritual beliefs, and psychological and phenomenological perspectives.

Derived from Lynch and Hanson's work, Table 2.1 outlines one way to understand the way of life of a people. This table juxtaposes the perspective of the dominant European-American culture versus perspectives more common to nondominant cultures. The dimension of study is not any one multicultural group per se. The focus is on way of life.

Suppose, for example, that you are a European-American counselor providing career counseling for an independent-minded Asian woman in her mid-30s. Your client is offered the job of a lifetime, but you are baffled by her

Table 2.1. Way of Life of an Ethnocultural Peoples: Primary Dimensions/Values/Concepts

DOMINANT CULTURE		NONDOMINANT CULTURE
Individual is primary/ competitiveness/ independence	SURVIVAL	Group is primary/collective orientation/interdependence
Personal power/ take charge attitude	CONTROL OF LIFE/ CONTROL OVER ENVIRONMENT	Fate/will of the Gods/harmony with nature
Time dominates/ carefully manageable	TIME	Human interaction dominates/ more oriented toward people
Nuclear family/ single-generation family more pronounced	FAMILY	Extended kinship networks/ parents may live with children
Youth oriented/beauty/ brains/talent	AGE	Elder oriented/elders have authority, wisdom, spiritual power/hierarchical roles
Carefully controlled/ reserved	FEELINGS	Highly expressive
Clearly designated/ male dominates	GENDER ROLES	Flexible/interchangeable, egalitarian
controlled/organized/ sequential	VERBAL COMMUNICATION	Call-response/fluid/highly expressive
Direct	CONFLICT RESOLUTION	Indirect/save face ritual
Professional services	HEALING STYLES	Indigenous healers

Source: Adapted from Lynch and Hanson (2004) and Sue and Sue (2008).

decision to fly home to Taiwan to discuss the opportunity with her parents before making her decision. This doesn't seem consistent with your prior conceptualization of this client's sense of independence, or for that matter her stage of life. A glance at Table 2.1 might help inform you that independence for an ethnic minority, such as an Asian American women, may have a different meaning than it would for European-American women. This client may indeed be independent minded (and may have already made her decision privately) but may go home to Taiwan out of respect for her parents and the filial piety that is expected in her family culture even from children in their mid-30s and older (Henderson and Chan, 2005).

Understanding Multicultural Group Variation by Intersections
The intersections of age, gender, sexual orientation, ability, socioeconomic class, size, religion, and gender create marginalization within the larger ethnic and racial groupings of African American, Asian American, Latin American, Native American, and mixed-race peoples. The multiple categories of intersections create countless numbers of potential subcultures within each larger ethnic/racial grouping, each with their own history, cultural depth and complexity, and psychological/phenomenological point of view. This begins to create a factorial number of subculture combinations and variations of identity with which any one individual might be grappling—hence the phrase *within-group variation is far greater than between-group variation.*

As the factorial number of cultural variation begins to boggle the mind, remember that one operative critical dimension is *salience.* What one must look for in attempts to fully understand another human being is not to necessarily quantify analytically the number and type of identity categories, but rather to be attuned on a process and content level to the saliency of one identity over another. Mental health care providers are encouraged to understand people and their identities in relative context to their life situation and living environments (Hays, 2001). People have the right to choose and may choose to identify and focus on one or two salient issues at a time. For a male Chinese gay immigrant engineer with degenerative arthritis, for example the saliency of race, immigration status, social class, and different ability may be more salient than sexual orientation for a number of years until the hurdles of racial discrimination, immigration status, and barriers to access for health services are mastered through securing adequate employment, H-1 visa, and health insurance. Once more financially stable and on the way to citizenship, he may decide to explore issues of coming out in the workplace.

Issues of saliency in multiple identities may involve for others an immersion into multicultural origins and family identity rather than a focus on occupation, social class, sexual orientation, gender, or size issues. Finally, class issues may become most salient as one moves into their own adulthood and are fighting for their own economic survival, particularly if they are fighting discrimination and/or struggling with emotional issues associated with emerging from a childhood marked by impoverished circumstances. A talented mental health professional will show flexibility in what multicultural identity and intersections they follow according to their clients needs.

This flexibility is enhanced through developing basic intellectual knowledge in each of the major intersection areas. To assist in the initial knowledge-building exercises, we list the major intersection categories with suggestions for key resources from which to start:

- age (Guidelines for Practice with Older Adults, 2004),
- gender (Taylor, Gilligan, and Sullivan, 1995),
- differently abled (Davis, 2007; Stone, 2004),
- religion (Ali, Liu, and Humedian, 2004; Holladay, 2006; Langman, 1999; Naber 2000; Schlosser, 2003, 2006; Schlosser et al., 2007),
- sexual orientation (Guidelines for Psychotherapy with Lesbian, Gay, and Bisexual Clients, 2000),
- size (Hirschfeld, 2007; Liu, Picket, and Ivey 2007; Spain and Spain, 2007; Wann, 1998), and
- socioeconomic class (APA Task Force on Socioeconomic Status, 2007; Nelson et al., 2006; Weisberg, 2005).

Key Topics in the Multicultural Literature
We recommend that one's knowledge-building process include the contemporary theoretical-psychological multicultural literature since 1980, with priority on keeping up with the most current literature. Key topics to watch are

- bias, prejudice, and racism (Ponterotto, Utsey, and Pedersen, 2006; Ridley, 2005),
- white privilege (MacIntosh, 1990; Neville, Worthington, and Spanierman, 2001; Rothenberg, 2008; Tuckwell, 2002),
- power and oppression (Liu and Pope-Davis, 2003; Sue, 2003),
- cultural trauma and empathy (Carter, 2007; Clark, 2003; Dyche and Zayas, 2004; Jenkins, 2001; Pedersen, Crethons, and Carlson, 2008),
- cultural transference and countertransference (Foster, 1998),
- psychological development theories for white and various multicultural groups (Ponterotto, Utsey, and Pedersen, 2006),
- immigration (Mahalingam, 2006),
- meaning of family (Bowe, 2006; McGoldrick, Giordano, and Garcia-Preto, 2005; The 21st Century Family, 2007), and
- body image (Wann, 1998).

Searching for Knowledge Through Literature and Film One can build an important base of knowledge through self-study with this new search perspective on how to understand a multicultural group's way of life in mind. Suggestions would be to read books that bust commonly held stereotypes, such as *Black Fathers: An Invisible Presence in America* (Connor and White, 2006); *Forgotten Founders: Benjamin Franklin, the Iroquois and the Rationale for the American Revolution* (Johansen, 1982); or *Black Stars: African American Women Scientists and Inventors* (Sullivan, 2001). Sometimes novels are windows on culture, as in *The Secret Life of Bees* (Kidd, 2002), *The Lost Language of Cranes* (Leavitt, 1987), *A Servant's Tale* (Fox, 2001), *The Guide* (Narayan, 2006), *The Wedding: A Novel* (West, 1995), and *Zami: A New Spelling of My Name* (Lorde, 1982) as can be historical fiction such as *Stone Butch Blues* (Feinberg, 2004).

Books by authors of multicultural groups of interests are powerful learning tools, especially those that also provide some historical background like *Catfish and Mandala* (Pham, 2002). This is an autobiography by Andrew X. Pham, a Vietnamese man who immigrated with his family by boat to the United States as a boy, and then later wrote his book about his bicycle pilgrimage back home to Viet Nam where he sought to understand his own identity and family experience. This book introduces the reader to different ways of life among Vietnamese people and how these ways change with acculturation from one generation to the next. Other powerful autobiographies are *The Autobiography of Malcolm X* (Haley, 1996), *An Autobiography: The Story of My Experiments with Truth* (Gandhi, 1993), and *Becoming a Visible Man* (Green, 2004). Biographies, such as *The Life of Rosa Parks* (Brinkley, 2000), can also be powerful learning tools. There are three excellent edited books, *Voices of Color* (Rastogi and Wieling, 2004), *Deconstructing Heterosexism in the Counseling Professions* (Croteau, 2004), and part I of the *Handbook in Multicultural Counseling* (Ponterotto et al., 2001), in which mental health pioneers of color and/or of gay, lesbian, bisexual orientation talk about their experiences in psychology that can be validating for multiculturally diverse students coming into the field.

Self-study can be facilitated by reading groups and book clubs. As an example, the first author once met with a group of eight European-American teachers in Missouri who met regularly to expand their cultural knowledge. Every month they read four books on African Americans, whether short stories, biographies, or fiction. Twice a month they had discussion meetings. Through this combination of individual study and group dialogue, this group of European-American women were trying to constructively learn about another culture intellectually and to engage with each other about their emotional experience as they learned and grew from the experience.

The following two books provide many movie and book recommendations for self-study: *Teaching Gender and Multicultural Awareness: Resources for the Psychology Classroom* (Bronstein and Quina, 2003) and chapter 10 in *Overcoming Our Racism: The Journey to Liberation* (Sue, 2003). Other excellent resources to consult are people running independent bookstores and librarians at public libraries. Ask them about books written by authors from the particular multicultural group of interest. The Internet has nearly endless resource listings for multicultural self-study. One example for films is from the Greenfield Intercultural Center website at the University of Pennsylvania (see Video Library, 2004).

Online or print magazines can be excellent resources for keeping up on current issues affecting particular cultural groups. Examples are

- *Ability* (www.abilitymagazine.com/),
- *Asia Week* (www.asianweek.com/),
- *Advocate* (www.advocate.com/),
- *Ebony* (www.ebonyjet.com),
- *Indian Country Today* (www.indiancountry.com/),
- *Indian Country News* (www.indiancountrynews.com/),
- *Latino Perspectives Magazine* (www.latinopm.com/),
- *Little India* (www.littleindia.com/),
- *Mainstream* (www.mainstream-mag.com/),
- *Native Peoples Magazine* (www.nativepeoples.com/),
- *Ragged Edge Online* (www.ragged-edge-mag.com/).

These media sources may also occasionally list the classic books within their cultural area (see *Sixty Years of Great Books*, 2005).

Popular and traditional folk music, multicultural dance, and storytelling are powerful expressions of how cultural life of a people has been passed down through one generation to the next. The cultural practices are particularly informative in that they give clues on indigenous healing styles, as well as core beliefs about spirituality and social mores. These art forms might be particularly informative about the social roles of healers (e.g., curandero, shamans) and healing practices ("laying on of the hands," "speaking in tongues," and "Santeria," which is an Afro-Cuban treatment of the spirit drawing on the Yoruba spiritual forces of ancient Africa).

Searching for Knowledge Through Courses, Conferences, Journal Literature, and the Internet   One can enhance the experience of movies and literature by going to lectures, auditing or enrolling in multicultural competency training courses, attending multicultural conferences such as the Winter Roundtable hosted by Teachers College (www.tc.edu/roundtable/) and the National Multicultural Conference and Summit (www.multicultural-summit.org/). Over and above, we cannot emphasize enough the importance of keeping up with at least two of the leading multicultural journals in psychology and education, such as the *Journal of Multicultural Counseling and Development*, *Cultural Diversity and Ethnic Minority Psychology*, *Journal of LGBT Issues in Counseling*, *Rehabilitation Psychology*, *Multicultural Education*, *Multicultural Review*, *Journal of Diversity in Higher Education*, and *Teaching Tolerance*.

Other ways to stay well informed are to join social action groups such as AF-FIRM (naples.cc.sunysb.edu/CAS/affirm.nsf), to join email listservs with APA (lists.apa.org/) and American Counseling Association (www.counseling.org/), and reading syllabi for multicultural courses available on the Internet.

Emotional Change Through Multicultural Dialogue

Dialogue groups offer tremendous opportunities for emotional growth. As a result of investing time in dialogue groups, change will most likely occur along five critical junctures:

- racial and multicultural self-awareness,
- perceptual gap,
- externalization of blame,
- introspection, and
- cultural empathy.

Each of these junctures is likely to be emotionally challenging and consequentially life changing. Whether concurrent to or sequentially after the conceptual/theoretical/intellectual change process, we challenge mental health professionals to reach toward other multicultural groups on a heart level through experiential dialogue and relationships. Multicultural learning takes on new meaning when one engages in dialogue with others.

How can one find opportunities for such dialogue? The National Multicultural Conference and Summits offer these opportunities through their "difficult dialogues," which are part of the conference design. Schlosser et al. (2007) offered the results from an encounter program designed to promote healing between African Americans and Jewish Americans. Similarly, one powerful way to pursue learning about culture and way of life on an emotional level is through study circles. Resources are available for those who would like to start dialogue or study groups. For example, Bill Clinton's Initiative on Race created a guide on starting dialogue groups (see One America Dialogue Guide, 1998). The Study Circles Resource Center (www.studycircles.org) provides excellent resources on how to start study circles, including topical discussion guides. The National Coalition for Dialogue and Deliberation (www.thataway.org/) provides excellent books, manuals, and videos on how to stimulate productive dialogue. Table 2.2 provides stimulus questions that the second author has for dialogues on race in workshops around the country.

Another way to stimulate discussion in classrooms or study circles is to show provocative videos, such as *Color of Fear* (Wah, 2004), *The Way Home* (Butler, 1998), *The Power of Harmony* (Martin, 2005), *Crown Heights* (Ka-

Table 2.2. Discussion Questions for a Multiracial/Multiethnic Dialogue

I. *Racial Self-Awareness*
   a. Who are you racially, ethnically and how did you come to be who and what you are?
   b. How would you characterize your ethnic background?
   c. When did you first realize that you were part of an ethnic group?
   d. Think about how you learned your ethnic heritage.
   e. In your neighborhood when you were growing up, how were people perceived who were ethnically or racially different?

II. Advantages and Disadvantages of *Ethnic Racial Group Membership*
   a. What are some of the advantages of being a member of your ethnic group?
   b. What are some of the disadvantages of being a member of your ethnic group?

III. *Critical Incidents and Life Experiences*
   a. Think about an incident in your life when you experienced the power of race/skin color.
   b. How did you feel about it at that time?
   c. I have been/have not been discriminated against on the basis of race, color, or ethnicity.

IV. *Perceptual Gap:* People of color see, perceive, and experience social reality differently. (Discuss example listed below.)
   a. Minister Louis Farrakhan of the Nation of Islam versus Colin Powell (especially before September 11, 2001).
       i. On a scale of one to five from favorable to unfavorable, how are these two men perceived by the American public?
       ii. How are they perceived by the black community?
       iii. Why are the reactions to these men so different?
   b. What do the people in the neighborhood you grew up in think about
       i. Affirmative Action?
           1. Why is Affirmative Action such a heated topic?
       ii. The O. J. Simpson verdict?
           2. Why is there such a big difference of opinion between blacks and whites on how the O. J. Simpson guilty verdict is perceived?

V. *Externalization of Blame:* Projection of blame outward.
   a. Who or what is responsible for the race problem in America or the residual of racism in American society?
   b. Who or what is responsible for the low number of blacks in senior positions in the corporate structure, university and college presidents, or head coaching positions in colleges and universities?
   c. Who or what is responsible for poverty and deteriorating living conditions on Native American reservations?
   d. Who or what is responsible for the low achievement levels of minority children in urban schools?

VI. *Introspection:* Looking within for responsibility for America's racial situation.
   a. Why is it difficult for people to talk openly and honestly about race in America?
   b. Why is it difficult for you to talk openly and honestly about race in America?
   c. In the past, I was exposed to racial stereotypes about people who didn't grow up in my neighborhood or live in a neighborhood near me.
   d. How did you handle these stereotypes?
   e. How have your feelings, thoughts, perceptions, or attitudes about racial matters changed over the years toward people from different ethnic groups?
   f. What helped you to change? Is there anything else you would like to change?

VII. *Cultural Empathy:* Struggling to understand the racial perspective or the worldview of persons from different racial and ethnic backgrounds.
   a. What needs to happen for you to increase your understanding of the perspective of others from different racial and ethnic backgrounds?
   b. Why is it difficult for us to reach across racial and ethnic boundaries to overcome resistance, enhance communication, and move toward mutual understanding, mutual enrichment, finding common ground, and racial reconciliation?

gan, 2004), and other similar films and engage in a heart-level dialogue after the film. Whether through discussing films, books, or current civic incidents, the important thing is to start engaging in dialogue with individuals of other multicultural groups in one way or another. This step will bring the intellectual learning to a heart level of experience.

It may be inevitable that a culturally isolated European-American person's first forays into experiential dialogue with persons from other multicultural groups may include self-consciousness. This is where the willingness to risk making mistakes will go a long way. Our advice is to roll up your sleeves, get involved, and burst through this stage of awkwardness as soon as possible. Through practice with dialogue on a heart level, this self-consciousness should ease up quickly.

Racial and Multicultural Self-Awareness

Theory and empirical research on multicultural identity development and its relationship to psychological health and adjustment has been growing since the 1970s. Many European-American mental health professionals still may not think of themselves as racial beings. It is more common for someone of the dominant culture to think of self-awareness in nonracial terms, such as self-esteem or self-concept within the dominant culture as conceived through psychoanalytic, humanistic, or developmental psychology (Baumeister, 2005). It is important that the mental health professionals expand and sometimes depart from monocultural perspectives and begin to see themselves and others in context of culture. Most people from nondominant cultures have not had the privilege to consider developing intrapersonally and interpersonally without prejudice, stereotypes, and racism impinging on the process of self-discovery and development (Guidelines on Multicultural Education, Training, Research, Practice, and Organization Change for Psychologists, 2003). Furthermore, many non-Western cultures do not conceive of self as a separate and independent construct from family and community as is prominent in European-American psychology (Henderson and Chan, 2005; Ivey et al., 2002; Lynch and Hanson, 2004; Parham, 2002; Sue and Sue, 2008).

As a challenge, we suggest that all mental health professionals undertake formal coursework and/or self-study through journal, book, and video literature on the latest multicultural models for

- general multicultural identity development (e.g., Phinney, 1990, 1992, 1995);
- specific models for European-Americans and the other major racial groups, persons with differing sexual orientations, and different religions (see chapters 4–7 in *Preventing Prejudice* by Ponterotto, Utsey, and

Pedersen, 2006; see also Cross, Parham, and Helms, 1991; Langman, 1999; Naber 2000; Schlosser, 2003, 2006; White and Cones, 1999; White, Parham, and Ajamu, 2007); and

• bicultural and multiracial identities through ecological models (LaFramboise, Coleman, and Gerton, 1993; Root, 1996).

Such study will lead to an understanding of differing worldviews and individual differences. Multicultural identity development is related to better psychological health, although the process can be emotionally tumultuous and often involve cycling through the stages many times over a lifetime (Guidelines, 2003; Helms, 1990; Parham, White, and Ajamu, 1999; White, Parham, and Ajamu, 2007).

Although people of color are more likely to be socialized toward some degree of racial self-awareness, multicultural identity theory emphasizes that people of all races are vulnerable to de-emphasizing their group membership to avoid distressing emotions in the early stage of their racial identity development (Cross, Parham, and Helms, 1991; Guidelines, 2003; Helms, 1990; Parham, White, and Ajamu, 1999; Ponterotto, Utsey, and Pedersen, 2006). To this end, *all* mental health professionals at whatever their stage of racial awareness are encouraged to cycle back to consider the following:

• Their characterizations of ethnic background with questions such as: *Who am I racially, ethnically, culturally, or as a person of different ability, size, gender, religion, social class, age, or sexual orientation? How did I come to be what I am? When did I first realize I was part of a racial, ethnic, or cultural group? How did I learn about my racial or ethnic heritage, religion, gender, social class, different ability, or sexual orientation? What messages did I receive from my family about my racial, ethnic, cultural, sexual orientation, different ability, social class, religion, age, and gender group versus other groups? How were people in my childhood neighborhood perceived according to their perceived category groupings? To what extent was I influenced by these beliefs? In what way have my beliefs changed? What influenced me to change my attitudes and beliefs?*
• The advantages and disadvantages of being a member of their racial, ethnic, and/or cultural group.
• Critical incidents when they have experienced the power of the dominant culture in terms of race, gender, social class, age, sexual orientation, able-bodiedness, size, religion, etc.
• Their life experiences when they have experienced discrimination, prejudice, exclusion, and/or emotional and physical persecution due to

race, ethnicity, culture, sexual orientation, gender, different ability, social class, religion, age, size, etc.

Perceptual Gap

There are perceptual gaps at the individual identity level. Consider how much the response to the question, *Who am I?* differs from the response to the questions, *How do others perceive me? What does society say that I am?* The perceptual gap is marked between European-Americans and people of color (Steele, 1997) but applies among many other multicultural groups as well (Kagan, 2004; Schlosser et al., 2007). There is an equally disparate gap between how individuals from different groups see the world and interpret events. The O. J. Simpson case was illustrative of the perceptual gap in evaluating televised broadcast of the courtroom events. The majority of European-Americans felt that Simpson was guilty, and the same majority of black Americans felt that he was not (Siegel, 1997). How could two sets of Americans watch the same courtroom proceedings and come to such different conclusions? Individuals can occupy different perceptual worlds. The movie *Crown Heights* (Kagan, 2004) portrays a similar story of how black and Jewish residents of New York City perceived another racial incident (Wertheimer, 1997) and the process by which two community leaders led community engagement and dialogue to help resolve perceptual differences.

Externalization of Blame

What are the ways in which each individual can ascribe responsibility for the racial divide in America? On one hand, as painful as it can be, European-American mental health professionals must remember, and in many cases learn, about how their European-American ancestors have impeded social justice, before, during, and after slavery and forward to today for Native Americans, African Americans, and many other diverse peoples (Edmonia and Highgate, 2003) through harmful policy and legal action. Examples are the genocide of our Native American population; participation in the slave trade leaving millions of Africans dead, brutalized, and enslaved on our own soil; historic immigration restrictions dividing families; Japanese internment; state restrictions on black voters; the one drop rule; segregation; police brutalization of the gay, lesbian, bisexual, transgender (GLBT) community before Stonewall; more controversially, the repeal of Affirmative Action; and the federal ruling for a fence across the southern U.S. border (Rodriguez, 1998; Guidelines, 2003). Although European-Americans today have not been directly responsible for these acts of violence, European-Americans can accept that they may be initially perceived as part of the socioeconomic and political power structure that have and are participating in these actions.

Many multicultural leaders have long advocated for (White and Cones, 1999) and participated in organizations that allow disenfranchised people to make progress in their self-determination. One excellent example of an organization working toward this goal is the African American Men's Project in North Minneapolis, Minnesota (http://northpoint.pcspeed.com/African AmericanMenProject/tabid/85/Default.aspx). The article, "Ten pocket tool kit: Encouraging entrepreneurship among people of color" (Henderson, 2006), is a source to many other organizations supporting wealth creation among multicultural groups, including young people.

Introspection
At this juncture, we challenge mental health professionals to introspect from two perspectives as recommended by Sue (2003) in *Overcoming Our Racism*. The first is to look within and begin to understand how one has contributed to problems of racism, sexism, classism, heterosexism, ageism, bias, and bigotry in America, by commission or by omission. Questions to stimulate this exploration are: In what ways am I more critical of European-Americans or of people of color? Are there biases and stereotypes about other aspects of diversity that I have not yet addressed? The following website provides excellent short online assessments to evaluate one's specific biases and stereotypes: implicit.harvard.edu/implicit/. Other important questions to explore from this first perspective are: How have my thoughts, feelings, perceptions, and attitudes changed over the years toward people for different multicultural groups? What else would I like to change? Am I harboring regrets about past behavior toward European-Americans or people of difference?

The second is to look toward the future with a self-challenge: How am I going to turn my regrets into more positive action in the present? What am I going to do to work toward a solution? The first line of internal exploration is likely to bring up many feelings, including embarrassment and regret when one comes across biases yet to be addressed. Once these biases are recognized, it is critical to move from the place of regret to positive action in resolving the biases toward more productive and inclusive attitudes and belief systems.

Cultural Empathy
When a European-American mental health professional begins to understand the worldview within which other people live, the door opens to begin to comprehend another person's emotional experience. The process of understanding a group's cultural trauma can help to build cultural empathy (Jenkins, 2001), which is regarded as one critical element in motivating antiracist behavior (Cruz and Patterson, 2005). When on this exploratory journey,

pay close attention to experiences with oppression, whether victim or perpetrator, and listen for emotions, attitudes, and values around the use of power in relationship, family, and in the larger community. Look for the strengths that have allowed people to rise up and out from under oppression, and conceptualize from what residual distress they are resolving. Through these activities, mental health professionals can develop both empathy and appreciation for the strengths of other races, ethnicities, cultures, and worldviews of those groups.

The process of learning about cultural trauma can be emotionally draining and troubling. It can be extremely difficult for mental health professionals to absorb the extent of cruelty that has taken place on American soil not to mention elsewhere in the world. People, caught by surprise by the intensity of their emotional experience, may respond either in defensive anger and retrenchment, or "guilt by association," and/or rejection of their own race (Drew, 1997; Huber, 1996). Techniques for healing at this critical point of resistance are now emerging. Empirical research (Drew, 1997; Helms et al., 2003; Huber, 1996) has suggested that good mentorship, education, and/or counseling from other progressive European-Americans and people of color can transform this resistance into a productive processing conducive to growth in multicultural competency. The process of teaching this dimension of multicultural competency can be most challenging for even the most experienced of instructors (Helms et al., 2003). When individuals are working through this stage of the M^{3}CB model—whether it is having difficulty with empathy toward another's experience or feeling overwhelmed by empathy for the extent of cultural trauma suffered—our advice is that they seek support from other colleagues and mentors. Sometimes it is working through this period of emotional distress that true possibilities open to engage in relationship with others, despite the forces that divide.

The key to understanding cultural trauma and developing cultural empathy is this: Culturally empathetic mental health providers understand that when they sit across from a client who is racially, ethnically, culturally different than themselves that they also sit directly across from the cultural trauma that has affected their client's life and cultural history. They also understand and are empathetic to the fact that their possible privilege is directly juxtaposed to that client's conscious or *unconscious* awareness of that cultural trauma (MacIntosh, 1990; Rothenberg, 2008). This positioning of privilege versus cultural trauma in the initial encounter may relate to the degree of uneasiness or distance that affects the initial rapport building process (Butler and Butler, 2006). The more that this process interference can be brought out into the open and discussed sensitively and productively, the less destructive power this process interference is likely to have on the therapeutic relationship.

There may be some sadness in this realization for European-Americans to comprehend that it may be decades before they can fully enter the world of the nondominant culture, due to the sociopolitical and exploitative forces that have been at work for generations preceding them (Butler and Butler, 2006). This unfortunate interference in the rapport building process may also apply to the process dynamics between two individuals from the non-dominant culture who are from two different nondominent groups with unequal levels of societal privilege. As a higher level of privilege is juxtaposed to one lower, a mental health provider can play a part in validating the injustice of that privilege or perpetuating it, depending on the multicultural competence of that provider. Consequently, when the injustice of unequal privilege is recognized and discussed openly, that mental health provider is in a strong position to recognize and honor the client's heritage of cultural strengths. This can be the source and platform for building a sense of group membership and positive cultural identity, about which the individual himself or herself may not be aware or tend to initially reject.

European-Americans, and all mental health providers, do have control over one important factor of influence to counteract the unfortunate societal divide that exists today. That is, each individual can maximize their multicultural competence making it much more likely for them to engage in actions that will facilitate healing, cooperation, and full participation of people inside and outside of the mental health setting.

Behavioral Change Through Multicultural Engagement

The behavioral interaction involves meaningful engagement with people who are different than you. By this we mean, meaningfully engaging with people in their own environments, on their own terms. People of color do this every day as they emerge from their community to go to work or school in the dominant culture. European-Americans in particular, but any mental health professionals in general, must follow suit by forcing themselves out of their comfort zone to seek out experience with people in nondominant cultures different from their own.

What are ways to do this? One might decide to attend a "get down" Baptist Church in a low-income area, spend time on a Native American reservation, visit a Latino community festival, arrange service learning in Asian communities through volunteering, attend a gay parade, volunteer at a GLBT activist event, volunteer at a rehabilitation center, etc. Basically, we suggest that one regularly engage in as many events as possible that force one out of one's comfort zone and out of one's own community. Immersion in what is different is the key to building new skills, which is the opposite of staying safe in one's own community of cultural isolation. While in an immersion experience, one can try to get a feel for the rhythms, social talk, speech patterns, gestures, interpersonal styles, interpersonal warmth, and psychological strengths of people who are multiculturally different. Our suggestion is to engage with others! Try it out!

Especially at black church gatherings, one can observe how openly people express powerful emotions like joy, sorrow, and affection. There is often a strong emotional/psychological connectedness within the congregation, which can be like an extended family, where nonrelatives are like brothers, sisters, elders, mothers, and fathers. At GLBT events, the closeness of the community support can carry tremendous meaning for so many individuals who have faced rejection from their own respective friends and family. For an excellent example of the latter, see the DVD documentary *Power of Harmony* (Martin, 2005). At Latino events, the power of the familia and the roles of comadres, copadres, tios, tias, mijas, elders, and curanderos can be a wonderful experience to engage in, especially if one integrates the themes in the music and observes the interactions that demonstrate traditions of respeto, simpatico, and personalismo.

As you accept this challenge, the ensuing experiences can be disorderly, lack sequence, cause some chaos, anxiety, and confusion personally and in relationship to others—this is all part of the process. Different meanings in body language may be difficult to interpret. It is much easier if one anticipates making cultural missteps; that way it is easier to recover and watch for clues on how to compensate for them. If one plans for this to happen, one may not be as caught off guard by feelings of awkwardness and moments of embarrassment and uncertainty. Although unpleasant, we suggest putting more weight on one's learning experiences than on the situational discomfort. Sometimes it is only through mistakes made over a nonlinear process that one can learn the nuance of customs, communications styles, and body language of diverse peoples. The big payoff for taking the risk to put oneself in new situations is the reward of meaningful cross-cultural connections.

Skill Building Integration of the Conceptual, Emotional, and Behavioral Changes

The skill building stage is the level where one's experiences at the previous levels begin to come together into concrete skills in engaging with others, professionally, clinically, or otherwise. One's change in knowledge and conceptual understanding joins with the emotional changes one has undergone through dialoguing and behaviorally engaging with others and results in an increased facility to work cross culturally.

At this point in the journey, one may be highly motivated to learn techniques in cross-cultural communication such as when it is appropriate to maintain eye contact or look away when talking, face each other when talking or stand side by side, self-disclose or keep a clinical distance, speak in clinical terms or terms more familiar, reflect feeling or cognition. These skills are addressed in multicultural microskills training based on the work of Allen Ivey, Daryl Wing Sue, Thomas Parham, Paul Pederson, among many other pioneers through the Microtraining and Multicultural Development website (www.emicrotraining.com/). Multicultural counseling skills are practiced in role play and improved through audio and videotaped client sessions (Ivey and Ivey, 2008). At this behavioral level, we recommend that you count on being uncomfortable, stumbling, feeling inadequate and frustrated, and trying again. Mastery in multicultural microskills comes after years of theoretical study, self-monitored practice, self-initiated learning, observation of experts, and supervisory critique. There is just no way around it; mastery takes commitment and effort.

Another way to begin to solidify one's skills is to participate in social justice action through teaching multicultural awareness in the community, writing and publishing articles on multicultural topics, and volunteering for organizations that are working toward social justice concerns. Research in multicultural psychology is still of paramount importance (Worthington, Soth-McNett, and Moreno, 2007). Finally, going back and working in one's own community to promote multicultural awareness is vital to the spread of multiculturalism and an excellent skill building exercise.

Conclusion

For a mental health professional desiring to begin their work on multicultural competency, an excellent start is to enroll in a course in multicultural diversity, but *don't stop there!* Let that first course be the conceptual starting line for a lifetime journey of continual learning and growth in multicultural psychology. Our multiracial/multiethnic/multicultural competency building model (M^{3}CB) is designed to offer suggestions for how to pursue change and growth along four levels: (1) conceptual/theoretical/intellectual, (2) emotional through multicultural dialogue, (3) behavioral engagement, and (4) skill building. As professionals infuse their experience of psychology with multicultural perspectives, they will naturally enrich their practices as researchers, directors, educators, clinicians, consultants, and in other roles mental health professionals assume.

The journey toward multicultural competency requires breaking the barriers of one's own cultural isolation, acquisition of knowledge about others different from oneself, engagement with people from other cultures on a heart level, introspection and review of one's own life experiences, facing the emotional roller-coaster of discarding old belief systems and adopting new ones, establishing and strengthening a new multicultural identity, and nurturing dimensions of a multicultural personality. Collectively, if every mental health student and professional were to take responsibility for their multicultural competency, we could together propel the field forward toward a paradigm shift that would position the field of psychology as a leader in global multiculturalism.

The Guidelines on Multicultural Education, Training, Research, Practice, and Organizational Change for Psychologists posited that

> Psychologists are in a position to provide leadership as agents of prosocial change, advocacy, and social justice, thereby promoting societal understanding, affirmation, and appreciation of multiculturalism against the damaging effects of individual, institutional, and societal racism, prejudice, and all forms of oppression based on stereotyping and discrimination (2003, p. 382).

Mental health professionals must recognize this challenge and the associated responsibility as they serve in multiple clinical, teaching, consultant, research, and activist roles. Mental health professionals are role models of multicultural competency in their professional occupations and in their lives; in this way, they are leaders to all individuals encountered.

A paradigm shift is under way. The issue is whether this paradigm shift will reach its full potential in psychology, in American society, and across the world.

Notes

1. Although it is not clear who coined the phrase "browning of America," we do want to mention its use in the works of Richard Rodriguez, a NPR reporter and writer of *Brown: The Last Discovery of America* (2003).

2. The fourth force refers to multicultural psychology as a movement coming after psychoanalytic, behavioral, and humanistic psychology. For further explanation, see Pedersen (1999).

3. For more on the concept of the tipping point, see Gladwell (2000).

4. The construct of *multicultural personality* has been developed by Ponterotto, Utsey, and Pedersen (2006).

5. More about Pearson and Bader's psychological perspective can be found on their website www.couplesinstitute.com/.

6. For more information on James Prochaska's stages of change, see www.uri.edu/research/cprc/Faculty/JProchaska.htm.

References

Adams, D. (2002). A metastructure for multicultural professional psychology education and training: Standards and philosophy. In E. David-Russell (Ed.), *The California School of Professional Psychology Handbook of Multicultural Education, Research, Intervention, and Training* (pp. 20–36). San Francisco, CA: Jossey-Bass.

Ali, S. R., Liu, W. M., and Humedian, M. (2004). Islam 101: Understanding the religion and therapy implications. *Professional Psychology: Research and Practice, 35*(6), 635–42.

APA Commission on ethnic minority recruitment, retention, and training in psychology task force (CEMRRAT2) Progress Report. (2007). Executive summary of major findings and priority recommendations. *Communique.* Retrieved November 3, 2007, from www.apa.org/www2/pi/oema/august_2007_communique.pdf.

APA Task Force on Socioeconomic Status. (2007). *Report of the APA Task Force on Socioeconomic Status.* Washington, D.C. Retrieved August 7, 2007, from www.apa.org/governance/cpm/SES.pdf.

Arrendondo, P., and Perez, P. (2006). Historical perspectives on the multicultural *guidelines and contemporary applications. Professional Psychology: Research and Practice 37* (1).

Baumeister, R. (2005). Rethinking self-esteem. *Stanford Social Innovation Review, 3*(4), 34–41.

Bennett, M. J. (1993). Towards ethnorelativism: A developmental model of intercultural sensitivity. In M. Paige (Ed.), *Education for the intercultural experience* (2nd ed., pp. 21–72). Yarmouth, ME: Intercultural Press.

Bowe, J. (2006, November 19). Gay donor or gay dad: An extended nuclear family? *New York Times.*

Brinkley, D. (2000). *The life of Rosa Parks.* New York: Penguin Group.

Bronstein, P., and Quina, K. (Eds.) (2003). *Teaching gender and multicultural awareness: Resources for the psychology classroom.* Washington D.C.: American Psychological Association.

Butler, S. (1998). *The way home.* Video. Oakland, CA: World Trust Educational Services.

Butler, S., and Butler, R. (2006). *Mirrors of privilege: Making whiteness visible.* Video. Oakland, CA: World Trust Educational Services.

Carter, R. T. (1991). Racial identity attitudes and psychological functioning. *Journal of Multicultural Counseling and Development, 19,* 105–14.

———. (2007). Special issue: Race-based trauma. *The Counseling Psychologist, 35,* 1.

Castillo, L. G., Brossart, D. F., Reyes, C. J., Conoley, C. W., and Phoummarath, M. J. (2007). The influence of multicultural training on perceived multicultural counseling competencies and implicit racial prejudice. *Journal of Multicultural Counseling and Development, 35,* 243–54.

Clark, J. (2003). Reconceptualizing empathy for culturally competent practice. In W. Shera (Ed.), *Emerging perspectives on anti-oppressive practice.* Toronto: Canadian Scholars Press.

Cokley, K., and Helm, K. (2007). The relationship between African American enculturation and racial identity. *Journal of Multicultural Counseling and Development, 35*(3), 142–53.

Connor, M. E., and White, J. L. (Eds.) (2006). *Black fathers: An invisible presence in America.* Mahwah, NJ: Lawrence Erlbaum.

Constantine, M. (1997). Facilitating multicultural competence in supervision: Operationalizing a practical framework. In D. Pope-Davis and H. K. Coleman (Eds.), *Multicultural counseling competencies: Assessment, education, and training, and supervision* (pp. 310–24). Thousand Oaks, CA: Sage Publications.

———. (2002). Predictors of satisfaction with counseling: Racial and ethnic minority clients' attitudes toward counseling and ratings of their counselor's general and multicultural competence. *Journal of Counseling Psychology, 49,* 255–63.

Constantine, M., and Ladany, N. (2001). New visions for defining and assessing multicultural competence. In J. Ponterotto, J. M. Casas, L. Suzuki, and C. M. Alexander, *Handbook of multicultural counseling* (2nd ed.). Thousand Oaks, CA: Sage Publications.

Cross, W. E., Jr., Parham, T. A., and Helms, J. E. (1991). Stages of black identity development: Nigrescence models. In R. L. Jones (Ed.), *Black psychology* (3rd ed., pp. 319–38). New York: Harper & Row.

Croteau, J. M. (2004). *Deconstructing heterosexism in the counseling professions: A narrative approach (multicultural aspects of counseling and psychotherapy).* Thousand Oaks, CA: Sage Publications.

Cruz, B. C., and Patterson, J. (2005). Cross-cultural simulations in teacher education: Developing empathy and understanding. *Multicultural Perspectives, 7*(2), 40–47.

D'Andrea, M., Daniels, J., Arredondo, P., Ivey, M. B., Ivey, A., Locke, D. C., et al. (2001). Fostering organizational change to realize the revolutionary potential of the multicultural movement: An updated case study. In J. Ponterotto, J. Casas, L. Suzuki, and C. M. Alexander, *Handbook of multicultural counseling* (2nd ed., pp. 222–54). Thousand Oaks, CA: Sage Publications.

Davis, R. (2007). The ABCs of disability rights. *Teaching Tolerance.* Retrieved October 30, 2007, from www.tolerance.org/teach/activities/activity.jsp?ar=872.

Drew, J. (1997). White racial identity in a multicultural society: A college course. Doctoral dissertation, California School of Professional Psychology, Los Angeles.

Dyche, L., and Zayas, L. H. (2004). Cross-cultural empathy and training the contemporary psychotherapist. *Clinical Social Work Journal, 29*(3), 245–58.

Edmonia, G., and Highgate, C. V. (2003). *Black teachers, freed slaves, and the betrayal of black hearts.* In Mjagkij, N. (Ed.), *Portrait of American life since 1865* (pp. 1–13). Wilmington, DE: Scholarly Resources Inc. See also Butchart, R. E. (no date). *The freedmen's teachers project* website. College of Education, University of Georgia. Retrieved May 28, 2007, from www.coe.uga.edu/ftp/.

Feinberg, L. (2004). *Stone butch blues*. San Francisco: Alyson Publishing.

Foster, R. P. (1998). The clinician's countertransference: The psychodynamics of culturally competent practice. *Clinical Social Work Journal, 26*(3), 253–70.

Fox, P. (2001). *A servant's tale*. New York: W. W. Norton & Co.

Gandhi, M. (1993). *An autobiography: The story of my experiments with truth*. Boston: Beacon Press.

Gladwell, M. (2000). *The tipping point: How little things can make a big difference*. New York: Back Bay Books.

Green, J. (2004). *Becoming a visible man*. Nashville, TN: Vanderbilt University Press.

Guidelines for practice with older adults. (2004). *American Psychologist, 59*(4), 236–60. Retrieved August 7, 2007, from www.apa.org/practice/adult.pdf.

Guidelines for psychotherapy with lesbian, gay, and bisexual clients. (2000). *American Psychologist, 55*(12), 1440–51. Retrieved August 7, 2007, from www.apa.org/practice/glbt.pdf.

Guidelines on multicultural education, training, research, practice, and organizational change for psychologists. (2003). *American Psychologist, 58*(5), 377–402. Also retrieved December 20, 2004, from www.apa.org/pi/multiculturalguidelines/homepage.html.

Haley, A. (1996). *The autobiography of Malcolm X as told by Alex Haley*. NY: Grove Press.

Hays, P. (2001). Entering another's world: Understanding clients' identities and contexts. *Addressing cultural complexities in practice: A framework for clinicians and counselors*. Washington D.C.: American Psychological Association.

Helms, J. E. (1990). *Black and white racial identity: Theory, research, and practice*. New York: Greenwood Press.

Helms, J. E., Malone, L. T. S., Henze, K., Satiani, A., Perry, J., and Warren, A. (2003). First annual diversity challenge: "How to survive teaching courses on race and culture." *Journal of Multicultural Development, 31*(1), 3–11.

Henderson, S. J. (2006). The ten pocket tool kit: Encouraging entrepreneurship among people of color. *Career Planning and Adult Development Journal, 21*(4), 90–102.

Henderson, S. J., and Chan, A. (2005). Career happiness among Asian-Americans: The interplay between individualism and interdependence. *Journal of Multicultural Counseling and Development, 33*, 180–92.

Hirschfeld, S. (2007). Introduction: The ABCs of size bias. *Teaching Tolerance*. Retrieved August 7, 2007, from www.tolerance.org/teach/activities/activity.jsp?p=0&ar=825&pa=1.

Holladay, J. (2006). The ABCs of religion in schools. *Teaching Tolerance*. Retrieved October 30, 2007, from www.tolerance.org/teach/activities/activity.jsp?ar=758&pa=1.

Howell, W. S. (1982). *The empathic communicator*. Belmont, CA: Wadworth Publishing.

Huber, J. M. S. (1996). Inter and intra-racial contact and affective reactions as aspects of recalled white racial identity socialization experiences. Doctoral dissertation, University of Maryland at College Park.

Ivey, A. E., D'Andrea, M., Ivey, M. B., and Simek-Morgan, L. (2002). *Counseling and psychotherapy: A multicultural perspective* (5th ed.). Boston: Allyn & Bacon.

Ivey, A. E., and Ivey, M. B. (2008). *Essentials of intentional interviewing: Counseling in a multicultural world.* Pacific Grove, CA: Thompson-Brooks/Cole.

Jenkins, P. (2001). African Americans "a culture of hope." Dissertation, California School of Professional Psychology, Los Angeles.

Johansen, B. (1982). *Forgotten founders: Benjamin Franklin, the Iroquois and the rationale for the American Revolution.* Boston: Harvard Common Press. Retrieved October 29, 2007, from www.ratical.org/many_worlds/6Nations/FF.pdf.

Kagan, J. (2004). *Crown heights.* Showtime.

Kidd, S. M. (2002). *The secret life of bees.* New York: Penguin Books.

LaFramboise, T., Coleman, H. L., and Gerton, J. (1993). Psychological impact of biculturalism: Evidence and theory. *Psychological Bulletin, 114*(3), 395–412.

Langman, P. F. (1999). *Jewish issues in multiculturalism: A handbook for educators and clinicians.* Northvale, NJ: Jason Aronson.

Leavitt, D. (1987). *The lost language of cranes.* New York: Bantam Books.

Lee, C. C., and Ramsey, C. J. (2006). Multicultural counseling: A new paradigm for a new century. In C. C. Lee (Ed.) *Multicultural issues in counseling: New approaches to diversity* (pp. 3–11). Alexandria, VA: American Counseling Association.

Liu, W. M., and Pope-Davis, D. B. (2003). Moving from diversity to multiculturalism: Exploring power and its implications for multicultural competence. In D. B. Pope-Davis, H. L. K. Coleman, W. M. Liu, and R. L. Toporek (Eds.), *Handbook of multicultural competencies in counseling and psychology* (pp. 90–102). Thousand Oaks, CA: Sage Publications.

Liu, W. M., Picket Jr., T., and Ivey, A. E. (2007). White middle-class privilege: Social class bias and implications for training and practice. *Journal of Multicultural Counseling and Development, 35*(4), 194–206.

Lorde, A. (1982). *Zami: a new spelling of my name.* Berkeley, CA: Crossing Press.

Lynch, E. W., and Hanson, M. J. (2004). *Developing cross-cultural competence: A guide to working with children and families* (3rd ed.). Baltimore, MD: Paul H. Brooks Publishing.

MacIntosh, P. (1990). White privilege: unpacking the invisible knapsack. *Independent School, 49*(2), 31–36.

Mahalingam, R. (Ed.) (2006). *Cultural psychotherapy of immigrants.* Mahwah, NJ: Lawrence Erlbaum Associates.

Marsella, A. J. (2007). Education and training for a global psychology: Foundations, issues, and actions. In M. Stevens and U. Gielen (Eds.), *Toward a global psychology: Theory, research, intervention, and pedagogy.* Mahwah, NJ: Erlbaum.

Martin, G. (2005). *Power of harmony.* DVD. AMS Production Group. www.amspg.com.

McGoldrick, M., Giordano, J., and Garcia-Preto, N. (Eds.) (2005). Ethnicity and family history (3rd ed.). New York: Guilford.

Mollen, D., Ridley, C., and Hill, C. (2003). Models of multicultural competence: a critical evaluation. In D. L. Pope-Davis, Coleman, H. L. K., Liu, W. M., and Toporek, R. L. (Eds.), Handbook of multicultural competencies in counseling and psychology (pp. 21–37). Thousand Oaks, CA: Sage Publications.

Murray, B. (2002). Psychology bolsters the world's fight against racism. Monitor on Psychology, 33(1). Retrieved October 21, 2007, from www.apa.org/monitor/jan02/bolsters.html.

Naber, N. (2000). Ambiguous insiders: An investigation of Arab American invisibility. Race and Ethnic Studies, 23(1), 37–61.

Narayan, R. K. (2006). The guide: A novel. New York: Penguin Classics.

Nasser, H. E. (2004, March 18). Census projects growing diversity. USA Today, p. 1.

Nelson, M. L., Englar-Carlson, M., Tierney, S. C., and Hau, J. M. (2006). Class jumping into academia: Multiple identities for counseling academics. Journal of Counseling Psychology, 53(1), 1–14.

Neville, H. A., Worthington, R. L., and Spanierman, L. B. (2001). Race, power, and multicultural counseling psychology: Understanding white privilege and color-blind racial attitudes. In J. G. Ponterotto, J. M. Casas, L. A. Suzuki, and C. M. Alexander (Eds.), Handbook of multicultural counseling (2nd ed., pp. 257-88). Thousand Oaks, CA: Sage Publications.

One America dialogue guide: Conducting a discussion on race. (1998). One America in the 21st century: The President's initiative on race. Washington D.C.: U.S. Government Printing Office. Retrieved January 1, 2005, from www.ncjrs.org/pdf-files/173431.pdf.

Parham, T. A. (Ed.). (2002). Counseling persons of African descent: Raising the bar of practitioner competence. Thousand Oaks, CA: Sage Publications.

Parham, T. A., White, J. L., and Ajamu, A. (1999). The psychology of blacks: An Afro-American perspective (3rd ed.). Upper Saddle River, NJ: Prentice Hall, Inc.

Peace Corps information collection and exchange T0087. (no date). Culture matters. The Peace Corps cross-cultural workbook. Washington D.C.: U.S. Government Printing Office. Retrieved July 9, 2007, from www.peacecorps.gov/library/pdf/T0087_culturematters.pdf.

Pedersen, P. B. (1991). Multiculturalism as a generic approach to counseling. In P. B. Pedersen, (Ed.) Multiculturalism as a fourth force in counseling [special issue]. Journal of Counseling and Development 70, 6–12.

———. (1999). Multiculturalism as the Fourth Force. Philadelphia, PA: Taylor & Francis.

Pedersen, P. B., Crethar, H. C., and Carlson, J. (Eds.) (2008). Inclusive cultural empathy: Making relationships central in counseling and psychotherapy. Washington, DC: American Psychological Association.

Pham, A. X. (2002). Catfish and Mandala: A two-wheeled voyage through the landscape and memory of Vietnam. New York: Picador.

Phinney, J. (1990). Ethnic identity in adolescents and adults: A review of research. *Psychological Bulletin, 108,* 499–514.

Phinney, J. (1992). The multi-group ethnic identity measure: A new scale for use with adolescents and young adults from diverse groups. *Journal of Adolescent Research, 7,* 156–76.

Phinney, J. (1995). Ethnic identity and self-esteem: A review and integration. In A. Padilla (Ed.), *Hispanic psychology: Critical issues in theory and research* (pp. 57–70). Thousand Oaks, CA: Sage Publications.

Ponterotto, J. G., Casas, J. M., Suzuki, L. A, and Alexander, C. M. (Eds.). (2001). *Handbook of multicultural counseling* (2nd ed.). Thousand Oaks, CA: Sage Publications.

Ponterotto, J. G., Utsey, S. O., and Pedersen, P. B. (2006). *Preventing prejudice: A guide for counselors, education, and parents* (2nd ed.). Thousand Oaks, CA: Sage Publications.

Pope-Davis, D. B., Toporek, R. L., Ortega-Villalobos, L., Ligiéro, D. P., Brittan-Powell, C. S., Liu, W. M., et al. (2002). Client perspectives of multicultural counseling competence: A qualitative examination. *The Counseling Psychologist, 30*(3), 355–93.

Rastogi, M., and Wieling, E. (2004). *Voices of color: First-person accounts of ethnic minority therapists.* Thousand Oaks, CA: Sage Publications.

Ridley, C. R. (2005). *Overcoming unintentional racism in counseling and therapy: A practitioner's guide to intentional intervention.* Thousand Oaks, CA: Sage Publications.

Rodriguez, R. (1998). *The browning of America.* PBS Online Newshour. Retrieved December 27, 2004, from www.pbs.org/newshour/essays/february98/rodriguez_2-18 .html.

———. (2003). *Brown: The last discovery of America.* New York: Penguin Group.

Root, M. P. P. (Ed.). (1996). *The multiracial experience: Racial borders as the new frontier.* Thousand Oaks, CA: Sage Publications.

Rothenberg, P. S. (2008). *White privilege: Essential readings on the other side of racism* (3rd ed.). New York: Worth Publishers.

Schlosser, L. Z. (2003). Christian privilege: Breaking a sacred taboo. *Journal of Multicultural Counseling and Development, 31,* 44–51.

———. (2006). Affirmative psychotherapy for American Jews. *Psychotherapy: Theory, Research, Practice, Training, 43*(4), 424–35.

Schlosser, L. Z., Talleyrand, R. M., Lyons, H. Z., and Baker, L. M. (2007). Racism, anti-Semitism, and the schism between blacks and Jews in the United States: A pilot intergroup encounter program. *Journal of Multicultural Counseling and Development, 35,* 116–28.

Siegel, R. (1997, February 5). Questions on race. *All Things Considered.* National Public Radio Transcript Archives. Retrieved October 20, 2007 from www.npr.org/transcripts/.

Sixty years of great books. (2005, November). *Ebony.* Retrieved October 19, 2007, from findarticles.com/p/articles/mi_m1077/is_1_61/ai_n15774364.

Spain, T., and Spain, L. (2007). Fat: What no one is telling you. PBS DVD. Twin Cities Public Television, Inc. www.shoppbs.org.

Steele, C. (1997). A threat in the air: How stereotypes shape intellectual identity and performance. *American Psychologist, 52*(6), 613–29.

Stone, J. (Ed.) (2004). *Culture and disability: Providing culturally competent services.* Thousand Oaks, CA: Sage Publications.

Sue, D. W. (2003). *Overcoming our racism: The journey to liberation.* San Francisco: Jossey-Bass.

Sue, D. W., Capodilupo, C. M., Torino, G. C., Bucceri, J. M., Holder, A. M. B., Nadal, K. L., and Esquilin, N. (2007). Racial microaggressions in everyday life: Implications for clinical practice. *American Psychologist, 62*(4), 271–86.

Sue, D. W., and Sue, D. (2008). Counseling the culturally diverse: Theory and practice (5th ed.). New York: John Wiley & Sons.

Sullivan, O. R. (2001). *Black stars: African American women scientists and inventors.* New York: John Wiley & Sons.

Taylor, J., Gilligan, C., and Sullivan, A. (1995). *Between voice and silence: Women and girls, race and relationships.* Cambridge, MA: Harvard University Press.

Toporek, R. L., and Reza, J. V. (2001). Context as a critical dimension of multicultural counseling: Articulating personal, professional, and institutional competence. *Journal of Multicultural Counseling and Development, 29*, 13–30.

The 21st century family. (2007). *Greater Good Magazine, 4*(2), 12–33. Retrieved from www.greatergoodmag.edu/greatergood/index.html.

Tuckwell, G. (2002). *Racial identity, white counselors, and therapists.* Philadelphia, PA: Open University Press.

U.S. Department of Health and Human Services. (2000). *Culture, race, and ethnicity: A supplement to mental health: A report of the Surgeon General.* Washington D.C.: U.S. Public Health Service. Retrieved November 12, 2007, from www.surgeongeneral.gov/library/mentalhealth/cre/execsummary-1.html.

Video Library (2004). Greenfield Intercultural Center. University of Pennsylvania. Retrieved on August 4, 2007, at www.vpul.upenn.edu/gic/videocat.php.

Wah, L. M. (2004). *Color of fear.* Berkeley, CA: Stirfry Productions.

Wann, M. (1998). *Fat? So!: Because you don't have to apologize for your size!* Berkeley, CA: Ten Speed Press.

Weisberg, R. (2005). *Waging a living.* DVD. New York: Public Policy Productions.

Wertheimer, L. (1997). Crown Heights verdict. *All Things Considered.* National Public Radio Transcript Archives, February 10. Retrieved on October 20, 2007, at www.npr.org/transcripts/.

West, D. (1995). *The wedding: A novel.* New York: Doubleday.

White, J. L., and Cones, J. H. (1999). *Black man emerging: Facing the past and seizing a future in America.* New York: W.H. Freeman & Co.

White, J. L., Parham, T. A., and Ajamu, A. (2007).*The Psychology of blacks* (4th Ed). Upper Saddle River, NJ: Prentice Hall.

Worthington, R. L., Soth-McNett, A.M., and Moreno, M. V. (2007). Multicultural counseling competencies research: A 20-year content analysis. *Journal of Counseling Psychology, 54*(4), 351-61.

PART II

PROMISING PRACTICES AMONG GRADUATE TRAINING PROGRAMS

CHAPTER THREE

~

Creighton University

Beyond the Conceptual: Diversity Education for Faculty

Patricia Ann Fleming, Erika L. Kirby,
G. H. Grandbois, Ngwarsungu Chiwengo,
Ashton W. Welch, and John Pierce

One of the great challenges the United States will face this century is a more racially and ethnically diverse culture, referred to by some experts as the "browning of America." This change, which Dr. Joseph White (2004) calls "the ultimate challenge," cries for a fundamental shift or paradigmatic change in the way faculty members interact with students and colleagues. In this chapter we detail the faculty development program—involving conceptual, dialogical, and interactional programming—that the College of Arts and Sciences at Creighton University adopted to foster a level of excellence in multicultural competency among the faculty.

The College of Arts and Sciences of Creighton University, one of twenty-eight Jesuit Catholic colleges and universities in the United States, revised its core curriculum in the early 1990s to integrate social justice, through diversity education, into key global and domestic courses. The college faculty defined "domestic diversity" in the new curriculum to include race, ethnicity, gender, and socioeconomic class. At the time of this revision, a request to include other forms of diversity, for example, religious diversity, disabilities, and sexual orientation, did not surface among the faculty. Since the 1990s questions have been raised about the exclusivity of the core definition of domestic diversity. The definition's expansion is tied to the revision of the core curriculum and there has been no movement in this direction. Hence, while the definition remains the same today as in the early 1990s, the initiatives sponsored by the Diversity Project have included some of these other forms of diversity. This curriculum innovation presented challenges, including the creation and implementation of faculty development training. These challenges were met through targeted hiring, a department-specific World Literature Program, and a college-wide Diversity Project administered by an advisory board.

The college-wide Diversity Project met with some success over the next eight years, particularly in numbers of faculty involved. However, the Diversity Project programs (Reading Groups, Student Voices Workshops, and Diversity Seminars) focused primarily on a *conceptual* approach to faculty development, emphasizing the intellectual content of courses and development of faculty primarily through the use of written materials and experts in academic fields of study. While it did include workshops intended to introduce classroom behavioral changes, this aspect of the project was underemphasized. After hearing our primary consultant Dr. Joseph White facilitate one of these workshops in April 2001, the college's new dean challenged us with the following questions: (1) do the programs sponsored by the Diversity Project tend to focus on issues only at an *abstract, conceptual* level? or (more aggressively), (2) do they also *encourage dialogue* among our diverse faculty and students on critical issues? or (most desirable of all), (3) do they include a *behavioral* component to bring participants face to face with the cultural differences within their respective groups and those of other ethnic communities? These challenges came at a time when certain anomalies of the conceptual paradigm, which had surfaced earlier, were increasing. Among these anomalies was increased distress among students of color regarding stereotypical treatment of them inside and outside the classroom, as evidenced in focus group interviews with African American, Hispanic, Native American, and Pan-Asian student groups.

Concomitantly, a new dean had assumed the reins of the college and the former director of the Diversity Project (lead author) had moved into college administration. The university also acquired a new president whose commitment to diversity was clear, concrete, and challenging from the time of his inaugural address (Schlegel, 2000). These changes in leadership juxtaposed to the inability of the conceptual paradigm to effectively meet the multifaceted multicultural competency development needs of faculty and students proved to be ripe conditions for a fruitful examination.

In this chapter we recount the development of the original Diversity Project by briefly discussing some of its successes as well as its various evolving revisions within the first eight years. The Diversity Project Advisory Board focused on the anomalies of the predominant conceptual approach of the original project. We then describe a new paradigm that incorporates the conceptual but is based on principles that move beyond it. Have our faculty shifted into this new paradigm? In answering this question, we share some early assessment of successes and challenges and some ways we have tried to address these challenges.

The Original Diversity Project

Success of the original Diversity Project became evident after the first two years of the program (the project began in 1996). The autonomy central to the program, the respect for academic freedom, the ease of acquisition of reading materials (delivered to faculty mailboxes), and the comfortable familiarity of a conceptual approach contributed to the program's popularity. College faculty members in departments whose chairpersons had predicted no involvement avidly participated. Academic connections among the faculty increased. These results were instrumental in creating and implementing interdisciplinary senior perspective courses in the new curriculum.

A survey was administered to the faculty (N = 52) who participated in the first seven reading groups, held from spring 1996 through spring 1997. Almost 70 percent (forty-six) responded to the survey. Across reading groups, a large percentage of respondents (67–91 percent) found the Reading Group Program personally useful and found that the program stimulated thinking about cultural diversity. They reported having a deeper appreciation of cultural diversity after completing a Reading Group. Respondents were satisfied with the interdisciplinary nature of the program and believed such a program supported the mission and goals of the university and of a liberal arts education.

The Diversity Project Advisory Board also discovered, however, a disproportionate participation by college divisions.[1] While 56 percent of the faculty participants were from humanities, the lowest percent was from the professional division, the smallest of the four divisions. More female than male faculty members reported that the Reading Group Program was personally useful, found the content and reading materials stimulated thinking, and acknowledged the importance of cultural diversity. More tenured faculty members reported that the Reading Group Program was useful professionally than nontenured faculty members who said that the program was "moderately" useful professionally. Clearly, there was more work to be done.

Through some "behind the scenes" recruitment efforts in response to the survey findings, the total number of faculty participating in the Reading Group Program increased to 168, with thirty-nine faculty participating in a second or third reading group. The number of faculty from divisions other than the humanities increased and the number of untenured faculty rose. Of the 168 faculty participating in a Reading Group, thirty-one (18 percent) came from other schools and colleges at Creighton University. The total number of full-time faculty in the College of Arts and Sciences during this period grew from approximately 150 to 180 members.

Whatever its successes and failures, this program used a conceptual approach to faculty development in its emphasis on reading diverse texts. It would be too simplistic to suggest that no significant dialogue about differences among participants or no behavioral changes in intergroup relations resulted from the Reading Group Program. As faculty discussed differences, new relationships formed among the faculty, enabling the successful design of several interdisciplinary courses. However, because the dialogues were unstructured, they tended to be about disciplinary differences among faculty, or to be discussions of generic issues of diversity rather than entering into a reflective dialogue about personal experiences.

Over time, anomalies increased. Despite its popularity, the Diversity Project, except for its College Workshop, became so conceptual in design that other faculty needs and concerns continued to go unmet. Faculty members were increasingly concerned about incidents on campus and in the classroom that did not seem to be affected by the explicit changes in the core curriculum. Faculty whose fields focused on behavioral interventions began to seek other university-sponsored faculty development programs or directed their challenges to the Diversity Project Advisory Committee. As members of the committee became aware of the limited results of a popular program, the time for change was at hand.

The Diversity Project did initially plan a more experientially focused program. This program, the College Workshop, was designed to meet the specific *pedagogical* needs of the faculty considering the realities of teaching our predominantly European-American students. The Diversity Project Advisory Committee recommended that the College Workshop be revamped as a "Student Voices Workshop." This entailed working more closely with the office of Multicultural Affairs to assess the specific pedagogical needs of students. Transcripts of multicultural student focus group interviews were made available to some reading groups and diversity seminars. Faculty participants reported that the interviews were the most significant material they studied. The resulting workshop proved to be a turning point in the paradigmatic design of the Diversity Project.

The Revised Diversity Project

Dr. Joseph White's workshop facilitation had identified the source of anomalies in the original Diversity Project, particularly its dominant conceptual focus. Consequently, the Diversity Project Advisory Committee, with Dr.

White's assistance, undertook an intensive examination of the project. After a year of self-study and planning, the Diversity Project Advisory Committee shifted to our current three-phase model: (1) conceptual programming, (2) dialogical programming, and (3) interactional programming. The revolutionary change in the college's approach to faculty training and development on diversity comes in the creation of phases of dialogical and behavioral/interactional programming.

This shift was clearly in Kuhnian fashion (see Kuhn, 1967). During the first phases of the self-study, undertaken under the auspice of a diversity seminar, some members of the Diversity Project Advisory Committee insisted on assessing the old project before any changes were made. Although some assessment had taken place, these members judged that more assessment was needed to determine the future needs of faculty training. This desire for further assessment suggests that some committee members believed that a new model might *evolve* from a rationale exploration of the difficulties of the older, more conceptual model. However, by the third planning session, the Advisory Committee simply abandoned the exclusivity of the conceptual model. So many anomalies had surfaced over time that no amount of ad hoc remedies could redeem the old paradigm. Moreover, after hearing Dr. White's lecture and participating in the dialogic workshop, the committee "converted" to the new White paradigm, with its conceptual, dialogical, and interactional phases and new rules for developing faculty diversity awareness.

The revised project also articulated clear objectives for each of its components and a method for assessing the program outcomes. Except for its renewed emphasis on outcomes and the assessment of these outcomes, the conceptual aspect of the revised project endured in this new paradigm, including the Diversity Seminar and the Diversity Workshop initiated in 1999. The largest change to these programs was that, just as the Diversity Workshop was intended to be pedagogical in nature so as to change classroom practices, the Diversity Seminar also became more focused on classroom practices; faculty participants shared either their changed syllabi or changed units of one of their courses after the completion of a seminar.

Dialogical Programming: Intergroup Relations Dialogues

As we moved from conceptual to reflective dialogue examining interpersonal perceptions/beliefs, attitudes, and behaviors, an intergroup relations training program was developed. In these "Diversity Dialogues," participants were expected to (a) identify their individual social identities and how they are shaped by race/ethnicity, gender, economic status, etc.; (b) understand the forces and dynamics affecting intergroup relations in the United States, including diverse perspectives; (c) develop strategies for communicating and relating across cultural/economic/gender differences; and (d) develop pedagogical materials for inclusion in their respective courses.

To achieve these objectives, training sessions were held for capacity building purposes where seven faculty facilitators were trained in intergroup relations, facilitation/communication, conflict resolution, and application of the model to pedagogy. Well-trained intergroup relations faculty are now in place to provide training to groups of other interested faculty members, and three of these groups are planned for every academic year. Each dialogic group is composed of seven faculty members and a trained facilitator. A small group is essential in this type of training due to the potential for intense interpersonal interaction. Intergroup relations training sessions use a series of questions, designed by Dr. White and Dr. G. H. Grandbois, a social work professor/expert in intergroup relations and programming needs, to guide participant responses.

To determine whether participants had been affected by exposure to the intervention, the Advisory Board facilitated an impact analysis on all the participants (consisting of the first faculty facilitator trainees) of the first workshop. We used a combination of Likert-type instrumentation as well as self-report measures that were most conducive to obtaining participant reactions in their own words, which proved useful in measuring intrapersonal phenomena. Instrument construction was concordant with standard program evaluation protocol, resulting in operationalizing the Diversity Dialogue objectives and requesting respondents to rate their ability to understand and ability to apply the concepts.[2] Preliminary findings (ratings were from adequately qualified to excellently qualified) indicate that those faculty who were trained to conduct Diversity Dialogues were able to understand Dr. White's (2004) model of multicultural discourse as well as how to develop norms in a group setting; how to handle conflict when it arises in the classroom; and how race/ethnicity, gender, and class intersect. In addition, faculty members were able to increase their awareness and appreciation of the complexity of identity and were able to recognize and examine diversity within a group. Finally, faculty members were able to understand how to develop pedagogical materials and techniques suitable for inclusion in their respective courses. Thus, our capacity building was a success.

Interactional Programming: Extended Immersion

To further impact the transformation of faculty beyond concepts and dialogue, the revised Diversity Project incorporated voluntary, long-term immersion in a cross-cultural environment. This aspect of programming was designed to allow for a process of conscientization leading to a lifelong commitment to the promotion of social justice. The purpose of interactional programming was to develop a critical knowledge of the world and deep and close ties to others who are "different." Extended immersion experiences better prepare faculty members to address pedagogical issues of diversity and justice, values consistent with the mission of Creighton University. After participating in extended immersion, participants were expected to be better able to (a) recognize how cultural and individual experiences shape social identities, (b) understand the forces and dynamics affecting intergroup relations in the United States including diverse perspectives, (c) develop close ties with (and understanding of) others different from themselves, and (d) acknowledge and develop an appreciation for others as persons in order to understand and eliminate xenophobia.

The revised Diversity Project proposal recommended that the immersion process occur through (a) a variety of cultural events, such as weekend activities, communal living, and visits to local factories, meat-packing plants, soup kitchens, etc. as well as (b) more personal activities such as visits to each other's homes during holidays, vacations, birthday celebrations, or other family activities in the spirit of reciprocity. Immersions may occur in any environment, near or far away from the university setting. In approving the revised program, the newly installed dean of the college modeled this programming on a small sabbatical program, wherein a faculty member is given a course release to engage in such immersion.

Faculty members were eligible for application to this program once they completed *both* the conceptual and the dialogical programming phases. Two course releases were provided for the two successful applicants: one to a faculty member seeking to deepen her connection with a refugee community in the urban environment, and a second to a faculty member seeking to immerse himself in local churches in order to learn about them, their respective make-up, and their attitudes toward sacred texts.

Assessment was provided in two forms. A post-hoc self-report protocol (e.g., reflection journals) was completed by faculty participants to evaluate the personal and spiritual dimensions of their immersion. An open-ended questionnaire was designed to guide reflection so that participants addressed the same frame of experience. Furthermore, since it was necessary to assess the value of the immersion sites, tools were developed for assessing immersion experiences in a manner consistent with The Higher Learning Commission's (2003) guidelines on *Engagement for Service*.

Preliminary assessment of the extended immersion is largely anecdotal. The faculty member who immersed himself in various faith communities contributed to the creation of an Employee Development Program, entitled *World Religions—The Core of Diversity* delivered to faculty and staff of Creighton. The faculty member who immersed herself with Sudanese refugees reflected in her grant report that "Their vastly different tribal [sic] viewpoints and cultural differences have stretched greatly my abilities to tolerate a tremendous amount of diversity." Subsequently, this faculty member was awarded the Points of Light award for her work with the refugees by the Omaha area United Way in April 2006. To this point, then, we have experienced moderate success in the realm of interactional programming with those who have participated in the program. Our biggest struggle has been garnering faculty interest to apply for an immersion; some faculty have asserted that adding "immersion" to their list of activities simply adds a fourth dimension to their workload of teaching, research, and service; so even though a course release is provided, it is not always an attractive option.

Early Results on Paradigm Shift Assessment

Despite these successes in capacity building for dialogical programming and with the first two immersions, in May 2005, the Diversity Advisory Committee held a meeting because the revised program had at that point been less "revolutionary" among the faculty than had been anticipated. When the program was opened for faculty participation in spring 2004, the first major challenge of the new Diversity Project emerged. While a widespread effort was made to recruit faculty to participate in Diversity Dialogues using a threefold approach of (1) announcing the effort through mainstream media outlets such as the college listserv, (2) personal invitations to faculty who had done a reading group in the prior project, and (3) written invitations sent to department chairs and promulgated by the college dean, faculty interest was remarkably low. The two scheduled Diversity Dialogues for the semester did not have enough committed participants to take place. Initially, it was presumed that faculty would be more than willing to participate as an ideological obligation; yet further analysis showed that there was little personal or professional incentive for faculty to participate in the dialogue series. In addition, informal assessment of faculty views revealed some confusion as to how the new Diversity Project differed from the original; for example, some faculty felt they "had done that before."

Furthermore, early in 2005 the college's Faculty Senate articulated an overriding sentiment that intellectual diversity of ideas would be a sufficient standard for which to strive in terms of diversity. Members of the Senate expressed concern that "diversity" siphons resources from real scholarship. Thus, the Diversity Project Advisory Committee's May meeting was designed to devise ways to increase interest (and hopefully participation) in the Diversity Project—to achieve a more fully revolutionary potential through participants' "conversions" resulting from the conceptual to the behavioral and interactional structure.

To enhance faculty participation in the program, the Diversity Advisory Committee developed an approach based on pre-existing college-oriented groups, including academic units/departments, new faculty groups, and members of the Diversity Seminar (conceptual programming). In other words, to gain access to faculty and increase their involvement, the Diversity Project implemented a more systematic and explicit approach in the 2005–2006 academic year consisting of formal presentations to established college entities, such as the Council of Chairs and the College Faculty Senate (and its Executive Committee). In addition, the codirectors of the project made face-to-face appeals to department chairs and faculty. Plans were also made to conduct Diversity Dialogues with the college's New Faculty Orientation group. The phase of garnering faculty participation outside of the trained facilitators, therefore, is an ongoing challenge, but tangible results have been seen in faculty participation in the program. For example, the College Faculty Senate Executive Committee (nine faculty members) and the entire Education Department (twelve faculty members) completed the diversity training.

But perhaps the largest participation has come from faculty who are working with the revamped first-year experience. Concomitant to changes being made in the Diversity Project, a multi-year-long study on the first-year experience was brought to closure by the academic vice president and the vice president of Student Services. Together they issued a new plan for introducing the students to collegiate life with advising occurring solely by faculty in the first year and solely by professional advisors until the student applies and is accepted into a major. This new plan is based on the 1599 Jesuit "Plan of Studies" called the Ratio Studiorum. It utilizes faculty preceptors and decurions (junior and senior peer academic leaders) within a one-credit graded course, RSP 100 "Introduction to the Culture of Collegiate Life." In the second year, RSP 200 "Discernment and Decision" utilizes professionally trained premajor advisors and beadles (student liaisons for the majors).

One of the program's stated goals is to increase student awareness of and appreciation for diversity. This goal is integrated into the course objectives for RSP 100 as follows: "Students will engage in self-exploration and self-discovery, including awareness of and appreciation for their differences in ethnicity, gender, and socio-economic class." Since the College of Arts and Sciences already had in place the resources and partial funding for the Diversity Dialogues, the Ratio Studiorum program began with Diversity Dialogue dinners for the faculty preceptors (fifty seven) facilitated by the trainers in place. The same Diversity Dialogue dinners were held for the decurions. They were facilitated by the associate vice president of Student Learning (who had prior experience with Dr. White's model), the director of Multicultural Affairs, and the director of Counseling.

Although we have no formal results and plans are in place to assess the first year of the Ratio Studiorum program, the following anecdotes are worth mentioning. The associate vice president of Student Learning reports that the letters written to incoming freshman by the decurions contain attention to differences among students as experienced in the Diversity Dialogues. Some decurions express in their letters an understanding of the fears freshmen might face if they come from different ethnic and socioeconomic groups and try to reassure them that they are not alone in this experience. At the same time, the faculty preceptors have written the Ratio Studiorum planning board members emails thanking them for the Diversity Dialogue dinners, including a faculty member who formerly alleged that he would not participate in the programs of the new Diversity Project model.

The positive environment created among the faculty and students because of these Diversity Dialogue dinners and a deepening understanding of the process of discernment has led the Ratio Studiorum planning board to consider refocusing the students' first-year experience on the question "Who Am I?" but with attention to the multicultural, classed, and gendered differences that freshmen bring to college and will experience. The board is currently considering that the mandatory book read by freshman be one that emphasizes domestic diversity and enables self-exploration and self-discovery through this vehicle. While this may seem as a return to the conceptual model, it will be accompanied by many other experiences that will allow the student to dialogue and interact with difference.

After our experience in (originally) struggling to garner voluntary participation, a word about the use of applying appropriate benefits is in order. Rothman, Erlich, and Teresa (1981) argue that when individuals are provided appropriate rewards, this ultimately affects participation frequency and rates. These benefits/rewards can be instrumental and/or expressive. While instrumental rewards are those that provide *material* benefits to the participants, expressive rewards are more *psychologically* oriented. In applying these two types of benefits to Diversity Dialogues, it appeared that both instrumental and expressive rewards were applied with some success. Instrumental rewards have been acquired through participants learning how to promote student classroom interaction about diversity. Expressive benefits are seen in the promotion of conviviality among faculty participants through dinners and program activities. Yet until these rewards were explicitly acknowledged (versus expecting individuals to recognize them), the program was not seen as beneficial.

In addition to 2005–2006 becoming a year of more "grassroots" efforts to target pre-existing groups regarding diversity programming within the College of Arts and Sciences, there was also a much stronger move toward institutionalization within Creighton as a whole. In February 2006, Creighton's (all-university) Diversity Coordinating Committee held a forum on "Striving for a More Diverse Community," where one hundred thirty-five campus leaders from across all units of the university collaborated in working sessions. The goal for the day was to take the institutional priority of "creating a diverse human community of students, faculty, and staff" and begin to operationalize tactics and courses of action to achieve it in order to make diversity a permanent part of the Creighton culture.

This event was closely tied to current college initiatives in our move toward a more dialogic and interactional model in which Dr. Joseph White suggested the need for such a forum during one of his prior visits, and was one of two distinguished consultants (along with Dr. JoAnn Moody) who gave expert feedback on the tactics generated in the working sessions. Following the Diversity Forum, the tactics that were generated were combined and repeats were removed. The Diversity Coordinating Committee has thematized the strategies and has created action items for the president's cabinet. Thus, Dr. White's model of multiculturalism is informing the culture of Creighton as a whole, which will presumably only reinforce and strengthen the diversity program of the College of Arts and Sciences.

Lessons Learned

The difficulties originally encountered in advancing the revised Diversity Project on campus may be partially reflective of the Diversity Project Advisory Board's failures to advance diversity efforts more broadly. The revised Diversity Project emerges in a national environment where hostility or indifference to notions of inclusion and justice are celebrated. Indeed, in a supposedly "post-ethnic America" (see Hollinger, 1995), some analysts claim that minorities are no longer marginalized, yet articles in The Chronicle of Higher Education and popular media attest to the contrary. This climate raises concerns about the future "revolutionary" nature of the current diversity project, but especially affirms its necessity. This being the case, we close with lessons we have learned about garnering faculty involvement in diversity training.

During the Diversity Project's odyssey to integrate diversity into the Creighton College of Arts and Sciences curriculum and to create a more diversity-aware campus, it became evident that the implementation of diversity could not be achieved through the individual faculty members' willingness to change the university environment. Some faculty members, even those resistant to diversity projects, are willing, however, to participate when they are given resources and autonomy. The conceptual model, while relatively successful, in its early stages attracted mainly humanities and natural science faculty, and to a lesser extent females and tenured faculty. Without the "behind the scenes" recruitment, it remained unattractive to faculty members in the professional and social science divisions most in need of diversity training because of their interactions with diverse populations.

Because the conceptual model focused on disciplinary differences and generic diversity issues through the reading of texts, rather than self-reflective dialogues, it encouraged the development of interdisciplinary courses and resulted in curriculum changes that inevitably would not have a direct impact on the Creighton campus mainstream culture. This explains the Diversity Projects' need to move to the dialogical and interactional models. During this process the Diversity Project Advisory Board realized, after experiencing difficulties in getting the faculty to be involved in this process, that successful implementation of the dialogical model necessitates working with pre-existing college groups, giving formal presentations to established college entities, and making face-to-face appeals. Moreover, diversity can be integrated only with the institutionalization of diversity, the incorporation of student involvement, and assessment during the implementation process.

The conceptual component raises theoretical awareness of diversity. Pedagogical impact can be materialized through the organization of seminars empowering the faculty to include diversity in their offerings after having become more conversant and comfortable with the subject matter. Despite this conscious raising and these curriculum modifications, behavior changes must be integrated into the process through dialogue workshops, student/faculty interactions, and immersions if the campus culture is to change. Getting faculty to commit to the dialogic component is the most taxing feat; because of competing goods, social justice reasons alone do not suffice to foster the need for such engagement. Hence, rewards in the form of teaching credit on annual reviews, larger stipends associated with robust programs that integrate the dialogic component (e.g., Ratio Studiorum program), course releases, and immersion experiences are necessary in the initial phase of the implementation. The current national and intellectual climate that has sidelined diversity only makes it more imperative that we continue to raise awareness of, integrate, and question old and find new models of articulating diversity on our campuses so that our institutions of higher learning continue to be societal torches in tune with the realities of our world.

Notes

1. Departments are grouped in four broad divisions: humanities, natural sciences, social sciences, and professional.

2. For example, the first workshop objective was "Understand and apply appropriate norms for dialogic settings/groups." Thus, the corresponding assessment item was "I am able to understand the nature and scope of developing norms in the classroom;" the resulting self-reports were measured on a Likert scale from 1 to 5. Specifically, 1 = inadequately qualified, 2 = poorly qualified, 3 = adequately qualified, 4 = well qualified, 5 = excellently qualified, and 6 = don't know, no opinion.

References

Higher Learning Commission. (2003). *Engagement for service: The criteria for accreditation and operational indicators.* Retrieved December 20, 2004, from ncahigherlearningcommission.org/reconstructing/newcriteria/NewCriteria.pdf.

Hollinger, D. A. (1995). *Postethnic America.* New York: Basic Books.

Kuhn, T. S. (1967). *The structure of scientific revolutions.* Chicago: University of Chicago Press.

Rothman, J., Erlich, J. L., and Teresa, J. G. (1981). *Changing organizations and community programs.* Beverly Hills, CA: Sage.

Schlegel, J. P. (2000, September 15). *President's inaugural response: "Embracing the future together"* [online]. Retrieved December 30, 2004, from www.creighton.edu/President/Speeches/Inaugural.html.

White, J. (2004). *Browning of America.* Unpublished videotape; available through elmejia@uci.edu.

~

CHAPTER FOUR

Counseling Psychology at the University of Missouri-Columbia

The Development of an Integrative Multicultural Training Model

P. Paul Heppner, Helen A. Neville, and Lisa Y. Flores

For over two decades, counseling psychologists have articulated a number of paradigms to identify the key components of multicultural counseling competencies and aspects to promote these competencies in training programs (e.g., American Psychological Association, 2003; Manese, Wu, and Nepomuceno, 2001; Ponterotto, Alexander, and Grieger, 1995; Ponterotto and Casas, 1987; Sue et al., 1998). These frameworks have helped provide useful guidelines for programs in their efforts to train new professionals to attend to the changing diverse landscape of the United States. The University of Missouri-Columbia's (MU) counseling psychology training program has been influenced by the growth of the multicultural psychology movement, and that has gradually transformed its program from a Eurocentric paradigm to a multicultural model. The counseling psychology program at MU, continuously accredited since 1953, is one of the oldest counseling programs in the country. The program is located in a large Midwestern land-grant university that is situated in the central region of a primarily rural state, and is approximately one hundred twenty-five miles from two large urban cities. Although it is within commuting distance to these bigger cities, the university is located in a community that is isolated from an urban environment and that reflects little of the racial/ethnic diversity among its residents.

In this chapter we address the successes and challenges of MU's adoption of an Integrative Multicultural Training Model (IMTM), from Pre-Awareness (pre-1980) to Awareness (mid-1980s to early 1990s) to Action (mid-1990s to the present). As depicted in Figure 4.1, we see the development of the multicultural training program being influenced by a number of interactive factors, such as (a) departmental, university, and American Psychological Association (APA) support; (b) student and faculty multicultural interests and skills; all leading to (c) curricular, environmental, and policy change. These outcomes then subsequently affect the future recruit of multiculturally oriented students and faculty, and additional multicultural developments. Although we will present these factors individually, it is important to note that change was not a simple linear process, but rather a multidetermined bidirectional process. For example, both university and departmental support lead to successful recruitment of a critical mass of both students and faculty of color and multicultural allies, which in turn affected our training model; in addition, the training model, environment, and policy changes also then lead to the subsequent recruitment of more students and faculty committed to multicultural issues.

The road from Pre-Awareness to Action has been a long and challenging yet rewarding process that has spanned well over three decades. Our journey to the creation and implementation of an IMTM is intricately tied to the political conditions of our country and the developments of the field of psychology, and specifically the emergence and prominence of multicultural issues in psychology. Through self-initiation and institutional support, our work dovetailed and built upon the aforementioned external factors to radically transform our program from a traditional "color-blind" program that ignored or minimized diversity issues to one that systematically trains students to be multiculturally competent scientist practitioners.

The early years of the program reflected the larger discipline of psychology, and counseling psychology more specifically. The program faculty was primarily white men and the student body lacked diversity in terms of race and gender. Because of the lack of diversity in the faculty and student body in the program, and the limited inclusion of race and multicultural scholarship in texts, there was little attention to multicultural issues in the curriculum and training. There was little awareness of multicultural issues, little support for multicultural training, and little sensitivity for the difficulties experienced by the few racial ethnic minority students in the program during this time. Gay, lesbian, bisexual, and transgender (GLBT) issues were not widely accepted and were sometimes viewed as abnormal or deviant as was the norm across the country during this period. In sum, prior to the 1980s the program was the prototypic counseling psychology program of the time, demonstrating little awareness of, and commitment to, diversity issues.

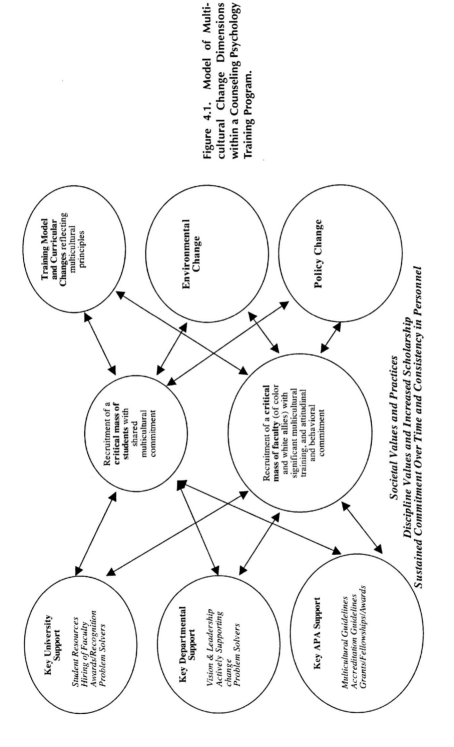

Figure 4.1. Model of Multicultural Change Dimensions within a Counseling Psychology Training Program.

An Integrative Multicultural Training Model

Strong Principled Leadership

Although we are not promoting hierarchical structures that solely rely on one or two figureheads, we recognize that vision and support from key leadership positions are needed to provide guidance and direction in the process of creating a strong multicultural training program. This requires leaders who are willing to be unpopular at times and remain principled in their fight to foster the necessary change. For example, departmental leadership that were supportive of and personally active in enhancing the program's diversity efforts greatly facilitated changes in faculty composition, student recruitment, curricular revisions, acquisition of space and other resources, as well as fostered a safe environment reflecting that support for diversity issues were instrumental. Administrative leadership also assisted in the merger of faculty housed in separate departments and colleges into one department, which increased the number of voices supporting diversity issues, and a critical mass then led to additional curriculum and training changes. Without guidance and unwavering commitment from a program director and/or department chair, it is unlikely that an integrated multicultural training model can be achieved.

Critical Mass of Committed Diverse Faculty

A large part of the impetus for change and innovation came from establishing a critical mass of multiculturally competent and committed faculty. For example, beginning in the early 1990s, six new faculty were hired: one white man and five women. The women (three white, one Chinese, one African American) were among the first substantial wave of women faculty hires and were the first international and U.S. racial ethnic minority hires. All six new hires brought an enhanced understanding of race, ethnicity, culture, gender, sexual orientation, and multicultural issues. Moreover, the new hires were able to effectively share their knowledge to promote the development of multicultural competencies with other faculty.

In 1998, a major event in the history of the counseling psychology program was the administrative integration of the counseling psychology faculty from the two sides of the joint training program into the department housed in the College of Education. This merger facilitated a number of outcomes; for the purpose of this chapter, the most important outcomes resulted in the increase in the number of voices supporting diversity issues, in essence a critical mass, which then led to additional curriculum and training changes.

In the past ten years, six faculty of color were added (three African Americans, two Latina/os, one Asian). Four of the latter hires were especially critical because they occurred during a period of budget cuts across the university; all of these hires were the result of creative leadership at the department chair level who negotiated new faculty lines and jointly funded positions, in conjunction with a great deal of support from the upper-level university administrators. As mentioned above, our developmental path has not always been linear. In both 1996 and 2000, for example, we took big steps backwards as an Asian assistant professor and an African American associate professor were lost to other institutions. This happened in large part due to the institution's inability to effectively solve spousal accommodation issues, underscoring the key role of university administrators in recruiting and retaining faculty of color.

With the diversification of faculty, the teaching, research, and training were broadened and deepened to reflect the multiple perspectives needed by counseling psychologists today. In addition, it was critical to have allies within the unit and on campus that supported and adopted similar viewpoints. In sum, a diverse faculty, most of who are committed to the broad mission of multicultural training, can assist in creating a new and continued mission for the program and recruiting a diverse student body.

Committed Diverse Student Body

Over the past fifteen years, the program slowly increased its emphasis on achieving a balance of diversity among students recruited into the program and changed its recruitment strategies to attract students who were interested and committed to the program's mission of training multiculturally competent professionals. Moreover, in 2000 we revised our doctoral application materials to evaluate the extent of cultural and diversity experiences related to various societal groups among doctoral applicants; and in 2005, the faculty adopted a training values statement that students are required to read and approve prior to entering the program that outlines the program's stance on diversity training. Subsequently, in the past seven years, 50 percent of the doctoral students represented a range of diversity, including racial or ethnic minority (25 percent), international (20 percent), and/or self-identified GLBT or students with disabilities (5 percent). Our recruitment strategies were significantly expanded during this time to include (a) repeated three- to five-day recruitment trips to historically black and Latino/a-serving institutions that were financially supported by the Graduate School dean and the department; (b) identifying and working with McNair Scholars and similar undergraduate research opportunity programs for students of color or first-generation college students interested in counseling psychology, and encouraging their application to our program; (c) recruitment of faculty and students at national conferences, especially culturally focused conferences such as the Winter Roundtable and the National Latino Psychological Association; and (d) networking with colleagues across the nation who have talented students seeking training that is consistent with our training goals. In 2003, three of our faulty (one white and two faculty of color) received a CEMRATT grant from the American Psychological Association to establish a program that provided mentoring, research experience, and professional socialization to Latino/a students interested in graduate study in counseling psychology, demonstrating another effort on the part of the program to increase the pipeline of counseling psychology graduate students of color at MU.

From our journey, we have learned that students are invaluable in the change process in a number of important ways, including (a) working with faculty to identify the strengths and areas of growth of the program's multicultural training, (b) playing a key role in helping faculty further develop its multicultural training mission, (c) helping to recruit the next cohort of diverse students and allies (e.g., completing recruitment trips, hosting students during campus visits, etc.), and (d) initiating and creating learning opportunities (e.g., starting an informal reading or film group). We have found it helpful to first establish a safe, collaborative learning environment, one that nurtures dissention and difficult dialogue between and within both faculty and students, and one that promotes and supports student initiatives. In essence, as more diverse students entered the program, the diverse students had an influence on the multicultural development of the faculty as well as the training program in general.

Multicultural Training Vision
Although the description of the growth of our training program initially may seem haphazard, there was some method to our efforts. In the Awareness phase of the program development, we provided faculty and students structured opportunities to reflect on our multicultural training and practice. For example, we established a Diversity Committee that assessed our multicultural training and climate and provided recommendations for enhancing our training efforts. We also addressed these issues during faculty retreats, and we held town hall meetings for both students and faculty on the topic. The changes in the faculty composition and interest areas in our program and in the field's depth of knowledge about multicultural training models helped us to create a more comprehensive and concrete mission. Through this reflec-

tion process, we were able to enter the Action stage in our development. One characteristic that differentiated the Action phase from the Awareness phase was the creation of a roadmap that helped guide us in our continued efforts to actualize our training objectives. Without clearly articulated short-term and long-range goals and objectives that were established through consensus, it would have been impossible to create an integrated model. Our training mission and the IMTM is not static; it is ever evolving to reflect the changing nature of our program, the field, and larger society. For example, in part due to some student value conflicts, two faculty (one white and one faculty of color) in the past year led the faculty in the development of a program values statement that all students sign upon entry into the program to underscore the importance of respect for individual differences. Likewise, in response to students' request for seminars on specific topics in the multicultural area, we developed a yearly specialty seminar series; the first seminar will be Native American Psychology.

Supportive, Culturally Sensitive, and Congruent Environment
The program holds the belief that it is not enough to admit students; it is also imperative to create a safe learning environment and to train students in areas that might be personally relevant to them as well as broaden their general understanding of the cultural richness in the United States and internationally. A number of structural events and programs have been implemented to foster a supportive, culturally sensitive, and congruent atmosphere for all students. First, the curriculum has been infused with multicultural perspectives. For example, in the past seven years we offered thirteen stand-alone diversity courses with some new additions such as multicultural counseling competencies, feminist therapy, applied multicultural interventions, and career development theories for women. Moreover, multicultural knowledge, awareness, and skill development are now central in at least fifteen courses and more thoroughly infused in foundation courses, such as the introductory counseling psychology course, introductory and advanced clinical assessment, ethical and professional issues, and career counseling. And perhaps more importantly, the number of faculty with advanced multicultural skills has affected the conceptualization of our primary training goals; no longer are multicultural skills seen as a special tool, an "add-on" or "something nice to have," but rather as one of our program's four primary training goals. Students' comprehensive examinations now have multicultural competencies as the sole focus in one learning domain and are woven throughout the other six major areas of study as well. Moreover, given our predominantly white campus, we have developed a number of practica and other

applied experiences in the university setting and surrounding community to provide exposure and training in working with racial and ethnic minorities, international students, women, and GLBT individuals.

Another significant structural curriculum change was the creation of a graduate minor in multicultural psychology and education. The goals of the minor are to (a) enhance graduate students' knowledge of multicultural theoretical and empirical research, (b) promote graduate students' development of multicultural competencies in research and practice, and (c) enhance graduate students' skills with training necessary to meet the psychological and educational demands of diverse populations. In essence, the minor not only serves to motivate students to acquire a deeper understanding of multicultural issues, but is also a reward for those who completed advanced study in this area.

In addition, the program also provides a host of other learning opportunities outside of formal courses related to multicultural issues, such as (a) colloquium speakers who address multicultural topics; (b) an international student support group, developed and lead by students within our program; (c) a language partners program, created by one of our doctoral students several years ago, which pairs international students with U.S. students, faculty, and staff to practice English language skills; (d) diversity-related research teams, where students and faculty work together on research projects that contribute to the multicultural literature; (e) brown bag seminars that offer students the opportunity to discuss cultural diversity issues important to research, theory, practice consultation, and professional development; and (f) multicultural events that offer students opportunities to discuss diversity and cultural issues as well as to strengthen their multicultural interests and skills. For example, the Graduate Student Network, our department graduate student organization, has instituted a multicultural committee that organizes and executes several multicultural events each semester, such as a multicultural film series and informal multicultural discussions lead by senior students to talk about the developmental process of becoming multicultural competent. In short, the program views retention as a critical activity and directly related to recruitment (that is, if our students are satisfied with their training, they are a major asset to our recruitment of other students).

In addition to expanding the curriculum and establishing a multicultural minor, we were interested in further institutionalizing our practice while increasing our efforts to provide systematic and integrative multicultural training experience for students. In 1998, two faculty members (one person of color and one white faculty) founded the Center for Multicultural Research, Training and Consultation. With the support of the department chair in 2001, the center was given space to house its activities and formalize its identity. As of this writing, the center is directed by two faculty members (one person of color and one white faculty), one associate director (a faculty of color), three faculty associates (three faculty of color), and two advanced doctoral students serving as assistant directors (students of color or international students). Through the years, the center has provided students with a broad array of multicultural training opportunities. For example, in the past three years the center has negotiated with university programs and outside agencies to fund up to twelve graduate student assistantships each semester; these assistantships allow students to practice and hone a wide range of multicultural skills. One example of these assistantships is with Academic Retention Services at MU where students work to promote retention efforts of racial/ethnic minority undergraduate students by conducting workshops and support groups aimed at a host of psychosocial issues experienced by students of color on a predominately white campus, as well as academic advising. In another example, university administrators have provided funds for our graduate students to lead support groups for international students, to offer an undergraduate diversity awareness class as well as American Sign Language courses, and to establish a new university service agency (International Students Career Services) to provide a wide array of career counseling services for international students. In addition, the center provides a host of other services, such as (a) multicultural consultations and workshops in the public schools; (b) multicultural research opportunities for students; (c) financial support to sponsor students to attend the Winter Roundtable at Teachers College, Columbia University; (d) sponsoring a MU Multicultural Speaker Series where nationally recognized multicultural scholars are brought to campus for two to three days to interact with our faculty and students and share their expertise; and (e) thesis/dissertation financial awards to support students' multicultural research. Finally, in 2005 and 2006 the center was influential in promoting the UM establishment of formal relationships with universities in Taiwan and China. Subsequently, in 2005 the center hosted fourteen graduate students from Taiwan in a cross-cultural immersion program; similarly in 2007, the center will organize a cross-cultural immersion trip to Taiwan for our graduate students and faculty interested in learning about professional counseling in a different cultural context. In short, the center has become an umbrella for many important multicultural research, training, and consultation training activities that involve many of our graduate students.

Institutional Support

MU is not alone among other universities in terms of the potential opportunities that exist at the institutional level to help implement a comprehensive multicultural training model. Throughout our developmental process, we established strong, stable relationships with key individuals and units on campus that have supported our mission. The combination of the vision and commitment of our leaders, faculty, and students coupled with institutional support significantly facilitated changes in the program's development in multicultural issues and training. For example, we created tangible support in collaboration with allies across campus (e.g., graduate research assistant positions, practicum training opportunities), which was critical in extending our applied training experiences in a predominantly white campus environment. In addition, in the late 1980s MU hired a new Graduate School dean who was committed to increasing racial and ethnic diversity on campus as demonstrated in his ability to secure funds to create (a) a number of competitive fellowships for racial and ethnic minority graduate students and (b) an active campus visitation recruitment plan for attracting racial and ethnic minority students to campus. Working closely with this dean's initiatives greatly facilitated our recruitment success. Moreover, the Graduate School dean was very helpful in problem solving difficult issues that we encountered in our recruitment efforts (e.g., securing competitive fellowship offers, spousal accommodation issues for students we were recruiting) and other obstacles (e.g., color blindness in admission criteria, differing worldviews of faculty) we encountered within the university. In essence, by having a vision we were able to work with university leaders and units to help us problem solve and achieve the type of support needed to implement an IMTM.

Entering the Campus, Community, and National Discourse

In the past seven years, nearly all of our faculty have published on diversity issues, most of which were coauthored with students, and they have consistently copresented on diversity-related issues with students at national conferences. Such coauthorship reflects both the diversity of training students are receiving as well as the students' multicultural achievements.

In addition, several of our faculty have grants that fund diversity-related research programs that provide important research training and graduate assistantships for our students; they have also elevated the program's multicultural contributions to the broader campus and the city and state levels through these visible projects. We will briefly highlight two such programs: one program centering on improving the educational outcomes of primary and secondary youth and the other a campus climate assessment.

One of our African American associate professors has been involved since 1999 in the program development, implementation, assessment and evaluation of the GEAR UP MU REACH Project (a seven-year $2.75 million school-based intervention program funded by the U.S. Department of Education), the Columbia PEAK Project (a four-year after-school community church-based tutor/mentor program), and the PEAK Institute (a training model for developing after-school programs). As a means to promote social justice and advocacy, each program has sought to serve low-income African American underachieving students attending public schools from grades 4 through 12, primarily in Kansas City, Columbia, and St. Louis. These programs have provided more than sixty-five assistantships for more than thirty-five to forty graduate students and other opportunities for over one hundred undergraduate students to develop a multicultural community-based approach to interventions with low-income African American students and effective collaboration with community and school systems. For example, as a part of the MU REACH and Columbia PEAK Projects, graduate students learned how to develop and adapt program services and interventions in a culturally appropriate manner to address critical academic, social, career, and cultural needs of low-income African American students. In the PEAK Institute, graduate students served as facilitators and trained over two hundred schoolteachers, counselors, and administrators to develop an effective after-school program using student-centered approaches to teaching and learning. As a part of the Columbia PEAK Project, undergraduate students primarily from the MU teacher education program served as tutor/mentors and developed effective cross-cultural interaction skills in the process of tutoring low-income African American students. The undergraduate students, mostly white females in the teacher education program, reported an increase in awareness, sensitivity, knowledge, and skills in working with African American students. Throughout the GEAR UP MU REACH Project, graduate students consistently expressed a sense of shock and disbelief about the quality of education received by African American students in the public school system, which has led to some students being motivated to become involved with their local school district, board, and system.

During the 1999–2000 academic year, a small group of faculty, graduate students, and professional staff began planning a comprehensive assessment of the campus climate for diversity at MU with regard to six groups: women, people of color, GLBT individuals, nonnative English speakers, persons with disabilities, and non-Christian religious minorities. One of our Latino faculty, an assistant professor at the time, became the principal investigator providing leadership to the group across the five phases of data collection and dissemination from nearly six thousand faculty, staff, students, and administrators at MU. The findings were prepared and disseminated in three volumes containing nearly five hundred pages of findings and information to top-level administrators across campus (including the chancellor's staff, the provost's staff, the deans' council, Student Affairs directors, and others). Findings from the research were integrated into the long-term diversity strategic planning for the university, and helped win the university a prestigious Ford Foundation grant under the Difficult Dialogues Initiative (again under the direction of the Latino faculty member). Moreover, the outstanding performance of the Latino faculty member led to a fellowship in the Office of the Deputy Chancellor to assist in the design and implementation of the diversity strategic plan for MU and he was subsequently appointed into the newly created chief diversity officer role.

These funded initiatives also provide a wealth of opportunities for our doctoral students to be involved in writing grant proposals and conducting research and service delivery with diverse populations; over the past seven years, a little over four out of ten of our doctoral students were involved in grant-funded research. All of these training opportunities have made our students highly marketable. For example, two-thirds of our racial and ethnic minority students and international students have taken faculty positions in universities in the United States and abroad, which we believe is perhaps one of the best ways of promoting the generation of MU's IMTM as these students then go on to build on what they learned here to train the next generation of counseling students.

Patience, Creative Problem Solving, and Persistence
Change is a long, slow process. For example, the transformation from Pre-Awareness to our current phase in the Action stage was a two-decade-long process. Through the process we had a number of significant critical turning events in the advancement of multicultural training (e.g., creation of fellowships, hiring of faculty) and at the same time we experienced a number of setbacks in the process (e.g., loss of key faculty, difficulty in obtaining suitable space to house the Multicultural Center). We have been able to make the type of sustained changes in our IMTM by (a) believing that the actualization of our larger training mission is possible and will be achieved over time, (b) remaining resolved to achieve the goals and objectives we have established, and (c) maintaining a focus even in the face of temporary challenges and stumbling blocks.

Conclusion

The MU counseling psychology program has gone through many significant changes in the past twenty-five years to enhance the multicultural training of the program. In essence, a number of distal (e.g., larger societal views about diversity, political movements, discipline-specific developments) as well as proximal (e.g., institutional polices and resources) factors affected the development of our training program. The cumulative effect over time of the factors depicted in Figure 4.1 has significantly affected the multicultural development of the MU counseling psychology program; however, the synergy of the interactive and bidirectional effects has allowed us to make the most significant and far-reaching multicultural changes in our program. Thus, we view our development as a training program as constantly changing and evolving and as one that requires a continued commitment to sustain our training goals. Whatever directions we pursue in the future, we are certain that our multicultural journey will contain joys and challenges as we continue to evolve, grow, and learn more about the different levels of multicultural training.

References

American Psychological Association. (2003). Guidelines on multicultural education, training, research, and practice, and organizational change for psychologists. *American Psychologist, 58,* 377–402.

Manese, J. E., Wu, J. T., and Nepomuceno, C. A. (2001). The effect of training on multicultural counseling competencies: An exploratory study over a ten-year period. *Journal of Multicultural Counseling and Development, 29,* 31–41.

Ponterotto, J. G., and Casas, J. M. (1987). In search of multicultural competence within counselor education programs. *Journal of Counseling and Development, 65,* 430–34.

Ponterotto, J. G., Alexander, C. M., and Grieger, I. (1995). A multicultural competency checklist for counseling training programs. *Journal of Multicultural Counseling and Development, 23,* 11–20.

Sue, D. W., Carter, R. T., Casas, J. M., Fouad, N. A., Ivey, A. E., Jensen, M., et al. (1998). *Multicultural counseling competencies: Individual and organizational development.* Thousand Oaks, CA: Sage.

~

CHAPTER FIVE

Alliant International University, Los Angeles

An Antidomination Paradigm Shift in the Training of Community-Clinical Psychologists

Carlton W. Parks Jr.

Ethnically and culturally diverse individuals are seeking culturally informed clinical services as the population in the United States shifts toward greater diversity. These individuals bring to treatment their cultural values, attitudes, and alternative belief systems concerning medicine as well as the healing process based on their diverse cultural backgrounds. Although progress has been made within the past several decades, it is clear that mainstream clinical psychology is still ill-equipped to provide large enough numbers of students with the necessary skills to provide culturally informed services.

The focus of this chapter is to propose an alternative model for training multicultural community-clinical psychologists in a manner that departs from the Eurocentric paradigm still dominating much of mainstream clinical psychology training. This particular model is unique given the inclusion of multicultural feminist theory, which has been neglected within graduate education in psychology. The antidomination principles of feminist theory (Brown, 1993) as well as the values and key concepts of community psychology (Brown, 1995) serve as the foundation for the paradigm shift that will hopefully occur during community-clinical psychology training and continue during the students' professional careers. Examples are the ecological levels of analysis, small wins (Weick, 1986), and multicultural community consultation. By forming long-term coalitions through their training with like-minded individuals with different worldviews, students become equipped to experience the different realities of ethnic and culturally diverse populations.

Antidomination Training Model

Assumptions

There are several assumptions that are at the foundation of this alternative training model (Brown, 1993). First, all members of our society, including those from the targeted group, are the products of an oppressive bias that impacts individuals affectively, behaviorally, as well as cognitively. Second, members of the dominant groups will make assumptions, and may take actions that presume the superiority of their own reference group over the minority group. Members of minority groups who are products of traditional training institutions frequently learn to collude, in their own oppression, through the expression of similar mainstream attitudes and actions. Third, challenging this pervasive bias is a constant. No one is ever fully finished with that process. Fourth, since this oppressive bias is expressed cognitively, affectively, as well as behaviorally, the biases must be addressed along these same dimensions. Finally, these unchecked biases interfere with the competent delivery of psychological services.

In these ways, antidomination training is a secondary intervention/prevention strategy that focuses upon the student's awareness and potential for change with respect to oppression and domination. These revelations can be painful and emotionally upsetting for students as the process unfolds. The beginning-level coursework therefore provides a supportive environment for students to embark upon this process and develops long-term coalitions with like-minded individuals that will hopefully last throughout their professional careers.

The Multicultural Community-Clinical Psychology (MCCP) Emphasis Area faculty strongly asserts that this perspective is critical in the development of culturally informed multicultural community-clinical psychologists. All of the training experiences are designed to reinforce this perspective as well as initiate the process of continual introspection within students enrolled in community-clinical psychology training that will hopefully result in either embracing substantive change, rather than maintaining and supporting the status quo with respect to the "isms" that persist in the communities we live and work in. One eventual goal of this process is that professionals will choose to live and advocate in the communities that they work in (Nelson, 1995).

Recruitment of Administrators, Faculty, Staff, and Students
The MCCP faculty has committed itself to training students who are increasingly aware of and sensitive to the intersections of race, gender, and sexual orientation as it expresses itself in individuals with multiple minority identities resulting in multiple oppressions. The students' keen awareness of multicultural feminism, as espoused by bell hooks (2000), has served as a catalyst for this growing commitment. bell hooks (1994) views education in the age of multiculturalism as a means of teaching the practice of freedom to disempowered individuals. In many respects, this is the primary function of community-clinical psychologists working with oppressed and stigmatized populations.

Along these lines, we have a growing appreciation of the presence of health disparities that exist in our society heavily and negatively influenced by race and socioeconomic status. Such realities foster a renewed commitment to training multicultural urban community health psychologists. Several MCCP faculty members have professional interest in multicultural urban community health psychology and are committed to training MCCP students in community-clinical psychology to become multiculturally competent health care professionals. The training models for training mental health professionals and health care professionals have considerable overlap (American Institutes of Research, 2002; Tervalon and Murray-Garcia, 1998). Recruitment of new MCCP faculty always seeks to build upon existing strengths within the Emphasis Area while simultaneously striking out into new training directions. At the cornerstone of the MCCP Emphasis Area faculty recruitment process is the documentation that applicants have behaviorally demonstrated their adoption of the antidomination philosophy in their professional activities in previous community agency settings.

The hiring, retention, and promotion of administrators, faculty, and staff need to involve individuals who genuinely reflect the current training program philosophy. In this respect, MCCP Emphasis Area faculty has committed themselves to this program training philosophy within the context of a much larger training program that is sensitive to the hiring, retention, and promotion of administrators and staff that are ethnically and culturally diverse.

Four characteristics that can guide the recruitment process include (1) valuing and recruiting applicants with previous life experiences working with oppressed populations; (2) recruiting applicants with diverse worldviews, attitudes/beliefs; (3) the recruitment of applicants with an awareness and appreciation of the antidomination paradigm; and (4) the recruitment of applicants with the ability to be thoughtful, reflective, and introspective about the world around them that directly impacts their overt and covert behaviors.

The ultimate goal here is to develop a critical mass of administrators, fac-ulty, staff, and students that form the core of the educational climate of the MCCP training program (Porsche-Burke, 1990, 1991; Olmedo, 1990). Pro-fessionals in training clearly benefit from continual interactions with ethni-cally and culturally diverse administrators, staff, faculty, and student col-leagues. Such interactions within an educational environment provide the arena for students to confront and challenge their biases, myths, and stereo-types about ethnic and culturally diverse populations separate and distinct from the clinical context. These interactions can also serve as a foundation for the clinical experiences that these students will encounter within the clinical arena.

Turning to the recruitment of students, there are inevitable tensions when one embarks upon the adoption of a nontraditional student admissions process. One such tension is often the tendency to place more weight upon traditional indices (e.g., standardized test scores, high GPAs, and matriculation at elite mainstream institutions). Instead, MCCP Emphasis Area faculty value nontra-ditional criteria (e.g., letters of recommendation from minority professionals, previous life and professional experiences within oppressed communities, com-mitment to serving the underserved demonstrated by sustained involvement within oppressed communities), although the latter can be perceived as being too "subjective." The MCCP Emphasis Area faculty finds these nontraditional criteria reflective of early endeavors into multiculturalism.

There are continual tensions concerning the adoption of traditional ver-sus nontraditional admissions criteria. Core faculty become more comfort-able with the use of nontraditional admissions criteria once they have seen several cohorts complete the program and enter the field. The development of "feeder institutions" has successfully provided the community-clinical doc-toral training program with candidates that are prepared to embark upon community-clinical psychology training (e.g., Historically Black Universi-ties, Predominantly Hispanic Serving Colleges and Universities). The cre-ation of alumni evenings where the alumni return to campus to interact with current students serves to empower students, faculty, and administrators con-cerning the efficacy of the program training philosophy. This is one potential outcome indicator to demonstrate the efficacy of a training program's admis-sions policies that can be included in ongoing institutional research data be-ing collected to evaluate the efficacy of the training program.

Curriculum

One of the outgrowths of program training philosophy is a curriculum that is multidisciplinary and cuts across the following topics: (a) community psychology, (b) multicultural social work, (c) developmental, (d) cognitive, (e) social, (f) counseling, (g) school psychology, (h) ethnic studies, (i) feminist studies, (j) sociology, and (k) community-clinical psychology. This multidisciplinary training is designed to cement the cognitive-affective-behavioral linkages through the use of didactic material as well as experiential training into the training process. The multidisciplinary nature of the curriculum also permits the incorporation of diverse worldviews into the predoctoral training experience. Most importantly, this multidisciplinary curriculum provides the trainee with strategies to access their own cognitive-affective-behavioral linkages, which can be extremely powerful for the student. Eventually, these linkages can be applied to the clinical arena when working with ethnically and culturally diverse clients (Walker, Wright, and Hanley, 2001).

Antidomination training is initiated during the first year in a yearlong course entitled Intercultural Processes/Human Diversity, which consists of both didactic as well as experiential coursework. This course is designed to serve as a catalyst for the first-year student to embark upon a lifelong process of introspection through role plays, journal entries, videos, and experiential exercises where students begin delving into their own biases and attitudes toward ethnic and cultural groups in a relatively safe environment where they can be vulnerable. Interactions with ethnically and culturally diverse students with multiple worldviews are an essential ingredient for substantive change to occur (Karumanchery, 2005). Students need to become aware of and able to manage their biases and attitudes toward racially and culturally different groups within professional contexts.

Two other courses, Seminar in Community-Clinical Issues as well as MCCP advanced clinical elective courses, provide students with the knowledge and skills necessary to facilitate their ability to conduct culturally informed work with oppressed populations based on MCCP values, theories, and methodologies. The potential abuse of power in the hands of a professional psychologist in their interactions with oppressed populations is ever present. Community-clinical training equips MCCP students to appreciate and address the potential abuse of power that psychologists must contend with on a daily basis and how to use their power in a more judicious manner. These courses are designed to set the stage for lifelong introspection among the faculty and studies concerning the judicious use of power as a professional psychologist.

Training in multicultural community consultation and community-based applied clinical research provides an additional layer of skills and techniques grounded in community psychology theory and methodologies that assist the community-clinical psychology trainee with the ability to empower oppressed populations. The goal of this training is to educate the trainee to relinquish the role of "expert" and instead embrace the paradigm shift associated with the adoption of the role of "consultant" within the contexts of community-based organizations. The applied clinical research consultant, based on a local clinical scientist model, seeks to ascertain the most optimal match between the research questions, generated typically by community leaders, and the methodologies that will yield ecologically valid data that will be of value to the community organizations and neighborhoods seeking answers to complex social problems (Nelson, 1995; Trierweiler and Stricker, 1992). The multicultural community consultation trainee receives training in program development and evaluation that empowers the trainee with the skills necessary to consult effectively with diverse organizations and neighborhoods desirous of substantive change at the group, organizational, and neighborhood levels.

Professional Field Training Experiences

Next, the combined didactic and professional field training experiences will assist the trainee with the abilities to interact with ethnically and culturally diverse populations who experience qualitatively different realities (Tinsely-Jones, 2001). The ability to hear and listen to these different realities is a major stepping-stone to effectively working clinically with ethnically and culturally diverse clinical populations within organizational settings.

Training in multicultural community consultation and community-based applied clinical research in the role of a local clinical scientist (Trierweiler and Stricker, 1992) serves to amplify the community-clinical psychology didactic training the trainee receives in the classroom. The goal of developing these distinct professional identities is to provide trainees with the skills necessary to serve as agents of social change. Trainees are then in a position to empower oppressed populations to address socially relevant problems through the implementation of "small wins" (Weick, 1986).

Similarly, professional field training experiences within a MCCP training program should provide the trainee with exposure to the full spectrum of psychiatric disorders. Professional field training in the diagnosis, assessment, and treatment of psychiatric disorders from a sociocultural/sociohistorical perspective is an essential component of community-clinical training. The careful selection and routine monitoring of these field training practicum and local internship sites need to occur to ensure that these settings reflect the core values and program training philosophy. There should be synchrony between the curriculum taught to trainees and the professional field training experiences they receive in the community. This goal can be accomplished by having the clinical supervisors become an integral component of the clinical training faculty and impact the direction of the training philosophy.

For instance, a subset of the MCCP Emphasis Area faculty is dialoguing with MCCP Emphasis Area students concerning multicultural issues and how it directly impacts the supervision process. This process is slowly evolving and several MCCP faculty have coined the phrase, "nonoppressive" multicultural clinical psychology supervision. There are three issues that have risen to the surface that impacts the quality of the supervision process: (1) Sociodemographic characteristics (e.g. race, gender, ethnicity, sexual orientation identity status, and socioeconomic status) have the potential of becoming a barrier to the process. (2) How one perceives differences in race, gender, ethnicity, sexual orientation identity status, socioeconomic status, etc. and the accompanying interpersonal dynamics can be a potent predictor of a professional's ability to engage in multiculturally competent interactions. All parties within the supervision process need to be consciously aware of this reality and be willing to openly explore these issues. (3) How one chooses to use their power within the context of their professional activities becomes critical (Friere and Ramos, 2002; Jackman, 2001; Tucker and Herman, 2002; Sidanius et al., 2001). One can use their power to either (a) oppress their clients through projecting their biases/myths/stereotypes upon their clients/supervisees that results in differential treatment, or (b) to gain a keener appreciation of what it feels like phenomenologically to be perceived as being "different."

These issues among others are beginning to rise to the surface within the MCCP Emphasis Area, in particular, the negative impact of the power imbalances that are inherent within the supervisor-supervisee relationship. Not surprisingly, across MCCP students, it appears that the perceived safety to explore these issues within the supervision process varies as a function of the settings that are involved. Multicultural quality clinical psychology supervision is clearly a topic that the MCCP Emphasis Area is just beginning to grapple within the twenty-first century in the following ways: (a) within the context of dialogues between faculty and students, (b) within the context of advanced seminars in clinical practice, and (c) within the context of national presentations and the development of manuscripts exploring the issue. The dialogue continues.

Mentoring

Mentoring culturally and ethnically diverse students should be conceptualized from life-span developmental as well as systemic perspectives. The process begins at the point that the applicant expresses interest in the program until the graduate establishes his or her professional identity several years following graduation. The mentor plays a pivotal role (a) in addressing the academic matters involved in becoming a doctoral student, (b) in professional socialization of the student into the profession of community-clinical psychology, and (c) as a sounding board for a myriad of concerns that runs the spectrum (Walker, Wright, and Hanley 2001). Mentees' concerns need to be conceptualized from a systemic perspective since mentors need to remember that their interventions are never involving the mentee in a vacuum. Rather, the mentors' interventions directly or indirectly impact the lives of the mentees' families, friends, as well as the significant others.

Given these realities, mentors themselves need to be willing to embark upon periodic introspection with respect to issues, such as identity issues and their impact on the mentor's role with diverse students. Questions that may arise can include: How do the changing composition of entering cohorts and the biases/stereotypes that still exist within the mentor that may appear on the scene negatively impact the professional responsibilities of mentors involved with incoming cohorts of students? How can mentors, as a collective, provide dynamic culturally informed professional psychology training experiences that will simulate real-world professional experiences following graduation?

The primary goal of the mentor should be to create a nurturing and supportive environment for students that assists them in their professional growth and development as community-clinical psychologists. Similarly, mentors need to be equipped to embrace the considerable heterogeneity that exists within ethnically and culturally diverse students entering training in psychology in the twenty-first century. Problems, independent of locale, will routinely emerge onto the scene challenging the antidomination model training philosophy. Routine faculty retreats can serve to empower the core faculty to address these issues in a timely manner. Faculty retreats can also serve as a catalyst to launch new training initiatives that carry the program in new directions.

Conclusion

It is important to recognize that programs differ in their ability to address all of these issues within a short period of time. At the cornerstone of evolving a training program into an environment that is open and receptive to incorporating multiculturally diverse administrators, staff, faculty, and student body is the incorporation of a program training philosophy that is consonant with those intentions. The program training philosophy must become a vibrant part of all aspects of the training program. It is much more than a statement included in brochures and catalogs. It is a program philosophy that is operationalized behaviorally into all aspects of the program.

Next, a critical mass of individuals who embrace this philosophy need to be created based on recruitment as well as long-term coalitions with professionals across departments/schools/colleges (i.e., feeder institutions). Given the political climate of the department where a program is located, the time frame for progress to achieve these goals can vary considerably. Realistic goals and a timetable to achieve these goals are essential components of this type of endeavor.

Substantive progress can occur with respect to the adoption of an antidomination training program philosophy independent of the locale of the university setting: urban, rural, or suburban. The steadfast commitment of administration, faculty, and staff to adopting a paradigm shift is far more critical than the locale surrounding the program. Support from the professional psychology community including practitioners and potential clinical supervisors located within community agencies can be invaluable in facilitating this process.

Likewise, the development of professional ties with programs that are further along in the process of establishing an antidomination program philosophy can be invaluable. Through attendance at multicultural professional conferences as well as networking with professionals with expertise in training issues involving multiculturalism, such connections and consultations should be created and nurtured. Moreover, the utilization of organizational consultants who are specialists in human diversity issues can also be quite helpful in navigating a training program toward a desired developmental trajectory that launches a training program in a new direction.

Finally, these suggestions about transforming a community-clinical psychology doctoral training program also apply to other professional psychology training programs (e.g., counseling and school psychology training programs). The same issues and strategies are relevant to all professional psychology programs. Likewise, the same process is likely to unfold in professional psychologists' attempts to achieve their training goals. Other professional psychology programs that have embraced an antidomination program philosophy can be consultants and collaborators for a training program just beginning this process.

Given the marked changes in the ethnic composition of the general population throughout the United States, and the relatively small numbers of ethnic minority professionals who are trained in professional psychology at the doctoral level, there is a pressing need to begin thinking outside of the box concerning the strategies necessary to train culturally informed community-clinical psychologists. Community-clinical psychology trainers will need to highlight more prevention work (i.e., primary, secondary, and tertiary) as well as utilize ecological levels of analysis in their curriculum resulting in the implementation of assessment and interventions strategies aimed at the individual, couple, family, group, organization, and neighborhood levels (Nelson, 1995).

It is now clearly evident that "one size does not fit all" and this fact needs to be at the foundation of any work designed to implement psychological interventions for specific populations (Bailey, 2006; Johnson, 1993). Particular care needs to be taken to ensure through qualitative methodologies that sociocultural influences are woven into the fabric of the school/counseling/clinical psychology interventions that are disseminated into ethnic and culturally diverse communities. There is considerable work for community-clinical psychologists desirous of providing culturally informed psychological services to stigmatized and oppressed populations in the twenty-first century.

References

American Institutes of Research (2002). *Teaching cultural competence in health care: A review of current concepts, policies, and practices, synthesis report.* American Institutes of Research (AIR) for the Office of Minority Health, U.S. Department of Health and Human Services. Retrieved November 4, 2007, from www.omhrc.gov/assets/pdf/checked/em01garcia1.pdf.

Bailey, E. J. (2006). *Food choice and obesity in black America: Creating a new cultural diet.* Westport, CT: Praeger Publishers.

Brown, L. S. (1993). Anti-domination training as a central component of diversity in clinical psychology. *Clinical Psychologist 46,* 83–87.

———. (1995). Cultural diversity in feminist therapy: Theory and practice. In H. Landrine, (Ed.), *Bringing cultural diversity to feminist psychology: Theory, research, and practice* (pp. 143–62). Washington, D.C.: American Psychological Association.

Friere, P., and Ramos, M. B. (2002). *Pedagogy of the oppressed.* New York: Continuum Press.

hooks, b. (1994). *Teaching to transgress: Education as the practice of freedom.* New York: Routledge.

———. (2000). *Feminism is for everybody: Passionate politics.* Cambridge, MA: South End Press.

Jackman, M. R. (2001). License to kill: Violence and the legitimacy in expropriative social relations. In J. T. Jost and B. J. Major (Eds.), *The psychology of legitimacy: Emerging perspectives on ideology, justice, and intergroup relations* (pp. 437–67). New York: Cambridge University Press.

Johnson, E. H. (1993). *Risky sexual behaviors among African-Americans.* Westport, CT: Praeger Publishers.

Karumanchery, L. (Ed). (2005). *Engaging equity: New perspectives on anti-racist education.* Calgary, Alberta: Detselig Enterprises.

Nelson, J. (1995). Working with inner city tribes: Collaborating with the enemy or finding opportunities for building community. In L. Combrinck-Graham (Ed.), *Children in families at risk: Maintaining the connections* (pp. 3–31). New York: Guilford Press.

Olmedo, E. L. (1990). Minority faculty development: Issues in retention and promotion. In G. Stricker, E. Davis-Russell, E. Bourg, E. Duran, W. R. Hammond, J. McHolland, et al. (Eds.), *Toward ethnic diversification in psychology education and training* (pp. 99–104). Washington, D.C.: American Psychological Association.

Porche-Burke, L. (1990). Minority student recruitment and retention: Is there a secret to success? In G. Stricker, E. Davis-Russell, E. Bourg, E. Duran, W. R. Hammond, J. McHolland, et al. (Eds.), *Toward ethnic diversification in psychology education and training* (pp. 131–36). Washington, D.C.: American Psychological Association.

———. (1991). Ethnic minority issues in clinical training at the California School of Professional Psychology, Los Angeles. In H. F. Myers, P. Wohlford, L. P. Guzman, and R. J. Echemendia (Eds.), *Ethnic minority perspectives on clinical training and services in psychology* (pp. 111–16). Washington, D.C.: American Psychological Association.

Sidanius, J., Levin, S., Federico, C. M. and Pratto, F. (2001). Legitimizing ideologies: The social dominance approach. In J. T. Jost and B. J. Major (Eds.), *The psychology of legitimacy: Emerging perspectives on ideology, justice, and intergroup relations* (pp. 307–31). New York: Cambridge University Press.

Tervalon, M., and Murray-Garcia, J. (1998). Cultural humility versus cultural competence. *Journal of Health Care for the Poor and Underserved, 9*(2), 117–25.

Tinsely-Jones, H. A. (2001). Racism in our midst: Listening to psychologists of color. *Professional Psychology: Research and Practice, 32*(6), 573–80.

Trierweiler, S. J., and Stricker, G. (1992). Research and evaluation competency: Training the local clinical scientist. In R. L. Peterson, J. D. McHolland, R. J. Bent, E. Davis-Russell, G. E. Edwall, K. Polite, et al. (Eds.), *The core curriculum in professional psychology* (pp. 103–11). Washington, D.C.: American Psychological Association.

Tucker, C. M., and Herman, K. C. (2002). Using culturally sensitive theories and research to meet the needs of low-income African-American children. *American Psychologist, 57*(10), 762–73.

Walker, K. L., Wright, G., and Hanley, J. H. (2001). The professional preparation of African-American graduate students: A student's perspective. *Professional Psychology: Research and Practice 32*(6), 581–84.

Weick, K. (1986). Small wins: Redefining the scale of social issues. In E. Seidman and J. Rappaport (Eds.), *Redefining social problems* (pp. 29–48). New York: Plenum Press.

CHAPTER SIX

~

University of California, San Diego, Student Counseling Center

Training for Multicultural Competence—
A Different Way of Knowing

Samuel S. Park and Jeanne E. Manese

The development of multicultural competence involves a comprehensive approach in conceptualizing, teaching, and assessing competence (American Psychological Association [APA], 2003). Training programs play a critical role in the growth of culturally competent professionals and should therefore actively strive to meet the evolving standards for multicultural training and education (Ponterotto, 1998). This requires multidimensional "outside the box" thinking and application that includes *active* and *continuous* efforts for individual awareness, growth, and empowerment through diverse training experiences (Suzuki, McRae, and Short, 2001). In short, training for multicultural competence is a way of being.

The predoctoral internship at Psychological and Counseling Services (PCS), the student counseling center at the University of California, San Diego (UCSD), is an example of a training program that has aspired since its inception to meet these expectations. The program was developed from a community psychology model of service delivery (Aponte and Bracco, 2000) and a strong commitment to multiculturalism. The training program adheres to an integrative and multicultural approach in training interns, not only in the awareness and knowledge of multicultural competence, but also its active application across several levels of populations, staff, and settings. Initial research evidence suggests that the program's efforts to increase multicultural competence in internship training and maintain it after internship appear to have been effective (Manese et al., 2001; Park, 2002). In this chapter we present the internship training model at UCSD: its philosophy, current applications, and future aspirations.

The Philosophical Foundations of the UCSD Internship Program

From its inception in the 1970s, the foundations of the internship and PCS were built upon innovative forms of training and service delivery. Part of this nontraditional approach stemmed from the community-based composition of the university, which is comprised of multiple undergraduate colleges and the graduate school. Accordingly, PCS was "decentralized" across the campus, with staff housed and linked to the undergraduate college communities. This model of service delivery thus required an equally inventive and diverse approach to training. In its development, humanistic and developmental philosophies were emphasized along with consistently multicultural and multidisciplinary sources of leadership. The historically diverse leadership and multidisciplinary nature of the training directors at UCSD manifested important characteristics of collaboration, acknowledgment of the multifaceted nature of healing, and sought out to represent individual and group differences. Over the next three decades, the internship program has continued to provide innovative training opportunities and experiences (e.g., college/university consultation, teaching, community outreach, and supervision of peer educators). This model was developed with a philosophical base that included a (1) systems orientation, (2) developmental orientation, and (3) cultural orientation.

From the *systems* orientation, the training program was based on the belief that the relationship between a client's capacity for environmental settings and social systems was vital. This philosophy led to a program that integrated, along with the more "traditional" forms of clinical service (such as individual therapy and psychological assessment), numerous outreach, preventative, and consultative interventions to the community. Use of a *developmental* orientation in the training program has been another fundamental feature. With this orientation, interns are trained to conceptualize comprehensive treatment approaches that include a combination of individual and group interventions to facilitate adult development and integrate the client to his/her community. A recent example of this effort has been the counseling center's investment in the research and implementation of a community-based group intervention, called "Goals in Action," designed to enhance the academic success of "at-risk" college students through strength-based interventions based on multicultural competency and positive psychology principles (Singley and Manese, 2006).

Finally, the training program was designed from its beginning to help new professionals enhance sensitivity and respect for *human diversity* arising from gender, ethnic, and cultural membership. PCS has a long-standing history of participation in campus-centered efforts to increase cultural awareness and competence—efforts that are largely experiential to promote advocacy and attention to social justice.

The philosophical underpinnings of *systemic, developmental,* and *cultural* orientations utilized in the 1970s still stand as fundamental and relevant today in our work at UCSD, and serves as a model of a diversity-based training program at the university. Beginning in the 1980s, congruent with the increased attention to multicultural issues in psychology, PCS incorporated a more comprehensive training curricula emphasizing formal skill and knowledge development for multicultural competency in training modules, supervision, and *research* of the internship program. In addition, recruitment for more diverse staff and interns increased, support for "affirmative action" procedures grew, as did efforts to engage in community-based projects that involved social justice and systemic change. These program features, which from its inception was implicitly and explicitly "known" to be important within our agency, have been recommended by Ponterotto, Alexander, and Grieger, (1995) in their "multicultural competency checklist" for training sites.

Multicultural Competence and Integration

Through the integration of theory, research, and applied practice within a growing college/university system, the training program has evolved into one that incorporates multiculturalism into *all* aspects of training: direct services, supervision, outreach, consultation, and research. It is the essential and primary ingredient in our current overarching training model, referred to as the multicultural integrative practitioner (MIP) model (Lane, 1999). The MIP embraces four types of integration: (1) *multiculturalism*, where culture is viewed as a central component of human nature; (2) the integrative use of *multiple theoretical models*; (3) *personal/technical integration*, in which interventions are chosen according to the unique characteristics of the clinician and client; and (4) *conceptual integration*, a more formal process in which two or more models are blended, sometimes with synergistic results.

Within this model, it has been understood that competence in psychological practice requires tolerance, flexibility, and judgment to deal with the complexity that accompanies a multicultural approach (Sue, 2001). As such, our internship program has long-standing traditions in practice that include multiple professional roles and the use of "indigenous healers" with members of the university community. For example, in the early 1970s, one African American staff psychologist served as the advisor to a campus-based student organization of African American men, was a group leader of the campus support group Campus Black Forum, while at the same time saw many of the same African American students who solicited counseling. Other examples include our multifaceted work with many units within Student and Academic Affairs (e.g., Residence Life, Academic Deans, Provost offices, Athletics), where our clinical staff and interns serve as consultants for campus community-related matters, are essential resources during times of crisis, and often work in therapy with students with whom we interact in other settings. Within PCS and the internship program, these examples reflect what has always been "known" to us as an essential outreach strategy: to promote fluid relationships between our staff and the university community in order to facilitate exposure and utilization of our services.

For its time (in the 1970s), this method of fluid professional roles presented a "cutting-edge" approach to counseling and training. Yet it was not until the publication of the APA 2002 Ethics Code did it become explicit that "multiple relationships that would not reasonably be expected to cause impairment or risk exploitation or harm are not unethical" (APA, 2002). Thus, preceding explicit written policy, ethical standards within our agency and training program, particularly those related to multicultural competence, were developed and carried out through essentially a "different way of knowing."

Another aspect of our approach to implementing multiculturalism into our work with the community has been our use of "indigenous healers," which has been repeatedly identified as important in the multicultural counseling literature (Lee and Armstrong, 1995). PCS has a long-standing history of utilizing and supervising "peer counselors," our version of indigenous healers. The work of these counselors, who are active students at the university, provides valuable "native" services to the populations they serve. Consistent with the diversity of our campus, our peer counselor programs strive to meet the wide range of needs of our student population, ranging from wellness and substance-use programs, to diversity-driven programs that address the unique issues of our female and lesbian, gay, bisexual, transgender student populations. Supervised by our senior staff and interns, they not only provide our program with the "pulse" of the student perspective, but they offer outreach, preventive, and remedial services directly to their peers—providing a level of credibility and accessibility to students who may not be as open or comfortable speaking directly with our professional staff. Now the Guidelines on Multicultural Education, Training, Research, Practice and Organizational Change for Psychologists (APA, 2003) actually specify that which has been our working mode of operation from the earliest days of our training program's history: "Psychologists strive to apply culturally appropriate skills in clinical and other applied psychological practices."

Evaluating Training of Multicultural Competency in our Interns

How do we know that our efforts to positively impact interns in multicultural competence are effective? Our answer to this important question involves continuous self-assessment of our training of competency skills of both our interns and staff. Like the "outside the box" philosophy from which our training program evolved, the assessment of our program in training for multicultural competence has been equally ambitious. To this end, we (1) provide continuous feedback and learning opportunities to interns, (2) seek continuous feedback from interns on our training on multicultural competence, and (3) engage in research and evaluation to assess the effectiveness in our training.

Intern, Supervisor, and Program Evaluation

Throughout our program's history, an extensive evaluation process has been a key component in providing and receiving feedback to enhance both intern and program development in multicultural competence. A 360-degree model of evaluation is used for both interns and supervisors, as both are viewed as significant components in shaping the course of our training program.

Interns receive continuous formal written and verbal feedback regarding their multicultural competencies throughout the training year. Development in multicultural competencies across all areas of training are assessed and discussed. Interns in these meetings are also encouraged to provide written and verbal feedback to the supervisors and the training director. This process is viewed as essential in modeling open dialogue and exchange of ideas to promote growth in multicultural competence for all parties.

Like our community psychology model would suggest, multicultural evaluation also comes from multiple sources within the university system: student peer educators (whom the interns supervise throughout the year), participants from diversity-based outreach programs or forums facilitated by our trainees, and informally from representatives from student and academic affairs. In addition, interns receive feedback continuously from clients, and later utilize this information for a self-study report of their own growth as a multiculturally competent and integrative practitioner. We believe these comprehensive methods of intern evaluation provide a format where interns can gain *awareness* of their strengths and growth edges with regard to multicultural competence, and can ultimately utilize this information to work toward increasing both *knowledge* and *skills*.

Along with our efforts to provide interns continuous evaluation in their multicultural skills, the staff at PCS engage in ongoing assessment of their own competencies. Like our interns, senior clinical and support staff are continuously provided formal and informal feedback regarding their multicultural competencies from numerous sources: clients, students, supervisors, campus departments, and fellow staff. However, intern feedback is viewed as among the most valuable and critical pieces of information needed to assess the effectiveness of our training, and has resulted in positive changes to our program and agency.

Furthermore, while normally it is the domain of the licensed doctoral staff to provide continuing education for psychologists, the training program recognizes that our interns can bring aspects of multicultural competence that may be less developed among the existing clinical staff. We encourage our interns to provide educational and experiential training to our staff in areas for the intern's and our own continued development. One example of this effort was when an intern and his supervisor, recognizing the need for increased training in working with transgender populations, provided direct feedback and actively worked with the center to provide this invaluable training to our entire clinical staff. Thus, within our model of feedback, we adjust, adapt, and/or change aspects of our training that will enhance our multicultural training informally on a continuous basis and formally at the end of each training year.

Empirical Evaluation

Our efforts to engage in empirical study of our internship is central to our mission to critically self-assess the effectiveness of our training. Recent studies on our interns have indicated that our internship training program positively increases their multicultural competence, as well as having an impact on their application of it after their internship year. Manese, Wu, and Nepomuceno (2001) conducted a pretest and posttest study of twenty-four former interns from 1990 to 1999. Participants were asked to rate themselves at the beginning and end of their internship year across three dimensions of multicultural competence: knowledge, awareness, and skills (using the Multicultural Counseling Assessment Scale B; Ponterotto, Sanchez, and Magids, 1991). The results revealed that by the end of their internship year, interns showed a significant increase in multicultural knowledge and skills from when they began their internship.

A follow-up study on twenty-three former interns from 1990 to 2000 was conducted to assess their evaluations of the PCS internship program, as well as their current application of multicultural counseling principles in their current work settings (Park, 2002). Results indicated that interns rated our program high in overall effectiveness, contributed to their development as professionals, and rated our training in multicultural competence (didactic and experiential training experiences) the highest among our various areas of training.

To assess the extent to which our interns engaged in multicultural practices after internship, participants in the same study were asked to describe their application of multicultural counseling competencies in their current work in psychology. Based on the three-dimensional model of multicultural counseling proposed by Sue (2001), we sought to assess how much our former interns recognized the multidimensionality of identity (dimension 1 of Sue's model); engaged in actions that included the ongoing acquisition of multicultural awareness, knowledge, and skills (dimension 2); and how much their work includes attention to social justice (dimension 3). In addition, we examined what our interns believed were aspects of our training program that distinguished itself as one that emphasizes multicultural competence.

Intern responses to the statement related to the multidimensionality of identity (dimension 1) revealed that our former interns strongly support this concept and attempt to utilize it through a blending of emic and etic principles within their current work. More specifically, they acknowledge attending to both individual and reference group aspects of identity. In addition, interns all acknowledged engaging in activities for the ongoing acquisition of multicultural awareness, knowledge, and skills (dimension 2), which included continuing education through seminars, conferences, and research; clinical practice experiences with diverse populations; consultation with supervisors and colleagues; immersion experiences; and ongoing reflection and self-awareness. Their responses also revealed that a large majority acknowledge and/or report to engage in actions that address social justice in their work (dimension 3). These actions are linked to providing active outreach to populations at risk/need, work in settings that emphasize equal access to services, and education on diversity issues at upper administrative and community levels—themes reinforced in our training program.

Responses to the final question, "What distinguishes the PCS Training Program as one that emphasizes multiculturalism?" indicated that having a *diverse clinical staff* was the most important factor in providing multicultural experiences for interns. The diversity in the staff, with over 70 percent specializing in working with diverse populations and issues (e.g., racial, ethnic, cultural, gender, spiritual, sexual orientation), is reflective of our emphasis on not only teaching about multiculturalism, but also embracing it as an essential way of being. In addition, beyond what takes place in our campus-based training, many of our clinical staff are actively involved in regional and national professional organizations devoted to the advancement of multicultural issues. This commitment to multiculturalism is not tied solely to organization memberships, however. Several of our staff make concerted efforts to research, publish, and present on topics related to multicultural counseling and training. Recent examples include an edited book on working with biracial populations (Gillem and Thompson, 2004), publications on Asian American men (Park, 2006) and ethical issues with diverse populations (Manese, Saito, and Rodolfa, 2004), and numerous presentations on multicultural counseling in training (Manese, 2005) and supervision (Park, 2002; Park and Manese, 2006). In addition, over the past four years, two staff members, as well as several former interns, have received national recognition for their efforts in multicultural training and research.

Areas of our training program that interns identified as reflective of our commitment to multiculturalism were (in descending order): (1) diverse clinical staff, (2) diverse student population, (3) diversity training seminars, (4) varied supervision experience, (5) existence of multiple diversity-oriented support/therapy groups, (6) outreach to underrepresented populations.

These data suggest that our efforts to enhance multicultural competence in our interns are effective, and that this influence extends beyond their internship training year. Thus the answer to "How do we know we are engaging in successful multicultural training?" is based on continuous assessment of our interns and ourselves through qualitative and quantitative means. These qualities of our training program, as well as our diverse staff composition, parallel Ponterotto's (1998) charge that effective multicultural training environments have at their core (1) a commitment to multiculturalism, (2) a emphasis on recruiting and developing multiculturally diverse staff and trainees, and (3) a process of ongoing assessment such that all parties can gain self-awareness and knowledge for their own multicultural development.

Future Directions, Trends, and Challenges

Current trends in the multicultural counseling literature provide many challenges to training programs: There are calls for more comprehensive approaches to multicultural assessment (Ridley, Li, and Hill, 1998), greater empirical efforts to assess effectiveness in multicultural training (Ponterotto, 1998), further development and application of the multidimensional nature of multicultural competencies (Sue, 2001), use of nontraditional or indigenous forms of therapy (Lee and Armstrong, 1995), consistency of diversity training in both academic and internship programs (Carter, 2001), and attention to social justice (Speight and Vera, 2004). As Sue (2001) suggested, the area of multicultural counseling is constantly evolving. However, such evolution or change cannot take place without socially active efforts to change or adjust existing (and long-standing) models of psychology training. With devoted efforts to instill multiculturalism across multiple systemic and societal levels, it is essential that training programs both teach and model the spirit of multiculturalism and diversity.

Such efforts are not likely to succeed without difficulties, however. As the history in our field suggests, meaningful change is attainable, but slow. To work to become a multiculturally competent unit often means working to affect existing, well-entrenched systems (Reynolds and Pope, 2003). As training programs work to integrate traditional and nontraditional approaches to education and service delivery, committed efforts to maintain multiculturalism across all levels of training, even if/when there is resistance, must be upheld (Ponterotto, 1998). Our goal at PCS is to continue facilitating the development of culturally sensitive, ethical, and competent practitioners. To do this, we realize that we will need to continuously adjust and *actively contribute* to change in order to meet the growing diversity of our student population, our interns, staff, and the university community. This change must occur at multiple levels and systems: from the agency (defining "services" to be more multidimensional), staff (diverse staff and intern recruitment), programmatic (evaluation and outcome research), and community (outreach, prevention, consultation, advocacy, and use of indigenous healers).

How will we know that our efforts will continue to embody the spirit of multiculturalism? It seems vital that integrating past history with current strengths, along with an active willingness to innovate and think out of the box, will lead us in a positive direction. With this strategy, the future involves a continued commitment to multiculturalism that will both honor *and* influence the ever-evolving landscape of our field. As the chapters in this volume suggest, multicultural competence involves not only reacting to the trends in our field, but actively initiating cutting-edge (or nontraditional) methods to teach, practice, and live multiculturalism. We believe that as the PCS internship training program has evolved over the past thirty years, we

have been able to meaningfully contribute to the areas of multicultural training and research with this very approach. Our goal is to stay committed to
this mission.

References

American Psychological Association. (2002). Ethical principles and code of conduct.
American Psychologist, 57(12) 1060–73.

————. (2003). Guidelines on multicultural education, training, research, practice,
and organizational change for psychologists. *American Psychologist*, 58(5),
377–402.

Aponte, J. F., and Bracco, H. F. (2000). Community approaches with ethnic populations. In J. F. Aponte and J. Wohl (Eds.), *Psychological intervention and cultural diversity* (2nd ed., pp. 131–48). Needham Heights, MA: Allyn & Bacon.

Carter, R. T. (2001). Back to the future in cultural competence training. *The Counseling Psychologist*, 29, 787–89.

Gillem, A., and Thompson, C., Eds. (2004). *Biracial women in therapy: Between the
rock of gender and the hard place of race*. Binghamton, NY: Haworth.

Lane, R. (1999). *Internship training manual: Psychological and counseling services*. Unpublished document. University of California, San Diego.

Lee, C. C., and Armstrong, K. L. (1995). Indigenous models of mental health intervention: Lessons from traditional healers. In J. G. Ponterotto, J. M. Casas, L. A.
Suzuki, and C. M. Alexander (Eds.), *Handbook of multicultural counseling* (pp.
441–56). Thousand Oaks, CA: Sage.

Manese, J. (2005, August). Training for multicultural competence: A different way of
knowing. In J. White and S. Henderson (Cochairs), *Best practices in multicultural
competence training: Initiating change in graduate psychology*. Symposium conducted
at the meeting of the American Psychological Association Convention, Washington, D.C.

Manese, J. E., Saito, G., and Rodolfa, E. (2004, January). Diversity based psychology:
What practitioners and trainers need to know. *California Board of Psychology BOP
Update*, 11.

Manese, J. E., Wu, J. T., and Nepomuceno, C. A. (2001). The effect of training on
multicultural counseling competencies: An exploratory study over a ten-year period. *Journal of Multicultural Counseling and Development*, 29(1), 31–40.

Park, S. (2002). *The effectiveness of integrative multicultural training: A follow-up study*.
Paper presented at the annual meeting of the Association of Counseling Center
Training Agencies, Santa Fe, NM.

————. (2006). Facing fear without losing face: Working with Asian American men.
In M. Englar-Carlson and M. Stevens (Eds.), *In the room with men: A casebook of
therapeutic change* (pp. 151–73). Washington, D.C.: American Psychological Association.

Park, S., and Manese, J. E. (2006, June). *The art and science of clinical supervision*. Continuing education seminar presented at the University of California, San Diego.

Ponterotto, J. G. (1998). Charting a course for research in multicultural counseling training. *The Counseling Psychologist, 26*(1), 43–68.

Ponterotto, J. G., Alexander, C. M., and Grieger, I. (1995). A multicultural competency checklist for counseling training programs. *Journal of Multicultural Counseling and Development, 23*, 11–20.

Ponterotto, J. G., Sanchez, C. M., and Magids, D. M. (1991, August). *Initial development and validation of the Multicultural Counseling Awareness Scale (MCAS)*. Paper presented at the annual meeting of the American Psychological Association Conference, San Francisco, CA.

Reynolds, A. L., and Pope, R. L. (2003). Multicultural competence in counseling centers. In D. B. Pope-Davis, H. L. K. Coleman, W. M. Liu, and R. L. Toporek (Eds.), *Handbook of multicultural competencies in counseling and psychology* (pp. 365–82). Thousand Oaks, CA: Sage.

Ridley, C. R., Li, L. C., and Hill, C. L. (1998). Multicultural assessment: Reexamination, reconceptualization, and practical application. *The Counseling Psychologist, 26*(6), 939–47.

Singley, D., and Manese, J. E. (2006). *Goals in action: Fostering excellence at UCSD*. Research Reports 01–06). San Diego: University of California, San Diego Psychological and Counseling Services.

Speight, S. L., and Vera, E. M. (2004). A social justice agenda: Read, or not? *Counseling Psychologist, 32*(1), 109–18.

Sue, D. W. (2001). Multidimensional facets of cultural competence. *The Counseling Psychologist, 29*(6), 790–821.

Suzuki, L. A., McRae, M. B., and Short, E. L. (2001). The facets of cultural competence: Searching outside the box. *The Counseling Psychologist, 29*(6), 842–49.

~

CHAPTER SEVEN

University of California, Irvine, Student Counseling Center

Lessons Learned Through

Commitment to Multiculturalism

Mary Ann Takemoto and Thomas A. Parham

The challenge of diversifying the professions of psychology and counseling has fallen to both the academic and the applied domains of these disciplines (Sue, Ivey, and Pedersen, 1996; Sue and Sue, 2003). Educational institutions have certainly borne their share of the scrutiny in examining whether and how they have properly trained students to effectively intervene in the mental health challenges that culturally different clients face. And yet, academic education without sound clinical or counseling experiential training does not produce the most competent professionals. In fact, training programs like the University of California, Irvine (UCI), have found themselves providing specific critiques around the multicultural competency of interns' academic programs. This reciprocal exchange of information has placed counseling centers in a position of not only evaluating their students, but also of directing and recommending curriculum modules that academic programs need to implement in their training of graduate students before the students are sent on internship.

What aspects of a clinician's experiential training are likely to be the most beneficial in helping him/her develop the skills necessary to be a competent professional? The UCI Counseling Center was founded by Dr. Joseph L. White in the early 1970s and has had an American Psychological Assocation (APA) accredited internship program for over twenty-five years. UCI is well known for the strength of its multicultural competency training. In this chapter we seek to answer the above question by acquainting readers with the internship training program at UCI and the components of its training program and legacy, allowing readers to then compare for themselves its features with programs with which they are familiar.

Institutional Context

Unquestionably, the establishment of a multiculturally focused counseling center does not occur in a vacuum. Indeed, such organizations, like the personnel who manage and service them, exist within a broader institutional and social context. Sue and Sue (2003) help us to appreciate this notion by reminding us about the "domains of advocacy" that must be traversed in order to become a multiculturally competent organization. Individuals work in and for organizations and agencies that in turn exist within institutional boundaries and protocols, which operate within a social context. Each of these domains (individual, organizational, institutional, and societal) is a key component in helping to achieve multiculturally oriented services that are capable of meeting the needs of a diverse population. In a similar way, the institutional culture of UCI provided the proper environment to nurture the multicultural aspirations of a counseling center striving to operationalize that vision.

In retrospect, there were several key ingredients that characterized this "institutional culture." The first of these was a geographic location in a state like California that was already diverse (and increasing in diversity) beyond what most states in the union could claim. Essentially, the demographics of the state were such that ethnic and racial diversity was a reality every institution had to address. Second, the institutional culture was impacted by the *demands for inclusion* from many of the racial/ethnic groups who were represented in the population demographics, but not within the institutions of higher learning's organizations or practices. Third, the institutional culture manifests *little resistance to multicultural progress*. This is not to suggest that the institution in and of itself was that progressive. Rather, "support" is sometimes measured not by the assistance it provides, but by the absence of resistance to an agency's attempt to become more multiculturally focused. Fourth, UCI experienced a change in the vice chancellor for Student Affairs, himself a psychologist of African American descent. His vision for a more multiculturally robust Student Affairs division was an ideal climate in which to operationalize the Counseling Center's multicultural aspirations.

Features of the Program

Outreach Focus

The internship program began with a strong emphasis on a proactive, developmental approach to working with students, in addition to a strong multicultural focus. Staff members of the Counseling Center have had a strong tradition of active involvement in outreach, teaching, and other prevention-oriented activities, especially given that many ethnic minority students would not seek out traditional mental health services on campus, a finding that has been corroborated by previous research (Giordano and Giordano, 1977; Tseng and McDermott, 1981; Terrell and Terrell, 1984; Lee and Richardson, 1991).

The UCI Counseling Center has worked closely with residence halls and other campus units for many years including sponsoring joint programs and peer programs with the Cross Cultural Center, Lesbian Gay Bi-sexual Transgendered (LGBT) Center, Center for Women and Men, and other units. We have found that these outreach activities help bring diverse students into the Counseling Center to receive services. In addition, these outreach services also assist our intern trainees in learning a broader range of intervention strategies. This outreach also provides a forum for the intern trainees to explore the biases and assumptions they carry about the populations with which they work. This is the foundation of the multicultural competency paradigms now embraced by the disciplines of psychology and counseling.

Recruitment of Staff and Interns

There is a deep commitment to and long-standing tradition of recruiting a diverse team of interns and staff at UCI. This tradition has persisted despite the implementation of California's statewide assault on affirmative action known as Proposition 209. One of the important issues that serves as a conceptual anchor for our program is related to our commitment to diversity. While we have embraced and defined diversity across dimensions of race, ethnicity, sexual orientation, gender, age, religion, and disability status, we are aware of the multiple identities that interns have and the limitations of categorizing them along a single demographic line. We have been, and currently are, interested in recruiting interns who have interests and experiences working with multicultural populations, and the focus is more on their competencies and proficiencies, rather than the demographic status they represent. We especially have been interested in including European American interns and staff in our multiracial dialogue, and recent work in the area of white racial identity has been a valuable addition to our discussion and training. This point is particularly important because we recognize that the majority of ethnic minority clients will be seen by white practitioners. Furthermore, we have long since recognized as a center that there is a difference between skin color and consciousness; thus while appropriate training cannot change an individual's racial composition, we can impact their worldview perspectives, as well as culture biases and sensitivities they bring with them into therapeutic spaces.

When the Association of Psychology Postdoctoral and Internship Centers implemented the computer-match system several years ago, we were concerned about the impact on diversity of our intern group. Prior to the computer match, we were able to have more control over maintaining a balance in the group in terms of gender, race, ethnicity, academic program, and other factors. We felt that it would be difficult to ensure this diversity if we submitted a single list of candidates to the computer match, so we made a decision to submit multiple lists (one for each of our four positions). Each list emphasizes different strengths and competencies of the intern candidates, and this approach has been helpful in allowing us to recruit a diverse intern group. Although we still cannot control what the exact composition of our intern group will be, this system has worked reasonably well for us in achieving our goals of recruiting highly qualified intern candidates, and a diverse group who come to our agency with a reasonable base of cultural competence.

Typically, we receive as few as 110, and as many as 150 applications for our four positions. Members of the selection committee review each application, and the pool is narrowed down to about thirty applicants who will be interviewed. The selection criteria include counseling/clinical contact hours, individual and group therapy experiences, a background in outreach and workshop delivery, as well as interest and experience in multicultural issues. All interviews are conducted by phone, and questions about diversity issues are included in the interview. Candidates are then ranked according to our assessment of their application, experience, interview, and overall fit for the program.

Operationalizing Diversity

Unlike many other centers and agencies around the country, the UCI Counseling Center never defined its commitment to diversity solely in terms of demographic representation. Rather, the diversity sought at UCI challenged the center to change the policies and practices of the agency, as a function of the changes in the demographics (Loden and Rosener, 1991). Accordingly, the internal culture of the center had to wrestle with policies around commitments to hiring personnel, performance expectations of staff, outreach targets and strategies, training priorities, preparation of public information and marketing materials, and commitments to professional development that was and is multiculturally oriented. Each of our staff, as well as trainees, is socialized in ways that underscore the importance of operationalizing real diversity.

The development of a multicultural emphasis in our training program required an organizational shift in our Counseling Center. We believe that the culture of the center has changed, as well as the dynamics within it. These changes go well beyond the institution of our "multicultural potlucks" and include integrating multicultural perspectives in the leadership and management of the center.

There has also been a shift in the way that leadership positions are assigned. In the early years of the internship program, the director, Clinical Services director, and training director positions were assigned on a rotating basis. Since the majority of the professional staff was relatively young, this model provided an opportunity for different staff members to serve in the leadership role within the center, including training director. The time period designated for a rotation was three years, although there was some flexibility in extending it a year or two. There are a few other counseling centers that continue to have a rotating training director position.

There were, however, some negative aspects to the rotating training director model at UCI. The first issue concerned the personnel classification of the training director's position and feedback from our Human Resources Department. The training director position was viewed as an administrative position and a promotion from that of staff psychologist. It involved an increase in salary as well as classification level. At the end of the rotation period, the training director would return to the staff psychologist level. However, Human Resources viewed this as problematic. They strongly encouraged us to make a permanent appointment that would not change every three years. In addition, there were concerns about the continuity of the internship program if the training director changed every few years. Incoming interns expecting to work with one training director might be disappointed to find they would be working with someone different. A change was made to have a permanent training director in 1993, three years after the current director came on board.

We realized that we would have to be flexible to meet the needs of a changing student population. In the early 1980s, one of the specific program objectives for internship training was providing services to ethnic minority students (called "third world students" at that time). In 1982, there were approximately 12,000 students enrolled at UCI, and 33 percent were ethnic minority. Within the Counseling Center, there was an Ethnic Minority Affairs Task Force. This committee had oversight over the "Third World Peer Counselor Program" that aimed to provide innovative services to culturally different students. Interns worked closely with this program.

In the late 1980s and early 1990s, there was a change and revamping of the earlier task force, which was renamed the Multicultural Task Force. This group was responsible for coordinating the multicultural training for interns and also sponsored a peer program for UCI undergraduate students called REACH (Reaffirming Ethnic Awareness and Community Harmony). Interns played a crucial role in the development and administration of this program. The REACH Program was cosponsored with the campus's Cross Cultural Center, and in the mid-1990s it was relocated from the Counseling Center to the Cross Cultural Center on a permanent basis. The Multicultural Task Force stopped meeting as a formal group when many of its recommendations and goals were met.

Within the past few years, a "Diversity Dialogue" group was suggested by several of the interns. The goal of this discussion group was to provide an open forum for interns and staff to discuss diversity issues of interest. This group met weekly for approximately two years.

Integrating Multicultural Content

Multiculturally oriented training programs begin with a diverse staff, who themselves represent the important demographic the center needs to address, and who display the level of competence necessary to upgrade the rigors of the training program. While many programs offer a single "multicultural seminar" for their interns, UCI has made a concerted effort to integrate multicultural issues in all aspects of training and supervision. Diversity issues are integrated in assessment training, case conceptualization, outreach and consultation, teaching, and developing culturally relevant clinical interventions. In addition, many of the professional development programs the center has for the entire staff have focused on multicultural topics (e.g., African American women's issues, family therapy with Asian Americans, working with Muslim clients, multicultural competence). As a center, we have a strong commitment to ongoing training on diversity issues, and that diversity focus extends to conceptualizing clients from different theoretical orientations, testing and assessment, differential diagnosis, issues in ethics, and treatment planning. Staff is encouraged to attend national and regional conferences such as the Multicultural Summit, Winter Roundtable on Cross Cultural Counseling, the national convention of the Association of Black Psychologists, and other meetings to advance their multicultural knowledge. Attendance at these meetings has also served as a useful recruiting tool for prospective interns.

Having a diverse team of interns and a diverse staff are essential for the opportunity to engage in a multiracial dialogue. While it provides rich opportunities for multiple perspectives, there is also the potential for conflict or differences of opinion. The ability to tolerate these differences and to facilitate a meaningful discussion around them is critical. We acknowledge that we may not always agree on issues, but are committed to creating an environment of respect for individual opinions.

It was essential for us to expand our appreciation of diversity beyond race and ethnicity to include other factors such as gender, sexual orientation, social class, religion, and disability status. These factors could not be looked at in isolation, but rather, how they interacted with each other to produce complex multiple identities. These multiple identities have allowed us to gain a stronger appreciation of respect for various demographic variables, but they have also helped us manage a social justice and advocacy agenda that is more inclusive and affirming of all. This is particularly important in recognizing, as others have before us (Lee and Richardson, 1991; Parham, White, and Ajamu, 1999; Parham, 2002; Sue and Sue, 2003), that many of the problems culturally different clients present with are not exclusively intrapsychic, but are sociocultural and environmentally influenced. Thus, the training interns receive includes both traditional therapy, as well as expanded roles of advocacy across the university environment that helps to translate client issues into systemic ones.

The sensitivities to broader issues of diversity were an important step in further operationalizing the Counseling Center's multicultural agenda. However, plain sensitivity without a more specific agenda of service delivery proved insufficient to meet the growing demands for greater inclusion from "diverse" groups who perceived themselves as on the margins of significant multicultural progress made by racial ethnic groups. Nowhere was this more apparent than with populations in the lesbian, gay, bisexual, transgendered, and queer (LGBTQ) and disabled communities. UCI was quick to further diversify its staff and hired one of the first openly gay and lesbian psychologists in the mid-1970s. Beyond the advocacy of individual staff, no single incident or event was any more important than the publication of the "Guidelines for Working with Lesbian, Gay, Bi-Sexual, Transgendered, and Queer Populations."

In addition to providing an important framework, this document helped crystallize the profession's commitment to multicultural issues where LGBTQ populations are concerned. This document also serves as a testament to the years of struggle and advocacy by LGBTQ professionals and allies who desired a more focused template for framing how therapeutic services should be delivered to that population.

The focus on disability issues has been equally challenging to our center, as we sought to better operationalize that commitment. While the center has enjoyed the services of part-time staff with disabilities, from time to time, we continue to request additional funding for a permanent, full-time staff member to represent the disabled community. While additional funding has been slow to materialize, the center's commitment to serve that community, as well as the LGBTQ community, has not wavered. The center has developed strategic alliances with the Disability Services Center and the Lesbian, Gay, Bi-Sexual, Transgendered Resource Center, and collaborated with their staff to provide psychological support that is both clinically and programmatically focused. Important too has been the inclusion of the "Guidelines for Multicultural Counseling," as well as the collaboration with the university's Cross Cultural Center to ensure that clinical counseling services, outreach and consultation, and programming and workshops are delivered in a skillful and effective way.

Encouraging Trust and Mutual Understanding

During the orientation period, interns spend a significant amount of time together. One of the group activities that they participate in involves sharing aspects of their cultural upbringing, class background, worldview, and self-identity with the other interns. This provides an opportunity for interns to become better acquainted with each other, as well as to recognize the various perspectives that each of them bring to the internship program. Since the interns will be working closely together through their seminars and group supervision, it is extremely important to have a foundation of trust and mutual understanding. In addition, this serves as a model for discussion of future clinical cases in group supervision. Interns are expected to present relevant information on a client's race, ethnicity, acculturation level, class background, sexual orientation, disability status, and counselor preference, etc. when they present cases. Over the year, we typically see an increasing level of sophistication in the interns' ability to integrate this information into client conceptualization and treatment plans.

Collective Survival

One of the cultural values we share at UCI is the notion of collective survival. Our belief in this principle is translated into a creation of a family atmosphere, where attachments take on elements of personal as well as professional bonds. These bonds do cross space and time as connections to trainees do not stop at the end of their internship, or because they relocate to other positions around the country. Staff and former interns have worked jointly on projects such as publications and conference presentations, participation in professional organizations and committees, and consultation work. In addition, they continue to have mentoring relationships after the training year ends. The culture of intimacy infused into the training program also fosters a level of collaboration between former interns of different classes, who themselves find common ground from which to engage collaborative initiatives.

We have been fortunate to have some outstanding interns go through our training program. Perhaps one of the indications of this reality is to look at the current professional positions former interns hold. Four of our former interns are currently directors of university counseling centers. Two former interns are training directors of internship programs and two currently serve as training directors of academic programs. A large number of former interns serve as faculty members in academic institutions, as well as staff in counseling centers and other clinical settings. Many of our former interns have commented that the multicultural training they received at UCI has been valuable to them and has influenced the work they have done at other academic institutions. As we maintain contact with a number of former interns, we have a sense of pride in seeing their professional development and accomplishments in the area of multicultural counseling.

UCI was one of the first counseling centers on the West Coast to receive APA accreditation for its internship training program. The program has been through over six site visits since its inception and has received positive feedback about the multicultural training offered to interns over the past three decades. We have observed that as the APA has struggled to operationalize how multiculturalism should be evaluated, the criteria for assessing multiculturalism have become more sophisticated and multifaceted over time. The early site visits were not as effective in evaluating one of our strengths as they tended to focus more on the demographics of staff and interns.

We are fortunate to have individuals on staff at UCI who are prominent within APA and leaders within specific psychological associations that are focused on multicultural issues. This has allowed us to stay ahead of the "normal curve" in terms of operationalizing diversity in our center and internship program. Our hope is that one day some of the specific ethnic psychological associations will develop certification and accreditation processes that would allow programs and agencies to seek their validation on the training they provide.

Lessons Learned

There are a number of important lessons that we have learned over the past two decades of intern training. One of the lessons was that we could not rely on the professional discipline of psychology itself to develop a training model relevant to multicultural and diversity issues. As we began to see rapid demographic changes in our student population in the late 1980s and early 1990s, especially in the Asian American community, we realized that we would have to develop our own training model. We included in our training seminar topics such as cross-cultural supervision issues, the psychology of African Americans, Asian Americans, and Chicano/Latinos, the intersection of ethnicity and sexual orientation identities, and issues related to the increasing population of biracial and multicultural students. In the early years, we found that many of our interns were coming to us without much background in multicultural training. This prompted us to send out letters to training directors of academic psychology departments in the early 1990s, advocating for increased training and skill development around multicultural issues. We are pleased to see that there has been some progress in this area, although this has varied across programs.

Pockets of Resistance

Without question, one of the most significant challenges our center has faced in operationalizing our commitment to multiculturalism is addressing the pockets of resistance. By this, we mean to suggest that the road to greater diversity has not been without some elements of controversy. Ironically, one would expect resistance and controversy to a multicultural agenda in an institution that was not fully committed to the principle. What was more difficult to recognize were the subtle pockets of resistance that were reflected in the attitudes of some staff members who outwardly appeared firmly committed to the idea of multiculturalism. In essence, the lesson learned here was the recognition that resistance is not simply "between group" (i.e., a counseling center struggling with its own institution), but can also be "within group" (i.e., that which emerges from within the center itself, among the staff).

Some of the challenges that we have dealt with over time have stemmed from characteristics of individual intern groups and their group dynamics. One of the things we have noticed is that there may be differing levels of multicultural competence among the interns, which partly reflects the differential training they received in their graduate training program. As some interns may choose to come to UCI to fill gaps they have in their training, it is not surprising that these differences exist. Geographical differences, political differences, and differences in worldview and life experiences are all factors that can impact individual interns and their group interactions. Tensions can exist because of the personality dynamics of the groups themselves or because of the multiple identities that interns have. Interns may choose to affiliate with one community more than another (LGBT, racial or ethnic community, etc.), or others may have preconceived expectations of them that are not met.

Conclusion

There is no doubt that the struggle inherent in advancing a multicultural agenda to get our center where it is today was well worth the price. Clearly, our staff had to manage issues of cultural pride, cultural comfort zones, and even staff tensions. Yet, by committing to the course of operationalizing true multiculturalism within the context of our center's policies and practices, we have achieved a level of comfort that is anchored in genuine awareness, knowledge, and skill of ourselves as cultural beings in a diverse world. And through our example, we hope to inspire other centers that still struggle with diversity issues, to embrace the concept of multiculturalism and trust the process. For in trusting the process, we find no guarantees of specific outcomes; we find only increases in the probability that you may achieve your desired goals.

References

Giordano, G. P., and Giordano, J. (1977). *The ethno cultural factor in mental health: A literature review and bibliography.* New York: Institute on Pluralism and Group Identity.

Lee, C. C., and Richardson, B. L. (1991). *Multicultural issues in counseling: New approaches in diversity.* Alexandria, VA: American Counseling Association.

Loden, M., and Rosener, J. (1991). *Workforce America.* Homewood, IL: Business One Irwin.

Parham, T. A. (2002). *Counseling persons of African descent: Raising the bar of practitioner competence.* Thousand Oaks, CA: Sage Publications.

Parham, T. A., and Whitten, L. (2003). Teaching multicultural competencies in continuing education for psychologists. In D. Pope Davis, H. Coleman, W. Liu, and R. Toporek (Eds.), *Handbook of multicultural competence in counseling and psychotherapy*. Newberry Park, CA: Sage Publications.

Parham, T. A., White, J. L., and Ajamu, A. (1999). *The psychology of blacks: an African centered perspective*. Englewood Cliffs, NJ: Prentice Hall.

Sue, D. W., and Sue, D. (2003). *Counseling the culturally different* (4th ed.). New York: John Wiley & Sons.

Sue, D. W., Ivey, A., and Pedersen, P. (1996). *A theory of multicultural counseling and therapy*. Pacific Grove, CA: Brooks/Cole.

Terrell, F., and Terrell, S. L. (1984). Race of counselor, client sex, cultural mistrust level, and premature termination from counseling among black clients. *Journal of Counseling Psychology, 31*, 371–75.

Tseng, N. S., and McDermott, J. F. (1981). *Cultural mind and therapy: An introduction to cultural psychiatry*. New York: Brunner/Mayed.

PART III

TRAINING AND MENTORING NEW GENERATIONS OF SCHOLARS

CHAPTER EIGHT

~

Training the Next Generation of Ethnic Minority Multicultural Researchers

Kevin Cokley

As the United States becomes an increasingly diverse country, psychology graduate programs continue to espouse a commitment to diversity and multiculturalism through the training of ethnic minority students. Indeed, a perusal of many counseling psychology graduate programs reveals student cohorts that are usually characterized by racial, ethnic, and cultural diversity. In many instances these individuals, upon graduation, go on to have productive and satisfying careers in counseling centers, private practice, community mental health agencies, hospitals, higher education, and other applied areas. However, relatively few ethnic minority students choose to solely pursue an academic career in a "publish or perish" environment. In one study, Pope-Davis, Stone, and Nielson, (1997) surveyed 118 ethnic minority students representing fifty training programs in counseling psychology. Results indicated that 6.8 percent endorsed an academic career goal, 19.5 percent endorsed a practitioner career goal, while the majority (73.7 percent) endorsed a combination of academic and practitioner career goals. In my conversations with students, this has usually meant that they want to primarily pursue a practitioner career goal while having the possibility of teaching on the side. It has been suggested that the reality is that most ethnic minority students are interested in direct service, not research and teaching (Atkinson, 1993). Atkinson goes on to argue that this trend will continue until European American professors assume a greater responsibility in involving ethnic minority students in research.

As an academic entering the midphase of my career, I continue to be concerned and frustrated about the low numbers of ethnic minority students, especially African American and Latino/a students, who express a strong interest in pursuing an academic career. In my years of reading applications while serving on admissions committees, I have not observed any discernable differences between ethnic minority applicants and majority applicants in expressing an interest to conduct research as an important component of their professional responsibilities. In light of the scientist-practitioner training model, many applicants are savvy enough to communicate an interest in conducting research. With a preponderance of counseling psychology programs embracing multiculturalism as important to their training missions, increasingly applicants express an interest in conducting research related to issues such as race, ethnicity, gender, and sexual orientation. Of course, faculty can only speculate whether applicants truly intend to pursue a career in research-related activities.

Giving the benefit of the doubt to the applicants, perhaps they truly are interested in making multicultural research an integral part of their professional activities, but at some point become disinterested, discouraged, or turned off from the prospects of becoming multicultural researchers. I submit that this loss of interest occurs in large part because of three reasons. These reasons fall broadly under the categories of (1) mentoring relationships (Davidson and Foster-Johnson, 2001), (2) the research training environment (Gelso, 1993), and (3) the hegemony of a positivist research paradigm (Paul and Marfo, 2001). While these reasons are not necessarily mutually exclusive, due to space constraints, I focus on mentoring relationships and offer suggestions for creating mentoring relationships that are more responsive to the "browning of America" that will ultimately produce more ethnic minority multicultural researchers.

Mentoring Relationships

In a comprehensive article on mentoring graduate researchers of color, Davidson and Foster-Johnson (2001) argue that a critical factor in determining the successful completion of graduate programs is the cultivation of mentoring relationships between graduate students of color and professors. Among other reasons, they suggest that mentoring relationships can assist students in acquiring core research competencies. Additionally, these mentoring relationships can result in opportunities to present research findings at academic conferences and to publish. However, for students of color, there is often a lack of close mentoring relationships. They cite a study by Smith and Davidson

(1992) of African American graduate students who reported receiving no guidance or support in their programs. We distinguish between advising relationships and mentoring relationships in that advising relationships tend to focus more on informing students of program, department, and university procedures and academic policies while mentoring relationships tend to be more intimate in that they involve more emotional and psychological support and role modeling. Of course, the two are not mutually exclusive, but it has been my observation that advising relationships, which all students have, do not necessarily involve a mentoring component or turn into mentoring relationships. In some programs this is by design, whereas in other programs this is a result of incompatibility of interests and personalities.

In my own graduate experience, I can recall that several doctoral students in my cohort had developed close relationships with faculty. These close relationships led to informal research teams that resulted in numerous opportunities for these students to make presentations at conferences and publish in journals. As I observed these wonderful opportunities, there was one consistent observation that I made: the majority of the students were white, and all of the faculty were white. As much as I tried to deny it, I could not help but become envious of the opportunities of my white classmates and other fellow students as I reflected on my perceived lack of similar opportunities. Sadly, years after this observation, I continue to have conversations with African American students who report similar experiences.

Cross-Cultural Mentoring Relationships

In those instances when ethnic minority students are able to develop a mentoring relationship, it is likely that the mentoring relationship is interracial or cross cultural. Anaya and Cole (2001) stated that race is a salient factor that can contribute to the dynamics of these relationships. One important issue that counseling faculty need to be aware of is that a one-size-fits-all approach of mentoring is inadequate and in some cases harmful because it does not take into consideration developmental and cultural differences between students, nor does it consider how differences in racial socialization can impact the mentoring relationship. Davidson and Foster-Johnson (2001) identify personal and cultural communication styles as essential to daily interactions in graduate school. When the mentor and protégé come from different cultural backgrounds, it is quite likely that their communication styles are different. In some instances, different communication styles can result in miscommunication. To the extent that mentors and protégés exhibit similar communication styles, regardless of cultural background, the likelihood of a more positive mentoring relationship is increased.

For example, European Americans tend to have a more cautious and re-served communication style (Davisdon and Foster-Johnson, 2001) and tend to use more low-context communication, which is characterized by very explicit, direct, and precise communication where interpretation of their words comes from the literal meanings of the words themselves (Gudykunst, 1988; Lustig and Koester, 1999). European American faculty from low-context cultures may assume that ethnic minority students who do not explicitly express an interest in becoming more proficient as researchers and/or wanting to get published are not interested in research. However, for ethnic minority students, many of whom may be first-generation students, the norms and culture of graduate school are usually quite foreign. Being inexperienced in a graduate school environment where low-context communication is the prevailing norm and feeling overwhelmed by the demands of the environment, it can be very intimidating for ethnic minority students to proactively seek additional research opportunities.

While European American culture and European American predominated institutions are usually characterized by low-context communication, it has also been pointed out that in the majority of the world's cultures (particularly non-European), high-context communication is the norm (Tannen, 1994). In high-context cultures such as Asian American, African American, and Latin American cultures, the meaning of words does not come from the words themselves as much as they come from the communicator's internalized beliefs, values, and norms (Lustig and Koester, 1999). High-context communication is usually understated, ambiguous, and indirect (Gudykunst, 1988). Ethnic minority students from high-context communication will often rely more on what European American faculty do not say rather than what they say. They will especially derive meaning from the nonverbals of European American faculty.

For ethnic minorities such as African Americans, whose communication styles are sometimes stereotyped as loud, aggressive, and acrimonious (Hecht, Larkey, and Johnson, 1992), issues of race are especially salient, and interactions with European American faculty will often be racialized. For example, when certain students are getting opportunities to publish or present with faculty, some African American students may see this as an example of a racialized environment that caters to students from certain racial or ethnic backgrounds and is unsupportive of the career development of African American students. Not being asked to be a part of research opportunities can stigmatize ethnic minority students by activating feelings of racial self-doubt. As an African American student once told me, she was never asked to join any research team, and she wondered if it had anything to do with doubts about her ability as a black woman. This was one of several experiences that contributed to her not pursuing a research-oriented career in academia.

Using Marcia's (1966, 1967) model of ego identity status as a conceptual framework, we can conceptualize that the process of forming a research identity for many African American students and other students of color starts off in a state of moratorium as students search for a defining professional identity. They have not made a commitment to a professional identity beyond being a counseling psychologist. The lack of research opportunities (perceived or real) to work collaboratively or under the guidance of a faculty member and the lack of encouragement, support, and mentorship by faculty to conduct research can undermine the research self-efficacy of students of color and can result in students becoming foreclosed in their professional identities, where being a researcher is never seriously considered or explored as a viable career option.

When European American mentors find themselves in cross-cultural and interracial mentoring relationships, they should be sensitive to subtle racial dynamics that can undermine or compromise their ability to provide critical feedback that could facilitate an ethnic minority student's research self-efficacy. As Cohen, Steele, and Ross (1999) point out, the ability to provide scholastic feedback that is potentially threatening to ethnic minority students becomes a dilemma given the negative stereotypes that exist about certain minority groups' intellectual capabilities. These situations create an "attributional ambiguity" whereby students do not know whether the lack of invitations to be a part of research teams and the critical feedback from a mentor are because of academic shortcomings or racial bias.

In an experimental study, Cohen and colleagues compared the responses of black and white students to critical feedback about a writing task. Students were randomly assigned to one of three conditions: (1) *unbuffered criticism*, where a reviewer provided a general critique of the student's performance using statements such as "your letter was vague and rambling—long on adjectives and short on specific illustrations"; (2) *wise criticism*, where the aforementioned general critique was prefaced by comments such as "the comments I provide are quite critical but I hope helpful . . . based on what I've read in your letter, [I think] you are capable of meeting the higher standard I mentioned"; and (3) *positive buffer*, where the aforementioned general critique was prefaced by such comments as "Overall, nice job. . . . You have some interesting ideas and make some good points. . . . I've provided some specific feedback and suggested areas that could be improved." Consistent with the hypotheses, results indicated that black students receiving unbuffered criticism rated the reviewer more biased than white students. Also consistent with the hypotheses, when the critical feedback was accompanied by the combination of high standards and assurance, black students rated the reviewer as less biased than did the white students. There was not a significant difference in the positive buffer condition. This study underscores the challenges European American mentors face when providing critical feedback to ethnic minority students, with the implications being that critical feedback is more likely to be positively received by ethnic minority students when it is placed in a context of high standards and the mentor's belief that the student has the capacity to reach them. Additionally, the mentor should actively support the student in reaching the higher standards, and be willing to process feedback with the student if necessary.

Another underexamined aspect of the mentor relationship that may discourage ethnic minority students' interest and participation in research concerns a lack of compatibility and expertise of research interests. We believe that multicultural research should be grounded in the "lived experiences of those whose lives we investigate" (Morrow, Rakhsha, and Castaneda, 2001, p. 575). Relatedly, research interests of the researcher are often driven by personal experiences. It should come as no surprise that ethnic minority students often choose thesis and dissertation topics and have research interests that reflect a phenomenological (lived experience that allows a first-person perspective on the object of study) point of view.

The overwhelming majority of ethnic minority students that I have worked with have chosen thesis and dissertation topics that usually reflected either an aspect of their personal experience or a culturally specific phenomenon related to their ethnic group. They usually pursue these topics because, like other students, they do not want to spend a significant amount of time writing a thesis or dissertation on a topic that they are not invested in. Additionally, dissertations are mandatory to receive a doctorate, so students have to engage in the process of writing one.

However, when it comes to additional research activities that are not required as a part of the program of study, a fledgling research interest in a culturally specific topic can be extinguished when that interest is not shared or nurtured by a faculty member. Even in instances when a faculty member expresses a willingness to guide or direct an ethnic minority student's culturally specific research interest, a lack of expertise in the topic might render the faculty member ineffective. In the true spirit of multiculturalism, we believe that these instances create learning opportunities for faculty. Thus, there is a win-win situation where the faculty teaches the methods and process of conducting research while becoming familiar with the multicultural literature, as the student learns the process of conducting research while teaching multicultural knowledge.

Who Speaks For Multicultural Research?

We are reminded of the passionate and at times heated discussion over ten years ago around the issue of who speaks for multicultural counseling research. Ponterotto (1990) organized a symposium around the topic of white researchers in multicultural counseling. By most accounts, the most memorable moments of the symposium came when Parham (1990) addressed the audience using the theme "Do the Right Thing: Racial Discussion in Counseling Psychology." Essentially, Parham sought to challenge white researchers in examining their own roles in contributing to the racial tensions across America. Parham (1993) later expanded on his initial remarks by stating that many white researchers are not qualified to speak on multicultural research issues (it is not clear if he meant not qualified to conduct multicultural research) because they do not have the (a) life experience, (b) graduate/clinical training, (c) certification by ethnic-specific bodies such as the Association of Black Psychologists, or (d) the real commitment to multicultural issues. While Parham's intention was certainly not to categorically dismiss all the efforts and important contributions of white researchers doing multicultural work, we believe that an important implication of his position is that "doing the right thing" has to include a commitment to training more ethnic minority researchers.

Even though the question "Who speaks for multicultural research?" may seem parochial, it is a question that has to be asked. Atkinson (1993) made the distinction between theory and research, where he argued that it is understandable why it would be considered inappropriate for European American individuals to theorize about the psychology of ethnic minority groups. However, he argued that multicultural research should not be solely conducted by ethnic minority researchers because (a) culture is a factor in all human behavior and should always be considered in counseling research, (b) there is a decline in published research on mental health issues, and (c) the small numbers of ethnic minority faculty have essentially not changed over the past ten years. I agree with him on this point. However, what is disconcerting is that because of the aforementioned issues related to mentoring, especially cross-racial mentoring, ethnic minority students are unwittingly being discouraged from pursuing multicultural research as a career option, which leaves potentially important gaps in our collective multicultural knowledge.

There are simply some research questions that even the most competent and committed white researchers are unlikely to ask because of an experiential lack of awareness that a problem or phenomenon even exists.

Lest I am misunderstood, I am not arguing *against* white multicultural researchers; I am arguing *for* the importance of more ethnic minority multicultural researchers. In many ways, the ability to produce ethnic minority multicultural researchers becomes an issue of multicultural training competence. In that spirit, I offer four recommendations regarding mentoring relationships that can contribute to increasing the numbers of ethnic minority multicultural researchers.

Recommendations

First, we recommend that faculty reach out to ethnic minority students to give them opportunities to be involved in research. If professors have research teams, there should be a concerted effort to invite ethnic minority students to join these teams. Similarly, if professors are working on research projects, ethnic minority students should be asked if they would be interested in working on these projects. Professors underestimate the impact that simple acts such as these have on the self-efficacy of ethnic minority students. In preparing this chapter, I asked several ethnic minority students for feedback, and I was met with complete surprise by their responses because they were flattered that I, a tenured professor, believed that they could provide me valuable feedback. While this was not an example of a collaborative research effort per se, it underscores the importance of communicating a belief in an ethnic minority student's ability to contribute, even in a small way, to a professor's scholarly activities.

A second recommendation related to enhancing students' multicultural research self-efficacy is to provide more opportunities for exposure to multicultural issues. Faculty should actively encourage students to take multicultural classes and to attend multicultural conferences, workshops, and presentations. Of course, encouraging students to take multicultural classes would necessarily involve increasing the number of multicultural courses that are offered.

In a recent study, Liu, Sheu, and Williams (2004) found that the number of multicultural courses taken and the students' perceived multicultural counseling competence were positively related to confidence in their multicultural research ability. Interestingly, Liu et al. also found that perceived multicultural counseling competence was positively related to multicultural research anxiety. They suggested that this finding could be related to students becoming aware that there are complex cultural dimensions in conducting multicultural research. They also suggested that it could be related to a more general anxiety that many students have related to feeling competent in their practitioner skills but not in their research skills. They recommended that research not be confined to statistics and research classes, but also be taught in multicultural classes. The more exposure students have to multicultural issues, the more opportunities they have to critically think about and discuss these issues, which can lead to an increased interest in conducting research on multicultural issues.

A third recommendation would be for faculty to develop multicultural research interests and expertise that would be appealing to ethnic minority students. Through my conversations with ethnic minority students I have come to realize that an important factor that prohibits their pursuit of research experience is not being interested in or feeling connected to the research interests of faculty. While I am not suggesting that faculty have to change their entire research programs to engage or involve ethnic minority students, I am suggesting that incorporating *some* multicultural interests, and advertising these interests, will likely be more attractive for many ethnic minority students.

A final recommendation is to expose students of color to successful ethnic minority multicultural researchers. This is important for all students of color, but it is especially critical for Native Americans, Latino/a Americans, and African Americans who are often underrepresented as producers of multicultural research. Social cognitive career theory states that the personal characteristics of a person such as race, ethnicity, and gender can play important roles in the career development of individuals (Lent and Brown, 1996). Verdugo (1995) has stated that the mere presence of Chicana/o faculty communicates to Chicana/o students that they can also succeed academically. Along this same line of thinking, I submit that exposing students of color to ethnic minority faculty who have successfully navigated the rigors of academia and the challenges of conducting research will positively motivate students of color and increase their self-efficacy about being able to conduct research.

In summary, I believe that counseling psychology stands at the helm of the multicultural movement. Some of the most vocal proponents of multiculturalism representing various cultural and ethnic backgrounds have argued for the importance of training culturally competent professionals. I believe that an equally compelling professional issue is to increase the numbers of ethnic minority researchers who will be equipped with the research skills to go into their respective communities to conduct much-needed research that will ultimately benefit their communities. It is incumbent upon all of us to "do the right thing" and be more intentional in our training of ethnic minority multicultural researchers.

References

Anaya, G., and Cole, D. G. (2001). Latino/a student achievement: Exploring the influence of student-faculty interactions on college grades. *Journal of College Student Development, 42*, 3–14.

Atkinson, D. R. (1993). Who speaks for cross-cultural counseling research? *Counseling Psychologist, 21*(2), 218–24.

Cohen, G. L., Steele, C. M., and Ross, L. D. (1999). The mentor's dilemma: Providing critical feedback across the racial divide. *Personality and Social Psychology Bulletin, 25*, 1302–18.

Davidson, M. N., and Foster-Johnson, L. (2001). Mentoring in the preparation of graduate researchers of color. *Review of Educational Research, 71*(4), 575–611.

Gelso, C. J. (1993). On the making of a scientist-practitioner: A theory of research. Training in professional psychology. *Professional Psychology: Research and Practice, 24*, 468–76.

Gudykunst, W. B. (1988). *Bridging differences, effective intergroup communication* (3rd ed.) London: Sage.

Hecht, M. L., Larkey, L. K., and Johnson, J. N. (1992). African American and European American perceptions of problematic issues in interethnic communication effectiveness. *Human Communication Research, 19*(2), 209–36.

Lent, R. W., and Brown, S. D. (1996). Social cognitive approach to career development: An overview. *The Career Development Quarterly, 44*(4), 310–21.

Liu, W. M., Sheu, H, and Williams, K. (2004). Multicultural competency in research: Examining the relationships among multicultural competencies, research training and self-efficacy, and the multicultural environment. *Cultural Diversity and Ethnic Minority Psychology, 10*(4), 324–39.

Lustig, M. W., and Koester, J. (1999). *Intercultural competence: Interpersonal communication across cultures* (3rd ed.). New York: Addison Wesley, Inc.

Marcia, J. (1966). Development and validation of ego-identity status. *Journal of Personality and Social Psychology, 3*, 551–58.

———. (1967). Ego identity status: Relationship to change in self-esteem, "general maladjustment," and authoritarianism. *Journal of Personality, 35*, 118–33.

Morrow, S. L., Rakhsha, G., and Castañeda, C. L. (2001). Qualitative research methods for multicultural counseling. In J. G. Ponterotto, J. M. Casas, L. A. Suzuki, and C. M. Alexander (Eds.), *Handbook of multicultural counseling* (2nd ed.) (pp. 575–603). Thousand Oaks, CA: Sage.

Parham, T. A. (1990, August). Do the right thing: Racial discussion in counseling psychology. In J. G. Ponterotto (Chair), *The white American researcher in multicul-*

tural counseling: Significance and challenges. Symposium presented at the 98th Annual Convention of the American Psychological Association, Boston, MA.

———. (1993). White researchers conducting multicultural counseling research: Can their efforts be 'Mo Betta. *The Counseling Psychologist, 21*(2), 250–56.

Paul, J. L., and Marfo, K. (2001). Preparation of educational researchers in philosophical foundations of inquiry. *Review of Educational Research, 71*(4), 525–47.

Ponterotto, J. G. (1990, August). Overview and the white scholar's entrance into minority issues in research. In J. G. Ponterotto (Chair), *The white American researcher in multicultural counseling: Significance and challenges.* Symposium presented at the 98th Annual Convention of the American Psychological Association, Boston, MA.

Pope-Davis, D. B., Stone, G. L., and Nielson, D. (1997). Factors influencing the stated career goals of minority graduate students in counseling psychology programs. *The Counseling Psychologist, 25*, 683–98.

Smith, E. P., and Davidson, W. S. (1992). Mentoring and the development of African American graduate students. *Journal of College Student Development, 33*(6), 531–39.

Tannen, D. (1994). *Gender and discourse.* Toronto: Oxford University Press.

Verdugo, R. R. (1995). Racial stratification and the use of Hispanic faculty as role models: Theory, policy, and practice. *Journal of Higher Education, 66*, 669–85.

CHAPTER NINE

~

Multicultural Mentoring

Anne Chan

The many benefits of mentoring have been well researched and documented—some of these major benefits include greater career satisfaction (Allen, Poteet, and Eby 2004; Burke, Burgess, and Fallon, 2006; Murphy and Ensher, 2001), more promotions (Scandura, 1992), higher salaries (Allen et al., 2004; Chao, Walz, and Gardner, 1992; Scandura, 1992), less isolation (Schrodt, Cawyer, and Sanders, 2003), easier socialization (Chao et al., 1992; Feldman, Folks, and Turnley, 1999), greater productivity (Paglis, Green, and Bauer, 2006), and higher commitment to the organization (Allen et al., 2004; Koberg, Boss, and Goodman, 1998). In higher education settings, the data suggest that faculty mentors are highly influential in the research training of graduate students and play significant roles in the shaping of students as researchers (Boyle and Boice, 1998; Gelso and Lent, 2000; Hollingsworth and Fassinger, 2002). The quality of a doctoral student's relationship with faculty and advisor has been shown to be critical in terms of student satisfaction (Loo and Rolinson, 1986; Lyons, Scroggins, and Rule, 1990) and successful completion of the doctoral degree (Girves and Wemmerus, 1988). A personal relationship with a mentor is vital because many critical skills needed to complete a doctorate cannot be gleaned from books or peers, but must be learned from the personal guidance and wisdom of more experienced colleagues (Dedrick and Watson, 2002).

For ethnic minority students, mentoring is an even more critical piece of the equation for academic and professional success. Given that ethnic minority students and faculty are underrepresented in academia, ethnic minority students are likely to feel more isolation and estrangement from the academic world without the benefit of supportive, understanding relationships (Williamson and Fenske, 1998). A key component for success is *engagement* in the academic world—those with meaningful relationships and interactions with faculty and peers tend to persist more than those with lower levels of engagement (Tinto, 1998). Those who feel isolated and lack a sense of belonging are most at risk of quitting their programs—examples of such students include those of ethnic minority status who lack adequate representation and students who are first in their family to go to college (Girves, Zepeda, and Gwathmey, 2005; Terrell and Hassell, 1994). For ethnic minority students in particular, mentors can be critical in helping a student integrate into the academic world, persist, and succeed (Davidson and Foster-Johnson, 2001; Girves et al., 2005; Terrell and Hassell, 1994).

Barriers to Multicultural Mentoring

Despite the clearly demonstrated multiple benefits of mentoring, there are a number of significant barriers that make it difficult to provide effective multicultural mentoring for ethnic minority students. First, there is the lack of ethnic minority mentors for ethnic minority students. Given that mentors tend to choose protégés who are most like themselves, ethnic minorities are at a disadvantage in seeking and finding a mentor because of the lack of ethnic minority representation in positions of power (Bowman et al., 1999; Dreher and Cox, 1996; Smith, Smith, and Markham, 2000; Tillman, 1998). Not surprisingly, in predominantly white environments, many ethnic minorities are mentored or have to seek mentorship from whites, even when they have a preference for mentors who share their ethnicity (González-Figueroa and Young, 2005; Thomas, 2001). For instance, Thomas's (1990) study of corporate managers found that the white protégés had almost no mentoring relationships with persons of another race, whereas the black protégés formed many of their mentoring relationships with whites.

Cultural differences within mentoring relationships can also pose another barrier against effective multicultural mentoring. The findings on this subject of diversified mentoring relationships are somewhat inconclusive. While a few recent studies have given some tentative indications that cross-race and cross-cultural mentoring can be successful (Bordes and Arredondo, 2005; Tillman, 1998), the results from other studies are much less positive: several studies have found that protégés in cross-cultural mentoring dyads tend to re-

ceive less mentoring and psychosocial support than protégés who have mentors that are similar to them (Dreher and Cox, 1996; Feldman, Folks, and
Turnley, 1999; Ortiz-Walters and Gilson, 2005; Thomas, 1990). Thomas's
(1986) dissertation on cross-racial mentoring also found that white racial consciousness and black racial identity significantly influenced the dynamics of
cross-racial mentoring relationships. In addition, some studies on cross-gender
mentoring relationships have shown that they experience more difficulties
creating and maintaining their relationships than same-gender relationships
(Dreher and Ash, 1990; Feldman, Folks, and Turnley, 1999; Kanter, 1977).

The third barrier to multicultural mentoring is the paucity of research and
knowledge on effective multicultural and cross-cultural mentoring. One
study of mentoring books and guides found that there is very little material
available in the United States to guide faculty in effectively and successfully
mentoring women, minority, and international students (Dedrick and Watson, 2002). Indeed, our notions of mentoring are derived from primarily European American conceptions of mentoring behaviors, hence the applicability of these concepts to other cultures is questionable (Feldman, Folks, and
Turnley, 1999). For instance, collegiality is often assumed to be an important
component of mentoring relationships; however, one study comparing U.S.
and Chinese protégés found that the Chinese dyads assumed a more didactic
tone in their conversations, with the Chinese mentors tending to be more
dominant, particularly in initiating topics (Wang, Strong, and Odell, 2004).
Although this approach to mentoring goes against commonly held assumptions about the value of collegiality, it was not observed to impede protégé
learning. Another problem with existing research on ethnic minority mentoring is the frequent tendency to conflate all ethnic groups into a single category. Although this strategy is understandable for statistical reasons, it hides
and blurs potentially meaningful between-group differences and concerns.

Multicultural and Cross-Cultural Mentoring

The purpose of this chapter is to highlight research findings pertaining to
multicultural and cross-cultural considerations in mentoring graduate students of color. In chapter 2 of this book, White and Henderson propose a
multilevel multicultural competency model guiding change along conceptual/
theoretical/intellectual, emotional via multicultural dialogue, behavioral via
muticultural engagement and skill building integration. Using their model as
an organizing framework, this chapter provides a review of the research literature pertaining to multicultural and cross-cultural mentoring.

Conceptual/Theoretical/Intellectual Change

Not only are there many different types of mentoring (for instance, peer mentoring, group mentoring, cross-generational mentoring), there is also a plethora of definitions for mentoring (Crosby, 1999; Tentoni, 1995). The focus in this chapter is on the more traditional conception of a mentoring relationship as that between a more experienced, senior member (the mentor) and less experienced junior member (the protégé) of an organization or field for the purpose of developing, supporting, and enhancing the career of the protégé (Mullen, 1994). The roots of mentoring in the United States can be located in bestselling publications in the late 1970s, such as *Passages* (Sheehy, 1976) and *Seasons of a Man's Life* (Levinson et al., 1978). These books highlighted the centrality of mentoring in the lives of professional men and women and helped introduce and popularize the concept of mentoring in business settings.

The above introduction to the background of mentoring, although admittedly brief, points to the decidedly Western influences on present-day conceptualizations about mentoring. Indeed, even the very definition of mentoring, as stated above, is shaped by distinct cultural values and biases. This European-American worldview is often a pervasive, yet unexamined bias in the research and literature on mentoring. It has at times led researchers to assume that there is a one-size-fits-all model to mentoring (Benishek et al., 2004).

Theories and models of mentoring abound, with the most frequently cited being Kram's (1985) classic model of mentoring functions, derived from her groundbreaking study of mentor-protégé dyads in a large corporation. Kram identified two major types of functions of a mentor: career functions and psychosocial functions. Sponsorship, exposure and visibility, coaching, protection, and challenging assignments are cited as career functions. These enhance advancement in an organization and are possible because of the mentor's seniority and power. Psychosocial functions, on the other hand, promote the protégé's self-confidence, identity, and efficacy in a professional role. These functions include role modeling, acceptance and confirmation, counseling, and friendship. Kram's pioneering research has been an immeasurable contribution to the research and literature on mentoring, and her work has been especially invaluable for highlighting the processes involved in mentoring. However, a major omission in her 1985 work is the lack of attention paid to cultural variables. Although gender was addressed in her study, no other cultural or racial demographics were examined or even noted in her participant pool. Hence, although her findings were, and continue to be, greatly influential in the mentoring literature, it is not known how applicable or suitable they are to ethnic minority mentors and protégés.

Kram's model has been the basis and inspiration for other models of mentoring. Most relevant to this chapter is Fassinger's model of feminist mentoring, which she first presented at the Woman of the Year Award address at the annual meeting of the American Psychological Association in 1997. Fassinger (1997) provides a model of mentoring that embraces feminist principles, thus her model emphasizes mentoring processes such as rethinking of power, emphasis on relational, valuing of collaboration, commitment to diversity, integration of dichotomies, and incorporation of political analysis. Her model is distinct in its highlighting of diversity and power within the mentoring relationship. Drawing on Fassinger's model, Benishek et al. (2004) proposed a multicultural feminist model of mentoring that explicitly infused multicultural considerations into the dimensions identified by Fassinger. Both of these models are revolutionary in their incorporation of feminist and multicultural considerations within their frameworks and in providing an evaluation of the benefits to both mentors and protégés. However, a major limitation of these models is that neither was empirically derived or tested. Hence, the actual validity of these models is not known.

A unique contribution to the mentoring literature is Harris and Smith's (1999) Africentric model of mentoring that is centered on Africentric principles (unity, self-determination, creativity, purpose, convergence of "I" and "We," and faith). Their model is distinctive for its conceptualization of cultural values for the purpose of mentoring African Americans in a culturally congruent way. Indeed, all three models (Harris and Smith, Fassinger, and Benishek et al.) are exemplary and exciting in their incorporation of multicultural perspectives. However, all three models are in need of empirical validation to test for their robustness and applicability to minority populations.

Emotional Change through Multicultural Engagement

White and Henderson advocate open communication about race and other multicultural topics to develop self-awareness as well as understanding and empathy for others. Dialoging about race has hardly been explored in the mentoring literature. The few studies that have been done in this area provide tentative, but largely indirect confirmation of the value of multicultural dialogue in mentoring relationships.

Thomas's (2001) study of minority and white professionals at three U.S. corporations found distinct differences between the patterns of advancement and types of mentoring relationships experienced by the two groups. Thomas argues that cross-race relationships are particularly vulnerable to "protective hesitation" (p. 105)—the reluctance to address sensitive topics such as race and racism. Thomas recommends that organizations teach mentors how to communicate about racial issues, warning that the reluctance or avoidance to speak openly about race can undermine the relationship. His study found that minorities tended to advance further when their white mentors acknowledged and understood the impact of race on their protégés. He also found that dyads that discussed race openly usually experienced greater career development for the protégé, as well as a broader understanding in both parties. Likewise, a qualitative study of four mentoring relationships involving ethnic minority protégés found that open discussions about race contributed to the overall rapport, understanding, and support in the relationships (Chan and Fetterman, 2005).

The difficulty in having a multiracial/multicultural dialogue may be part of the reason why protégés of color with mentors of color tend to report more satisfaction and interpersonal comfort than those who do not have mentors sharing their race or ethnicity (Ortiz-Walters and Gilson, 2005) or gender (Allen, Day, and Lentz, 2005). Ortiz-Walters and Gilson recommend that:

> Mentors and protégés should try to find some common deep-level similarities before working together and that surface-level characteristics, while not influencing the perceptions of mentors, are still of consideration to protégés of color. What these findings suggest is that it may behoove both parties to spend some time getting to know one another and understand what is important value- and problem-solving wise before embarking upon a relationship (p. 472).

Behavioral Change through Multicultural Engagement

Since there is a lack of representation of minorities in academia, many protégés look to white mentors for guidance, hence necessitating cross-racial and cross-cultural behavioral interaction. Thomas's (1990, 2001; Thomas and Gabarro, 1999) research in this area is instrumental in highlighting the importance of mentors learning to become comfortable interacting with people of different races. In particular, he notes the importance of white managers being comfortable interacting with people of color:

> The difficulty in developing the psychosocial aspect of cross-racial relationships most likely contributes to and is caused by the lack of comfort that white and black managers feel with each other. The long term result may be that black managers and, for similar reasons, women managers are not given difficult and important assignments of the type that lead to high visibility and advancement, because those assignments imply greater risk to the sponsor or mentor (p. 489).

Thomas's research (2001) shows that mentors' behavioral interactions with ethnic minority protégés can be enhanced if mentors go beyond instructional mentoring, for instance, they do not simply focus on skill building. Certainly, it is vital that the mentor provide guidance and opportunities for growth in key areas such as networking, sponsorship, providing challenging assignments, and protection. However, Thomas's research indicates that the minority executives in his study benefited from having close, in-depth mentoring relationships with mentors who served in both counseling and coaching capacities, as opposed to focusing strictly on instrumental mentoring. Likewise, Valadez (1998) found that positive, constructive interactions between mentors and protégés are critical to mentoring relationships and Chan (2006) noted the importance of sharing personal stories and using humor in mentoring ethnic minority students.

Skill Building Integration

The available research on multicultural mentoring strongly suggests that mentors need to be trained to work effectively and sensitively with culturally different protégés (Thomas, 2001). In particular, mentors need to understand race and how it impacts their protégés:

> The mentor of a professional of color must also be aware of the challenges race can present to his protégé's career development and advancement. Only then can the mentor help his protégé built a network of relationships with people who can pave the way to the executive level (Thomas, 2001, p. 100).

In addition to having an in-depth understanding of race, mentors must also be perceptive and sensitive to other sociopolitical and other meta-level obstacles that can impede a mentoring relationship. These include, but are not limited to, mistrust of the majority culture, stereotype threat, and the model minority stereotype (Johnson, 2007). Davidson and Foster-Johnson (2001) further recommend that mentors introspect and become aware of their own prejudices, attitudes, and biases.

Not only do mentors have to possess multicultural knowledge, they also have to demonstrate sensitivity to cultural traditions that might be close to the heart of a protégé. For instance, a Native American student might have to take a leave of absence so that he or she can be involved in culturally and spiritually important ceremonies, such as attending traditional sweats or other community celebrations (Pavel, 1988). Mentors of Mexican American women might also have to be particularly sensitive to their protégés' struggle with balancing professional roles and family obligations (Valentine and Mosley, 2000).

Future Directions for Research on Multicultural Mentoring

The research on cultural concerns in mentoring is still in its early stages—clearly, this is an area in great need of much more extensive research, writing, and reflection. There are many directions that deserve attention for future research. These directions include research on diversified relationships in different settings (such as academic, community-based, and different types of corporations) and research on specific ethnic populations and how different cultural values and needs impact mentoring processes (for instance, the mentoring needs of Asian American as opposed to Hispanic/Latino populations).

One area that would be especially valuable for further research is the *type* of mentoring best suited for different ethnic groups. For instance, some groups might favor the more traditional hierarchical model of mentoring, while other groups might prefer a more egalitarian, peer-focused arrangement (Girves, Zepeda, and Gwathmey, 2005; Haring, 1997). Of particular importance is research on the processes of mentoring relationships, particularly pertaining to cross-cultural and cross-racial dynamics within such relationships. Qualitative/ethnographic studies would be especially helpful in providing in-depth, nuanced views of cross-race mentoring relationships (Thomas, 1990). In conducting such research, two considerations are especially important to keep in mind: the context of the mentoring relationships (Thomas, 1990) and the perspectives of both mentors and protégés (Allen, Eby, and Lentz, 2006; Russell and Adams, 1997).

Conclusion

There is much we do not know about the impact of race on mentoring processes and outcomes. A critical challenge for multicultural mentoring is to provide socialization into a field or organization without compromising, denigrating, or denying the racial, ethnic, and cultural identities and values of the protégé.

Despite the scarcity of research on this topic, the work that has been done thus far furnishes important insights for organizations, schools, training programs, advisors, and clinical supervisors who are instrumental in teaching and guiding the next generation of psychologists. In summary, the existing literature point to the following five guidelines as appropriate strategies for mentors of ethnic minority students:

- attentiveness and sensitivity to cultural variables in the lives of ethnic minority protégés;

- open communication about race and racism;
- awareness of personal and societal stereotypes, prejudices, biases, and attitudes;
- ease in interacting with people of color;
- focus on the personal as well as professional dimensions of the protégé.

In addition to these guidelines, the multilevel/multicultural competency building model proposed by White and Henderson further illuminate the multicultural competencies needed for effective, culturally sensitive mentoring. Specifically, mentors committed to working optimally with ethnic minority students should aspire toward change on the four levels of the change model: conceptual/theoretical/intellectual, emotional through multiracial dialogue, behavioral through multicultural engagement interaction, and skill building integration.

References

Allen, T. D., Day, R., and Lentz, E. (2005). The role of interpersonal comfort in mentoring relationships. *Journal of Career Development, 31*(3), 155–69.

Allen, T. D., Eby, L. T., and Lentz, E. (2006). Mentorship behaviors and mentorship quality associated with formal mentoring programs: Closing the gap between research and practice. *Journal of Applied Psychology, 3*, 567–78.

Allen, T. D., Poteet, M. L., and Eby, L. T. (2004). Career benefits associated with mentoring for proteges: A meta-analysis. *Journal of Applied Psychology, 89*(1), 127–36.

Benishek, L. A., Bieschke, K. J., Park, J., and Slattery, S. M. (2004). A multicultural feminist model of mentoring. *Journal of Multicultural Counseling and Development, 32*, 428–42.

Bordes, V., and Arredondo, P. (2005). Mentoring and 1st-year Latina/o college students. *Journal of Hispanic Higher Education, 4*, 114–33.

Bowman, S. R., Kite, M. E., Branscombe, N. R., and Williams, S. (1999). Developmental relationships of black Americans in the academy. In A. J. Murrell and F. J. Crosby (Eds.), *Mentoring dilemmas: Developmental relationships within multicultural organizations* (pp. 21–46). Mahwah, NJ: Lawrence Erlbaum Associates.

Boyle, P., and Boice, B. (1998). Systematic mentoring for new faculty teachers and graduate teaching assistants. *Innovative Higher Education, 22*, 157–79.

Burke, R., Burgess, Z., and Fallon, B. (2006). Benefits of mentoring to Australian early career women managers and professionals. *Equal Opportunities International, 25*(1), 71–79.

Chan, A. (2006, March). *Best practices mentoring ethnic minority students in psychology: Access to the inside story.* Paper presented at the California Psychological Association, San Francisco, CA.

Chan, A., and Fetterman, D. (2005, April). *Mentoring Up-Close and Personal: An In-Depth Look at Mentor Activities with Ethnic Minority Students.* Paper presented at the International Mentoring Association, Oakland, CA.

Chao, G. T., Walz, P. M., and Gardner, P. D. (1992). Formal and informal mentorships: A comparison on mentoring functions and contrast with nonmentored counterparts. *Personnel Psychology, 45*(3), 619–36.

Crosby, F. J. (1999). The developing literature on developmental relationships. In A. J. Murrell and F. J. Crosby (Eds.), *Mentoring dilemmas: Developmental relationships within multicultural organizations* (pp. 3–20). Mahwah, NJ: Lawrence Erlbaum Associates.

Davidson, M. N., and Foster-Johnson, L. (2001). Mentoring in the preparation of graduate students of color. *Review of Educational Research, 71*(4), 549–74.

Dedrick, R. F., and Watson, F. (2002). Mentoring needs of female, minority, and international graduate students: a content analysis of academic research guides and related print material. *Mentoring and Tutoring, 10*(3), 275–89.

Dreher, G. F., and Ash, R. A. (1990). A comparative study of mentoring among men and women in managerial, professional, and technological positions. *Journal of Applied Psychology, 75*, 539–46.

Dreher, G. F., and Cox, J. T. H. (1996). Race, gender and opportunity: A study of compensation attainment and the establishment of mentoring relationships. *Journal of Applied Psychology, 81*, 297–308.

Fassinger, R. E. (1997). *Dangerous liaisons: Reflections on feminist mentoring.* Paper presented at the American Psychological Association Convention, Chicago, IL.

Feldman, D. C., Folks, W. R., and Turnley, W. H. (1999). Mentor-protegé diversity and its impact on international internship experiences. *Journal of Organizational Behavior, 20*, 597–611.

Gelso, C. J., and Lent, R. W. (2000). Scientific training and scholarly productivity: The person, the training environment, and their interaction. In S. D. Brown and R. W. Lent (Eds.), *Handbook of counseling psychology* (3rd ed., pp. 109–39). New York: Wiley.

Girves, J. E., and Wemmerus, V. (1988). Developing models of graduate student degree progress. *Journal of Higher Education, 59*(2), 163–89.

Girves, J. E., Zepeda, Y., and Gwathmey, J. K. (2005). Mentoring in a post-affirmative action world. *Journal of Social Issues, 61*(3), 449–79.

González-Figueroa, E., and Young, A. M. (2005). Ethnic identity and mentoring among Latinas in professional roles. *Cultural Diversity and Ethnic Minority Psychology, 11*(3), 213–26.

Haring, M. J. (1997). Networking mentoring as a preferred model for guiding programs for underrepresented students. In H. T. Frierson, Jr. (Ed.), *Diversity in higher education: Mentoring and diversity in higher education* (Vol. 1, pp. 63–76). Greenwich, CT: JAI Press.

Harris, F., and Smith, J. C. (1999). Centricity and the mentoring experience in academia: An Africentric mentoring paradigm. *Western Journal of Black Studies, 23*(4), 229–38.

Hollingsworth, M. A., and Fassinger, R. E. (2002). The role of faculty mentors in the research training of counseling psychology doctoral students. *Journal of Counseling Psychology, 49*, 324–30.

Johnson, W. B. (2007). *On being a mentor: A guide for higher education faculty.* Mahwah, NJ: Lawrence Erlbaum Associates.

Kanter, R. M. (1977). *Men and women of the corporation.* New York: Basic Books.

Koberg, C. S., Boss, R. W., and Goodman, E. (1998). Factors and outcomes associated with mentoring among health-care professionals. *Journal of Vocational Behavior, 53*(1), 58–72.

Kram, K. E. (1985). *Mentoring at work: Developmental relationships in organizational life.* Glenview, IL: Scott, Foresman and Company.

Levinson, D. J., Darrow, C. N., Klein, E. B., Levinson, M. H., and McKee, B. (1978). *The seasons of a man's life.* New York: Knopf.

Loo, C. M., and Rolinson, G. (1986). Alienation of ethnic minority students at a predominantly white university. *Journal of Higher Education, 57*, 58–77.

Lyons, W., Scroggins, D., and Rule, P. B. (1990). The mentor in graduate education. *Studies in Higher Education, 15*, 277–85.

Morrow, S. L., Rakhsha, G., and Castañeda, C. L. (2001). Qualitative research methods for multicultural counseling. In J. G. Ponterotto, J. M. Casas, L. A. Suzuki, and C. M. Alexander (Eds.), *Handbook of multicultural counseling* (2nd ed.) (pp. 575–603). Thousand Oaks, CA: Sage.

Mullen, E. J. (1994). Framing the mentoring relationship as an information exchange. *Human Resource Management Review, 4*, 257–81.

Murphy, S. E., and Ensher, E. (2001). The role of mentoring support and self-management strategies on reported career outcomes. *Journal of Career Development, 27*, 229–46.

Ortiz-Walters, R., and Gilson, L. L. (2005). Mentoring in academia: An examination of the experiences of protégés of color. *Journal of Vocational Behavior, 67*, 459–75.

Paglis, L., Green, S., and Bauer, T. (2006). Does adviser mentoring add value? A longitudinal study of mentoring and doctoral student outcomes. *Research in Higher Education, 47*(4), 451–76.

———. (1993). White researchers conducting multicultural counseling research: Can their efforts be 'Mo Betta. *The Counseling Psychologist, 21*(2), 250–56.

Pavel, D. M. (1988). Developing faculty mentors for American Indian and Alaska Native graduate students. In H. T. Frierson, Jr. (Ed.), *Diversity in higher education: Examining protégé-mentor experiences* (Vol. 2, pp. 115–27). Stamford, CT: JAI Press.

Russell, J. E. A., and Adams, D. M. (1997). The changing nature of mentoring in organizations: An introduction to the special issue on mentoring in organizations. *Journal of Vocational Behavior, 51*, 1–14.

Scandura, T. A. (1992). Mentorship and career mobility: an empirical investigation. *Journal of Organizational Behavior, 13*(2), 169–74.

Schrodt, P., Cawyer, C. S., and Sanders, R. (2003). An examination of academic mentoring behaviors and new faculty members' satisfaction with socialization and tenure and promotion processes. *Communication Education, 52*(1), 17–29.

Sheehy, G. (1976). *Passages: Predictable crises of adult life.* New York: Dutton.

Smith, J. W., Smith, W. J., and Markham, S. E. (2000). Diversity issues in mentoring academic faculty. *Journal of Career Development, 26*, 251–62.

Tentoni, S. C. (1995). The mentoring of counseling students: A concept in search of a paradigm. *Counselor Education and Supervision, 35*(1), 32–42.

Terrell, M. C., and Hassell, R. K. (1994). Mentoring undergraduate minority students: An overview, survey, and model program. In W. A. Wunsch (Ed.), *Mentoring revisited: Making an impact on individuals and institutions* (pp. 35–45). San Francisco: Jossey-Bass Publishers.

Thomas, D. A. (1986). An intra-organizational analysis of differences in black and white patterns of sponsorship and the dynamics of cross-racial mentoring. *Dissertation Abstracts International.*

———. (1990). The impact of race on managers' experiences of developmental relationships (mentoring and sponsorship): An intra-organizational study. *Journal of Organizational Behavior, 11*, 479–92.

———. A. (2001). The truth about mentoring minorities: race matters. *Harvard Business Review, 79*, 99–107.

Thomas, D. A., and Gabarro, J. J. (1999). *Breaking through: The making of minority executives in corporate America.* Boston: Harvard Business School Press.

Tillman, L. C. (1998). The mentoring of African-American faculty: Scaling the promotion and tenure mountain. In H. T. Frierson, Jr. (Ed.), *Diversity in higher education: Examining protégé-mentor experiences* (Vol. 2, pp. 141–55). Stamford, CT: JAI Press.

Tinto, V. (1998). Colleges as communities: Taking research on student persistence seriously. *The Review of Higher Education, 21*(2), 167–77.

Valadez, J. S. (1998). The social dynamics of mentoring in graduate education: A case study of African-American students and their graduate advisors. In H. T. Frierson, Jr. (Ed.), *Diversity in higher education: Examining protege-mentor experiences* (Vol. 2, pp. 129–40). Stamford, CT: JAI Press.

Valentine, S., and Mosley, G. (2000). Acculturation and sex-role attitudes among Mexican Americans: A longitudinal analysis. *Hispanic Journal of Behavioral Sciences, 22*, 104–13.

Wang, J., Strong, M., and Odell, S. J. (2004). Mentor-novice conversations about teaching: A comparison of two U.S. and two Chinese cases. *Teachers College Record, 106*, 778–813.

Williamson, M. J., and Fenske, R. H. (1998). Relationships between mentors and Mexican-American and American Indian doctoral students. In H. T. Frierson, Jr. (Ed.), *Diversity in higher education: Examining protege-mentor experiences* (Vol. 2, pp. 59–90). Stamford, CT: JAI Press.

CHAPTER TEN

Managing Resistance

The Difference between Success and Failure of
Multicultural Competency Initiatives

John E. Queener and Shannon D. Smith

Over the past thirty years, researchers and theorists have argued for a multi-cultural perspective in psychology. It is commonplace to hear about the importance of taking into account contextual and cultural factors when assessing and providing psychological interventions to nonwhite populations (Atkinson, Morten, and Sue, 1998; D'Andrea and Daniels, 1995; LaFromboise and Howard-Pitney, 1995; Paniagua, 1998; Parham, White, and Ajamu, 1999). Moreover, numerous multicultural models and paradigms have been developed in order to aid our understanding of multiculturalism (Sue and Sue, 2003). In fact, the American Psychological Association adopted a set of multicultural guidelines for psychologists (American Psychological Association, 2003). These guidelines were developed to provide instruction to psychologists on how they can conduct their professional activities in a culturally relevant manner. In spite of the activities of many professionals to attempt to make the discipline of psychology more receptive to multiculturalism, some argue that racism and cultural biases still remain as significant impediments to developing multiculturalism as an integral part of psychology (Carter, 1995; Constantine, 2006; Guthrie, 1997, Mio and Morris, 1990; Ridley, 1995; Samuda, 1998; Sue and Sue, 2003). We believe that in order for multiculturalism to become an integral part of psychology, racism in the form of resistance to multiculturalism needs to be adequately understood. Therefore, the purpose of this chapter is to present a conceptual framework for understanding psychological resistance to multiculturalism.

To date, strategies for understanding resistance to multiculturalism have received scant attention in the literature. Mio and Awakuni (2000), however, insisted that resistance to multiculturalism has been an enduring aspect of the multicultural movement in psychology from the beginning and extends beyond students in the classroom to faculty and administrators, and the entire academy. Mio and Awakuni conceptualized resistance as emanating from covert unintentional racism, which they define as "a form of racism that comes about because of laws or traditions that are racist in nature, the protagonist is unaware of the racists roots of these laws and traditions" (p. 21). Feagin, Vera, and Imani (1996) argued that racism is an endearing aspect of the entire academy and creates an atmosphere of hostility at worst and an environment of discomfort at best for faculty, staff, and students of color. We postulate that resistance to multiculturalism in the form racism takes on three forms: individual, cultural, and institutional racism as conceptualized by Jones (1997).

Individual, Cultural, and Institutional Racism

Jones (1997) suggested that individual racism has three important components. The first component is that one believes that he or she is superior to other groups based on skin color. Second, he or she believes that attributes such as intelligence are distributed based on the possession of certain physical traits such as skin color. Third, he or she treats others in an inferior manner based on the assumption of superiority due to skin color. Jones argued that the important components of cultural racism were ethnocentrism, power, and the ability to perpetuate dominance from one generation to the next. Jones defined institutional racism as systematic ways of operating that produce racial inequities. Institutional racism can be overt or covert and intentional or unintentional. It is difficult for individuals socialized in America to completely avoid being affected by individual racism, cultural racism, and institutional racism. Although all these forms of racism influence the attitudes of professionals in psychology from embracing multiculturalism, Sue and Sue (2003) argued that it is the institutional and unintentional type of racism that is the most insidious.

We believe that one of the reasons that institutional racism is so insidious is that it allows some whites to feel good about what they do and how they do it without any awareness of how their actions negatively impact people of color. In other words, institutional racism allows the status quo to be maintained, allows administrators to administrate, faculty to teach, and staff to serve in a manner that does not hold them accountable for how their actions can offend, discriminate against, adversely impact, or otherwise damage nonwhite persons. In essence, institutional racism allows white administrators, faculty, and staff to deny any personal responsibility for racism in spite of evidence to the contrary.

Gaertner and Dovidio (1986) called those who perpetuate institutional racism aversive racists. They define aversive racism as covert, subtle forms of racism that continue to allow for the oppression of people of color. Moreover, aversive acts of racism are not seen as acts of racism because many whites are socialized to believe that racism is overt, blatant acts of discrimination such as not admitting students of color to graduate programs, purposely failing students of color on exams, or making statements about the intellectual inferiority of students of color. Aversive racists never consider the fact that they help create null environments or even hostile environments for students of color by never inviting them to participate in research projects, failing to provide students of color with the same academic assistance as aversive racists provide white students, and literally failing to acknowledge the existence of students of color and their culture. In contrast to being racists, Gaertner and Dovidio argued that aversive racists see themselves as espousing egalitarian values instead of resisting multiculturalism; aversive racists see themselves as proponents of multiculturalism.

This false belief in themselves keeps aversive racists in a state that can lead to at least two problems. First, when covert acts of racism are highlighted as those that go beyond the overt into more institutional types of racism, the aversive racists will tend to react defensively thereby blaming the messenger and avoiding the process of understanding the racist act itself. Second, the aversive racists' denial of this institutional type of racism prevents them from being introspective on how they perpetuate racism. This denial risks perpetuating the status quo and jeopardizes all opportunities to change policies and procedures that adversely affect people of color or to create programs or activities that can benefit people of color.

Blaming the Messenger

A common reaction of aversive racists to being told of unintentional racist incidents is to label the person delivering the message as the culprit. A case study illustrates the point: At one particular institution of higher education, several administrators set out to make a high-quality video that could be used to recruit students to their program. The video was shown to the entire staff of the program to which these administrators belonged. After the video was played, the administrators asked for feedback. An African American member of the program asked why no students of color were featured in the video. He discussed the implications of this in terms of recruiting students and mentioned how that might hurt any attempts to recruit students of color to the program. In spite of being informed of this, one of the creators of the video stated that if another video is made, an effort would be made to include students of color in the video, but this video was going to be used even though the participants were all white. This was a done deal. One of the two video creators continued expressing her irritation at the suggestion that she did not do her job, as she was the public relation specialist and did not need to consult with others on how she could have recruited students of color to participate in the video project. When the administrator critic of the video stated that it was not enough to think about the next video, as this current video with all white students was not acceptable, this critic then became the problem, not the video. Subsequent discussions focused on how the critic should have been less harsh in his statements about the video. Statements were made that he should have understood that this was the first time such a task was being undertaken and mistakes were going to be made. In essence, the creators of the video became upset and believed that it was not the video that was the problem, but it was the critic of the video that was the problem. Therefore, instead of focusing on the message that a video that included all white students might send to potential recruits, the focus was on the critic. Instead of focusing on why students of color may have refused to participate in the video, the focus was on the critic. We believe that blaming the messenger allows the aversive racist to deny the existence of racism and resist multiculturalism by failing to be introspective.

Denial of Racism

Constantine (2006) argued that racism in all its forms continues to be a part of the fabric of America. In spite of scholars documenting the existence of racism, aversive racists continue to deny the existence of racism in general and especially the existence of racism where they may be personally responsible for perpetuating it. In academic programs across the country, members of the faculty continue to talk about the importance of diversity, especially ethnic diversity. In spite of talking about the importance of diversity, ethnically diverse students continue to complain about academic environments that are devoid of racial sensitivity and lack cultural competence. Yet, students' complaints can often fall on deaf ears because administrators and faculty who deliver programs may deny the existence of racism. Furthermore, attempts to decrease institutional racism at the macro level through the creation of specific programs or through the change of polices are deemed as "unnecessary," "not needed," "not the best use of resources," or a myriad of other excuses are manufactured to serve as resistance to multiculturalism.

Constantine (2006) argued that faculty and administrators have a responsibility to understand how they knowingly or unknowingly perpetuate racism in spite of the complex and challenging nature of institutional racism. We believe that faculty and administrators need a strategy to understand their personal role in perpetuating resistance to multiculturalism and keeping intact institutional racism.

Below is a description of our attempt to identify how persons who see themselves as egalitarian maintain their resistance to multiculturalism through what we identify as psycho-emotional defensive mechanisms. These factors were developed in an attempt to understand resistance to multiculturalism of trainees in counseling-related programs. After we briefly describe the application of the model to counseling trainees, we discuss how a similar model can be applied to administrators and faculty in counseling-related programs. We believe that understanding this resistance can lead to strategies to overcoming the resistance by helping faculty and administrators understand how they might be playing a personal role in perpetuating racism.

Nonlinear Process of Resistance

Our model of psychological resistance is called the Circuitous Model of Multicultural Development (CMMD) and is based on the Circuitous Model of Trainee Multicultural Development (CMTMD). Below is a brief description of the CMTMD developed by Queener et al. (forthcoming). They conducted a qualitative study examining graduate students' resistance to multiculturalism. Participants consisted of twenty-eight graduate students enrolled in a counseling-related program at the master's level. The data collection resulted in a compilation of over six hundred typed pages of participant journal reflections on their perspectives on multiculturalism over a fifteen-week period. The data were analyzed utilizing grounded theory (Strauss and Corbin, 1990) and components of consensual qualitative inquiry (CQR) (Hill, Thompson, and Williams, 1997) in order to determine the factors that led to student participants engaging or resisting multiculturalism.

Upon completion of the CQR data analysis and grounded theory procedures, the research team formalized the research findings. One major discovery that emerged from the data was that trainee engagement and resistance to multiculturalism was best defined as a nonlinear process; we observed a circuitous process of engagement and resistance of multicultural development unfolding throughout the investigation. Students tended to vacillate between engaging and resisting the course material, versus being completely engaged or totally resistant to multiculturalism. Figure 10.1 displays this

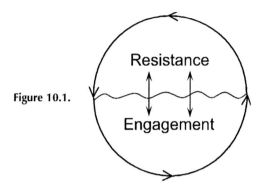

Figure 10.1.

circuitous process of resistance and engagement during multicultural development. The outer circle depicts the circular process of resistance and engagement, while the wavy middle line illustrates that there is not a distinct (solid line) boundary between each of them. The arrows point out that one can move back and forth between resistance and engagement to a greater or lesser degree.

The second major finding was the identification of four major themes that emerged from the data, which influenced the process of engagement and resistance to multiculturalism. We propose these themes in our CMTMD as facilitating factors involved in the process of engagement and resistance. They are (a) emotional expressiveness, (b) awareness of self and others, (c) avoidance, and (d) dissonance. The more students experienced themes (a) and (b), the more they tended to engage the material. The more the students experienced themes (c) and (d), the more they tended to resist the material. Each theme is defined and discussed below.

Theme 1: Emotional Expressiveness
Emotional expressiveness emerged from a wide range of emotions that the participants experienced during the course of study with respect to multicultural skill development. The range of emotions that were expressed was quite broad, including anger, frustration, happiness, joy, excitement, fear, worry, anxiety, guilt, shame, embarrassment, confusion, sadness, and depression.

Theme 2: Awareness of Self and Others
Awareness of self and others is related to the degree to which students were alerted to or developed knowledge of others and used this insight to facilitate their own growth. Student awareness emerged over the course of this investigation, particularly as participants were able to apply their new knowledge of alternative worldviews to their own worldviews, values, and beliefs.

Theme 3: Avoidance
Avoidance is the process or act of withdrawing or vacating from something. Avoidance was observed when students withdrew from the process of multicultural development when their thoughts or feelings created too much internal tension. A related subtheme of avoidance that was noted is the "retreat to universalism." This retreat signified the degree to which participants intellectualized or failed to acknowledge that cultural differences were significant in understanding human behavior. Typically, these students would minimize differences based on culture and focus only on individual differences or state that observed differences were due to some other demographic.

Theme 4: Dissonance
Dissonance is the degree to which there is inconsistency between the beliefs that one holds and between one's actions, as it relates to multiculturalism. Dissonance referred to the degree to which participants identified with ideal ingredients of the multiculturally competent counselor, yet they did not simultaneously identify inconsistencies within themselves.

The themes of emotional expressiveness, awareness of self and others, avoidance, and dissonance emerged as four major factors related to trainees' engagement and/or resistance to multicultural training. These four factors related to the process of engagement resistance are shown in Figure 10.2. The arrows of the outer circle suggest that the four factors are in constant circular motion. Each factor interacts with another as displayed by touching at each end. Furthermore, each factor is influenced by the other three factors to a greater or lesser degree throughout the process of resisting and engaging.

Based on these four factors derived from the CQR process, utilizing grounded theory, we formulated six theoretical statements that reflect aspects of multicultural development. These principles emerged from the data. They are as follows: (1) trainees engage in a circular process of engagement and resistance to multicultural development to a greater or lesser degree; (2) students express a wide range of emotions during multicultural development; (3) participants strive to become the "ideal" multiculturally competent counselor; (4) students express dissonance between the "ideal" multiculturally competent counselor and their actual multicultural counseling competencies; (5) subjects retreat to "universalism" when overwhelmed by their inadequacies or stress related to multiculturally development; and (6) trainees display a greater understanding of self and others as they develop increased awareness and competencies of multiculturalism.

Based on these six theoretical statements, we developed a preliminary model to reflect how these factors interact as a result of data and the participant

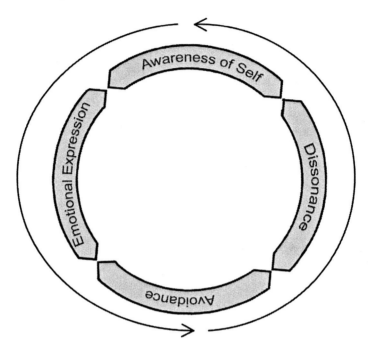

Figure 10.2.

experience from this investigation. Figure 10.3 combines both figures 10.1 and 10.2 by depicting a model of trainee development related to multicultural skills. This is the CMTMD. The circle illustrates that this process is circuitous, not linear. We propose that trainees have the potential to move between engagement and resistance. The figure illustrates this potential motion.

Each circle of Figure 10.3, the larger outer and the smaller inner circle, is depicted as being in constant circular motion. The inner circle of resistance and engagement illustrates that students oscillate between engaging and resisting multicultural development. The inner circle is located in the center of the figure, which demonstrates that the process of resistance and engagement is central or the primary process involved in trainee multicultural development. The four major factors associated with this process are positioned just outside of the inner circle, but remain within the larger circuitous model. The factors are depicted as rotating through the inner circle. The inner circle is seen as spiraling in a constant circular motion through each of these four factors. Thus, as students vacillate between resistance and engagement, they can experience each factor in a state of resistance or engagement to a greater or lesser degree.

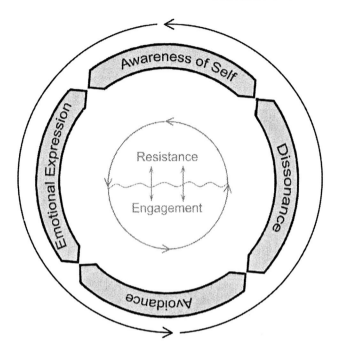

Figure 10.3.

Circuitous Model of Multicultural Development

The CMMD is a modification of the trainee model to fit the development toward multiculturalism of faculty and administrators. We believe that there are several similarities and several differences between the model for trainees and the model for faculty and administrators. We are not aware of any other faculty models that examine the psychological resistance to multiculturalism in the literature.

Similarities between the Models

There are several similarities between the student model and the adminis-trators and faculty model emerging from the data. First, for all groups, we be-lieve that the process of resistance to multiculturalism is a nonlinear process. That is to say that all groups are not totally for multiculturalism or totally against multiculturalism. Second, we believe that all groups use the psycho-emotional factors of emotional expressiveness, awareness of self and others, avoidance, and dissonance to manage multicultural resistance.

Differences between the Models

We believe that there are several differences between the models for trainees and the model for administrators and faculty. The most important difference is the power differential. Trainees tend not to be operating from a position of power. Therefore, they may engage issues related to multiculturalism due to more powerful administrators and faculty suggesting that trainees engage multiculturalism. However, administrators and faculty do not have this power differential at the same level as do student trainees. This means that strategies must be used at the macro level (D'Andrea, 2006; Vera, Buhin, and Shin, 2006), as well as strategies that can be used at the micro level (Pedersen, 2206). We also believe that administrators and faculty have been socialized for a longer period of time to resist multiculturalism. Therefore, resistance from faculty and administrators is much more sophisticated and ingrained than the resistance that can be experienced from trainees.

Implications

We view this discussion as the beginning steps in the process of examining resistance to multiculturalism. Further studies are needed to examine both the trainee model of resistance and the administrator and faculty model of resistance to multiculturalism. However, we think that it is very important for proponents of multiculturalism to understand resistance to multiculturalism at the macro level as it relates to institutional racism, as well understand resistance to multiculturalism at the micro level in terms of aversive racists. If we better understand the psycho-emotional factors that allow aversive racists to resist multiculturalism and perpetuate institutional racism, we will be better able to develop strategies to overcome the resistance.

Our preliminary findings suggest that, due to the nonlinear manner of resistance, an individual may be a proponent of multiculturalism in one instance and an opponent of multiculturalism in another instance. Therefore, as proponents of multiculturalism work to break down institutional racism that leads to resistance, it may be necessary to build fluid coalitions with people. That is to say, proponents of multiculturalism may disappoint themselves, if they conclude that once they identify an ally, that person will always remain an ally. Conversely, proponents of multiculturalism may find it surprising that a person, who is an opponent, may not always remain an opponent to multiculturalism.

We believe that future research can focus on the relationship between strategies for overcoming resistance and the four psycho-emotional defensive mechanisms. In addition, future research initiatives can explore the relationship between psycho-emotional defensive mechanisms and racial and cultural identity development models. Finally, we believe that resistance to other areas of multiculturalism needs to be explored such as gender, sexual orientation, and disabilities.

Conclusion

Many psychologists have defied monocultural traditions in psychology, by forcing the inclusion of multicultural theory, research, practice, and training. In spite of these efforts by psychologists, institutional racism and aversive racism remain in the form of resistance to multiculturalism. Theory and research must further explore resistance to multiculturalism, as the success or failure of our programs may depend on it.

References

American Psychological Association (2003). Guidelines on multicultural education, training, research, practice, and organizational change for psychologists. *American Psychologist, 58*, 377–402.

Atkinson, D. R. Morten, G., and Sue, D. W. (1998). *Counseling American minorities* (5th ed.). Boston: McGraw-Hill.

Carter, R. T. (1995). *The influence of race and racial identity in psychotherapy: Toward a racially inclusive model.* New York: John Wiley.

Constantine, M. G. (2006). Racism in mental health and education settings: A brief overview. In M. Constantine and D. W. Sue (Eds.), *Addressing racism: Facilitating cultural competence in mental health and educational settings* (pp. 3–13). Hoboken, NJ: John Wiley & Sons.

D'Andrea, M. (2006). In liberty and justice for all. In M. Constantine and D. W. Sue (Eds.), *Addressing racism: Facilitating cultural competence in mental health and educational settings* (pp. 251–70). Hoboken: NJ: John Wiley & Sons.

D'Andrea, M., and Daniels, J. (1995). Promoting multiculturalism and organizational change in the counseling profession: A case study. In J. G. Ponterotto, J. M. Casas, L. A. Suzuki, and C. M. Alexander (Eds.), *Handbook of multicultural counseling* (pp. 17–33). Thousand Oaks, CA: Sage.

Feagin, J. R., Vera, H., and Imani, N. (1996). *The agony of education: Black students at white colleges and universities.* New York: Routledge.

Gaertner, S. L., and Dovidio, J. F. (1986). The aversive form of racism. In J. F. Dovidio and S. L. Gaertner (Eds.), *Prejudice, discrimination and racism* (pp. 61–90). Orlando, FL: Academic Press.

Guthrie, R. V. (1997). *Even the rat was white: A historical view of psychology.* New York: Harper & Row.

Hill, C. E., Thompson, B. J., and Williams, E. N. (1997). A guide to conducting consensual qualitative research. *The Counseling Psychologist*, *25*, 517–27.

Jones, J. M. (1997). *Prejudice and racism* (2nd ed.). New York: McGraw-Hill.

LaFromboise, T., and Howard-Pitney, B. (1995). The zuni life skills development curriculum. *Journal of Counseling Psychology*, *42*, 479–86.

Mio, J. S., and Awakuni, G. I. (2000). *Resistance to multiculturalism: Issues and interventions*. Philadelphia: Brunner/Mazel.

Mio, J. S., and Morris, D. R. (1990). Cross-cultural issues in psychology training programs: An invitation for discussion. *Professional Psychology: The Theory and Practice*, *21*, 434–41.

Paniagua, F. A. (1998). *Assessing and treating culturally diverse clients* (2nd ed.). Thousand Oaks, CA: Sage.

Parham, T. A., White, J. L., and Ajamu, A. (1999). *The psychology of blacks: An African centered perspective* (3rd ed.). Englewood Cliffs, NJ: Prentice-Hall.

Pedersen, P. B. (2006). Five anti-racism strategies. In M.G. Constantine and D.W. Sue (Eds.), *Addressing racism: Facilitating cultural competence in mental health and educational settings* (pp. 235–50). Hoboken, NJ: Wiley & Sons.

Queener, J. E., Smith, S. D., Woodworth, J. G., and Stokes, S. C. (under review). *Factors Related to Trainees' Engagement or Resistance to Multicultural Training*. Manuscript submitted for publication.

Ridley, C. R. (1995). *Overcoming unintentional racism in counseling and therapy: A practitioner's guide to intentional intervention*. Thousand Oaks, CA: Sage.

Samuda, R. J. (1998). *Psychological testing of American minorities*. Thousand Oaks, CA: Sage.

Strauss, A. L., and Corbin, J. (1990). *Basics of qualitative research: Grounded theory procedures and techniques*. Newbury Park, CA: Sage Publications.

Sue, D. W., and Sue, D. (2003). *Counseling the culturally diverse: Theory and practice* (4th ed.). New York: John Wiley & Sons.

Vera, E. M., Buhin, L., and Shin, R. Q. (2006). The pursuit of social justice and the elimination of racism. In M. Constantine and D. W. Sue (Eds.), *Addressing racism: Facilitating cultural competence in mental health and educational settings* (pp. 271–87). Hoboken, NJ: John Wiley & Sons.

∽

CHAPTER ELEVEN

Challenging Dialogues

Working Through Resistance Toward Multicultural Understanding

Evelinn A. Borrayo

An empathic way of being with another person . . . means temporarily living in the other's life, moving about in it delicately without making judgments. . . . To be with another in this way means that for the time being, you lay aside your own views and values in order to enter another's world without prejudice . . . a complex, demanding, and strong— yet subtle and gentle—way of being.

—C. R. Rogers (1980, pp. 142–43)

Empathically understanding the worldviews and experiences of others requires us to temporarily suspend ours and to divest from the preconceived notions we might have of theirs. Such endeavor is difficult if we have been encultured in an individualistic society that has taught us to hold on to our own views and to think of our values as universal and equally applicable across cultures. Pedersen (2000) notes that the dominant culture and society in the United States conceives individualism, autonomy, and the ability to become your own person as healthy and desirable life goals. Notions of "mental health" are precisely formulated around this cultural framework, which inheritably leads one to prejudicially define other worldviews and experiences that do not capitalize on these values as deviating from what is acceptable and normal (Ivey, Ivey, and Simek-Morgan, 1997).

The training of mental health professionals in the United States has also been culturally bound to the ideological milieu of individualism and other

European American worldviews and values. Historically, the type of training that psychologists and other mental health professionals have received has ill-prepared them to work with individuals that come from non-European American cultural backgrounds (Sue and Sue, 2003). A wealth of evidence exists regarding the tendency of ethnic minority clients to drop out of mental health services due to the clashing of cultural values with mental health providers or the clients' perceptions of mental health services as irrelevant to their needs (Atkinson, Morten, and Sue, 1998).

Various efforts have been undertaken in the field of psychology to be more responsive to the need to train more multiculturally competent mental health professionals. The movement to revamp the training of counseling psychologists began in the early 1980s and continued through the 1990s with the inclusion of multicultural courses that were absent from most training programs (Hills and Strozier, 1992). Around this period, efforts were also launched to increase ethnic minority students' recruitment, admission, and graduation from psychology programs (Heppner et al., 2000). However, despite these efforts, the profession is behind with respect to fostering multicultural competence among counseling psychologists who will continue to serve an increasingly diverse U.S. population (Heppner et al., 2000).

A paradigm shift toward multicultural competency training in psychology is still likely to face the macro- and micro-level obstacles that have historically slowed its progress, such as the resistance that occurs in the teaching and clinical training of psychology graduate students (Mio and Awakuni, 2000). The present chapter will address resistance issues that arise in personal encounters between students who embrace dominant (Eurocentric) worldviews (with accompanying values, beliefs, and assumptions) and students who bring worldviews that diverge from these, by virtue of their ethnic/cultural background or experience with multiculturalism. Particularly, the chapter will introduce how to promote healthy, useful, empathic, but challenging discussions and interactions around topics and issues (e.g., oppression, discrimination, privilege) related to cultural, racial, and ethnic diversity facing the profession with the increasing "browning of America" (White, 2003). The goal of this chapter is to provide readers with ideas on how to help students work through resistance toward a higher level of awareness of self and others essential to becoming multiculturally competent psychologists.

Resistance to Diverse Worldviews

Each of us embraces a worldview that shapes how we perceive events in our lives and the meanings that we attribute to these, as well as how we react based on our evaluation and appraisal of the situation. The culture in which we were raised highly influences our worldviews through the attitudes, values, and beliefs that we learn from it. Various experiences that we encounter with people from other cultures further affect our worldviews (Ibrahim, 1985). The very nature of encountering new worldviews challenges individuals to move from a "relatively egocentric and cognitively simple state to a more other-centered and cognitive complex way of viewing themselves and the world in which they live" (Garcia, 1994, p. 429). The process by which an other-centered awareness and understanding unfolds, however, is not a simple one and often times involves both cognitive and affective struggles. At the cognitive level, many schemas and dynamics used to frame the world are challenged, and individuals are faced with the need to construct, deconstruct, and reconstruct their strongly held attitudes, beliefs, and values. Typically, these cognitive changes do not take place without resistance.

Resistance is a defensive behavioral and emotional reaction that occurs when one is challenged to modify or change one's worldviews. According to Jackson (1999), resistance in the classroom can interfere with the reciprocal communication between professors and students, and for that matter between students, when they communicate their worldviews to each other. Jackson proposed that classroom resistance interferes with learning in a way similar to how resistance interferes with the therapeutic process. Defensive behaviors are geared toward intentionally or unintentionally circumventing or sabotaging the learning process associated with diversity content, and may include challenging and/or questioning the teacher's expertise or the validity of the theories and content of the class (Williams, Dunlap, and McCandles, 1999).

Emotional reactions are closely linked to the cognitive dissonance experienced during the confrontation of students' worldviews with the diverse worldviews of others. When students begin to realize that some aspects of their worldviews are disconfirmed through experiencing the realities of others who are different, they may feel threatened (Garcia, 1994) and may react defensively with an array of emotions (Kirkham, 1999). Emotional forms of resistance include emotional withdrawal, fear, guilt, resentment, anger, and even rage (Jackson, 1999; Mio and Barker-Hackett, 2003). Although these feelings are at times verbally expressed, they can also be kept private or repressed. They can, however, be recognized through behavioral displays such as "denial, isolation, reaction formation, or projection toward the faculty, other students in class, or both" (Jackson, 1999, p. 29). Emotional resistance can be an impediment to students' learning, growth, and development, if it is not constructively processed and placed in context.

Kirkham (1999) encouraged instructors to explore the source and content of students' emotional and behavioral reactions that are triggered when their worldviews are challenged. This author explained that the best predictor of emotions underlying discussions of diversity topics is the criteria or implicit assumptions participants use to determine the legitimacy of a topic. "Ferreting out the core assumptions about legitimacy," explained Kirkham (1999), "enables the emotional intensity to be more richly explored for all involved in a discussion" (p. 49). As in other instances, students use their own lifelong held and supported worldviews to form these initial criteria or assumptions. When diversity topics framed along such criteria are challenged or treated perceivably unfairly, emotionally charged reactions predictably occur. Consequently, it is important for instructors to explore the set of assumptions that students bring into the classroom and to decipher how these might differentially influence the perceived legitimacy of topics related to cultural, racial, and ethnic diversity among students.

Worldviews and the Legitimacy of Diversity Topics

In the science and practice of psychology in the United States, the primary point of reference to evaluate the legitimacy of any topic tends to be dictated by the assumptions that are based on a Eurocentric worldview. "Self-concept" or personal identity, for example, is a legitimate topic of investigation given the high value placed on the individual. Moreover, most of the knowledge regarding "self-concept" has been obtained by research done almost entirely on Anglo-Americans (Dana, 1993). Because the concept of self for this population has been found to be self-contained individualism at the exclusion of other people, individuals who are more collective than individualistic in relationships tend to be labeled as dependent and even deficient in self-esteem. Other core concepts in psychology like personality, intelligence, and mental health have been equally derived from Eurocentric worldviews and are used as the gold standards to understand all people.

An implication of this dominant stance when introducing topics related to culture, race, and ethnicity in the classroom is that most of psychology's core concepts must be deconstructed and reconstructed to include a more diverse understanding of the human experience. Such understanding, however, is not accomplished without a struggle to establish the legitimacy of these topics. Another implication of the profession's dominant stance is that students who embrace a dominant Eurocentric worldview are at an unearned advantage to believe and present their perspectives as more legitimate than students who embrace a different worldview. In general, because students' worldviews often tend to be associated with their group's ethnic or racial background, their assumptions about and their responses to topics related to race, culture, and ethnicity are quite common and representative of members of their social group (Sue and Sue, 2003).

Using the value of individualism as an example, one similarity among students who hold Eurocentric worldviews, mostly white students, is that they "do not move quickly and comfortably back and forth between their *individual* identity and their identity *as a member* of a racial or gender group in this society" (Kirkham, 1999, p. 50). White students, for instance, tend to perceive discussing issues, such as how institutional racism oppresses minority group members, as illegitimate accusations to them personally because they are less prepared to identify with the common experience of members of their group. Perhaps it is this lack of fluidity that underlies the common defensive reaction among white students, when ethnic minority students bring up how institutional racism in higher education has affected their group. Majority students tend to personalize these kinds of observations and argue that they advocate for equal opportunity and thus are "not racist." In the process of defending themselves as individuals, they fail to recognize the oppression exerted by the social institutions created by members of the dominant and privileged ethnic group to which they belong.

Ethnic minority students in return can react defensively to arguments that to them provide additional evidence that others do not understand the *real* problems in society. At the lowest level of defensiveness, some ethnic minority students launch an attempt to educate their peers about the sociopolitical experiences of their oppressed groups that individuals from the dominant group do not seem to understand. For other students, the issue becomes more personal when their classmates' comments are experienced as another instance of oppression where the victim is blamed for its victimization and held responsible for remaining in this position. Although the minority students might have been able to personally overcome social obstacles, they can strongly identify with the discrimination suffered by other individuals when their view of the world is rooted in the concept of "groupness" (Parham, White, and Ajamu, 1999).

White students, on the other hand, are not typically socialized to be viewed as members of a group and to understand how that membership is associated with a dominant worldview and set of privileged experiences. In fact, a common reaction is that "there isn't anything like a white race" (Sue and Sue, 2003, p. 239), and thus, such a topic lacks legitimacy for discussion. Although there is validity to this statement, historically in the United States, the ethnicity (e.g., Irish, German) of white individuals is lost and the assimilation to a common Eurocentric worldview and lifestyle gives life to a new culture, which at a superficial level is identified by phenotypic appearances (e.g., white skin). Because of a lack of awareness and understanding of their racial/ethnic status, a majority of white students react defensively when, in their view, the illegitimate topic of what it means to be white is discussed. Initially, it can be challenging and threatening to comprehend how "whiteness" is associated with unearned privileges by virtue of its institutionalized normative features. Consequently, they tend to resist the idea that their group's privilege of power contributes to the oppression, prejudice, and discrimination of disempowered groups.

To ethnic minority students, their classmates' whiteness becomes more evident when "it is denied, evokes puzzlement/negative reactions, and is equated with normalcy" (Sue and Sue, 2003, p. 238). However, ethnic minority students often do not have the awareness and knowledge to recognize that the white students' beliefs have been inherited from their culture's dominant Eurocentric worldviews. Understandably, they tend to counterreact defensively to what they believe is also an illegitimate position. In their experience, many ethnic minority students are constantly reminded of being racially and culturally different from the majority of white individuals in the dominant environments such as academia. A lack of recognition of the meaning of whiteness (e.g., privilege) feels invalidating to ethnic minority students and many are hurt and even angry toward classmates that endorse predominantly Eurocentric worldviews.

Challenging Dialogues: Constructive Outcomes

Emotional and behavioral reactions from both ethnic minority and dominant group students become more easily triggered as the topics discussed tend to be viewed as illegitimate because of its content or because they reflect a lack of empathy for the others' experience of the world. A disruption in their communication appears to occur as a mutual understanding becomes harder to reach. As a result, constructive dialogue seems to fade, along with students' opportunity to broaden their worldviews and learn from each other. In most instances, instructors feel compelled to intervene in this exchange of opinions and burst of emotions to avoid a climate that can become out of control and harmful to those involved. However, Kumashiro (2000) invites instructors to allow challenging dialogues to take place even when these lead students to enter a form of *crisis* when confronting their own and others' emotions and life experiences. If discussions remain at the level of intellectual and detached conversations, students are not forced "to look within, to look back, to disrupt [their] memories, to contradict [their] worldview" (p. 7), and hence, they are not able to unlearn and understand multicultural issues at a deeper level. In other words, true learning around these topics takes place only through crisis.

As illustrated in the movies, *Crown Heights* (Kagan, 2002) and *The Color of Fear* (Mun Wah, 1994), instructors need to provide space for students to work through crisis so that they do not become stuck and unable to move to a place where they are positively transformed. An extensive literature exists regarding various methods to process students' crisis (e.g., Carter, 2003; Mio and Barker-Hackett, 2003). Of utmost importance during challenging dialogues is to utilize strategies that help students work through crisis and lead them to gain insight, break down their resistance, express empathy, and learn from each others' worldviews and life experiences (Timpson, Yang, Borrayo, and Canetto, 2005).

A climate of openness and safety during class discussion is essential for facilitating the courage needed for students to take on the complexities, ambiguities, and difficulties required to understand diverse worldviews, along with its accompanying cognitive and affective crises (Canetto et al., 2003). Openness invites the exploration of all students' ideas, including their views that are unrefined, blunt, or idiosyncratic. Safety provides an environment where contributors do not fear being ridiculed, attacked, or punished for their opinions. Both openness and safety should go hand in hand in order to facilitate challenging dialogues that bring about constructive outcomes. Nonetheless, they require a complicated and sometimes contradictory set of actions. Openness, for instance, demands that we listen to all students but safety may require that we interrupt a comment that might be potentially offensive to another student. Keeping this dynamic in mind, instructors should implement strategies that will support openness and safety simultaneously during challenging dialogues.

Appropriate self-disclosure is one useful strategy to model to students the open expression of ideas, biases, worldviews, and experiences. "Pick an upcoming topic, and begin class by recalling your earliest encounters with that material as a student—what was difficult for you to grasp, and what finally helped you to understand" (Timpson et al. 2005, p. 37). If instructors are uncomfortable talking about their experiences encountering difficult topics and their feelings in this regard, it is likely that students will not openly share their own and gain insight from these experiences. Conversely, it is also important for instructors to share with students how they have worked through their own biases or stereotypes and the importance of doing so within a safe environment. Once students realize that they can openly share their worldviews within a context of safety, they tend to express their issues more freely, including their resistance to the topics being discussed and to each other.

Although resistance makes classroom discussions more challenging, it should not be viewed as something to be avoided, but rather it should be viewed as a normal part of the learning process. It suggests that students are struggling with the issues and taking them seriously enough to be upset by them (Davis, 1992). If, however, resistance is not dealt with appropriately it can intervene with the learning process (Jackson, 1999), such as when dialogue stops and mutual understanding is lost. Dealing with resistance can begin by recognizing that it exists and that it is normal for discussions about multicultural issues to trigger pre-existing emotions and conflicts that are deep-seated and personal (Garcia and Van Soest, 1999). One way to facilitate this process is to warn students about possible emotional and behavioral reactions that they might encounter when interacting and dialoguing with each other. Normalizing resistant thoughts, emotions, and behaviors allows students to feel less threatened when these occur and better equipped to work through crisis when they experience resistance.

At the core of resistance to multicultural issues might be students' tendency to overpersonalize the topics discussed, precisely because of pre-existent emotions and conflicts. Teaching them how to approach and think critically about the issues that surge is a good strategy to help students learn to take an objective stance while keeping their emotions in check. Following Fried's (1993) suggestions, students can be taught three sets of skills: (1) to separate facts from their assumptions about those facts and their legitimacy, (2) to shift perspective, and (3) to differentiate between personal discomfort and intellectual disagreement. Although these skills can be introduced at the beginning of a course, it is not until students react defensively and enter crisis that they really learn them. Students need to be reminded about these skills and encouraged to persist in their efforts to implement them. These three sets of skills have the potential to be among the most helpful in aiding students to break down resistance and work through their crisis.

Another strategy to help students work through their resistance is to lead them to analyze the terms, concepts, and meaning of the language that they use to refer to multicultural issues. However, "when debates swirl around the language that people use to refer to this or that group, some will see a dampening effect on classroom discourse, an excessive sensitivity, and concern for political correctness" (Timpson et al., 2005, p. 20). Our choice of words is based on our worldviews and reflects how we think and feel about certain topics. Pay attention, for example, to how students discuss issues of "racism."

Historically, ethnic minority groups have been the targets of racism for centuries and many students might even be personally affected by it. To other students, primarily white students, the topic of racism might be purely historical. These students are likely to use politically correct language when discussing racism or argue that "they do not know why minorities keep moaning and complaining about it or that minorities cry racism all the time to get their way when it does not really exist" (Mio and Barker-Hackett, 2003, p. 15). When the instructor or fellow classmates point out that these beliefs and attitudes are at the core of the problem in race relations, these students tend to perceive that they are being label, "racist," even though they do not view themselves as such. As expected, they are likely to respond defensively with further arguments that can turn heated by pain, anger, and shame, or some students simply withdraw from such discussions in fear of being further perceived as racist.

In an effort to avoid alienation and work through crisis, it is important to break down what has been said and how and analyze underlying beliefs. Instructors could facilitate the discussion of racism, for example, by examining unearned white privilege. Through this route students might be able to understand that the consequences of racism in their lives are as invisible to them as their skin color privileges. Stopping to reflect, to analyze, and to assess terms can begin to remove students' resistance and lead to more precise and socially sensitive thinking.

The task of involving students in challenging dialogues and working through crisis would not be successful if this journey did not lead to constructive outcomes such as the students' ability to be empathic toward and learn from each others' worldviews and life experiences. As students begin to discover the origin of some of their resistances to multicultural issues and to lay them aside, they begin to create a cognitive and affective space to better understand others. Learning to do so in the midst of emotional and behavioral reactions is a valuable and fundamental skill as students are likely to encounter these dynamics when working with clients of diverse cultural and ethnic backgrounds.

The use of "self" can also prove helpful for modeling empathy to students. Throughout challenging dialogues, it is important to resort to strong communication skills (e.g., reflecting feelings, clarifying views, summarizing ideas) to facilitate students' discussions around multicultural topics and to help them better understand each other's views and experiences. Eventually, there is less need for the instructor's intervention as students begin to use these skills to dialogue among themselves. Communicating in this manner leads them to develop the kind of empathy that Carl Rogers described, which is best evidenced when students begin to recognize that other worldviews can be as legitimate as theirs and to exercise understanding and acceptance toward others. It should be recognized that not all students are able to work through their crisis and achieve this level of empathy by engaging in challenging dialogues alone. Other methods such as journaling, experiential exercises, field research, change projects, cultural autobiographies, and the like undoubtedly provide a holistic approach (Pence and Fields, 1999; Timpson et al., 2005). Engaging in challenging dialogues, however, can lead to very constructive outcomes and instructors can facilitate this process by using some of the strategies described in this chapter.

Summary

Training programs in psychology can serve as practice arenas for mental health professionals to learn about their own worldviews and those of diverse others. Ideally, such educational opportunities should occur throughout the various components of students' training: formal coursework, clinical experience and supervision, mentoring, and research (American Psychological Association, 2003). Training programs should be multicultural environments where individuals from diverse cultural backgrounds interact and learn from one another. Nonetheless, in psychology graduate programs the vast majority of faculty and students are white (Pate, 2001)—thus the importance for continued efforts to significantly increase faculty and students from underrepresented ethnic groups (e.g., black, Latino, Native American, Asian American) that will enrich graduate training programs in psychology.

With the increasing diversification of psychology, conflict, at times irresolvable, is likely to arise to the extent that our worldviews diverge and we lack the skills to empathically understand and react to one another. To avoid irresolvable conflict, it is of critical importance that psychologists are keenly aware of the worldviews they possess and how these are likely to influence their interpersonal transactions with those who hold a different set of worldviews. Engaging in challenging dialogue around topics related to culture, race, and ethnicity provides an opportunity to learn about our diversity of worldviews and be positively transformed by this interaction. Academia is an ideal setting to introduce mental health professionals to challenging dialogues because it can afford the openness, safety, and empathy that are needed to work through the crisis that result from the exchange of diverse worldviews. More importantly, learning from these kinds of experiences prepares us to interact and competently serve the increasing multiethnic/multiracial population of the United States (U.S. Census Bureau, 2004).

References

American Psychological Association. (2003). Guidelines on multicultural education, training, research, practice, and organizational change for psychologists. *The American Psychologist, 58*(5), 377–402.

Atkinson, D. R., Morten, G., and Sue, D. W. (1998). *Counseling American minorities: A cross-cultural perspective* (5th ed.). Boston, MA: McGraw Hill.

Canetto, S. S., Timpson, W. M., Borrayo, E., and Yang, R. (2003). Teaching about human diversity: Lessons learned and recommendations. In W. M. Timpson, S. S. Canetto, E. Borrayo, and R. Yang (Eds.), *Teaching diversity: challenges and complexities, identity and integrity* (pp. 275–94). Madison, WI: Atwood.

Carter, R. T. (2003). Becoming racially and culturally competent: The Racial-Cultural Counseling Laboratory. *Journal of Multicultural Counseling and Development, 31*(1), 12–30.

Dana, R. (1993). *Multicultural assessment perspectives for professional psychology.* Boston: Allan & Bacon.

Davis, N. J. (1992). Teaching about inequalities: Student resistance, paralysis, and rage. *Teaching Sociology, 20*, 232–38.

Fried, J. (1993). Bridging emotion and intellect: Classroom diversity in progress. *College Teaching, 41*(4), 123–28.

Garcia, B., and Van Soest, D. (1999). Teaching about diversity and oppression: Learning from analysis of critical classroom events. *Journal of Teaching and Social Work, 18*, 149–67.

Garcia, J. E. (1994). Reflections on teaching diversity. *Journal of Management Education, 18*(4), 428–31.

Heppner, P. P., Casas, J. M., Carter, J., and Stone, G. L. (2000). The maturation of counseling psychology: Multifaceted perspectives, 1978–1998. In S. D. Brown and R. W. Lent (Eds.), *Handbook of counseling psychology* (3rd ed, pp. 3–49). New York: John Wiley & Sons.

Hills, H. H., and Strozier, A. L. (1992). Multicultural training in APA-approved counseling psychology programs: A survey. *Professional Psychology: Research and Practice, 23*, 43–51.

Ibrahim, F. A. (1985). Effective cross-cultural counseling and psychotherapy. *The Counseling Psychologist, 13*, 625–38.

Ivey, A. E., Ivey, M. B., and Simek-Morgan, L. (1997). *Counseling and psychotherapy: A multicultural perspective* (4th ed.). Boston: Allyn & Bacon.

Jackson, L. C. (1999). Ethnocultural resistance to multicultural training: Students and faculty. *Cultural Diversity and Ethnic Minority Psychology, 5*(1), 27–36.

Kagan, J. P. (2002). *Crown Heights* (videotape). Showtime Entertainment.

Kirkham, K. (1999). Teaching about diversity: Navigating the emotional undercurrents. *Organizational Behavior Teaching Review, 13*(4), 48–67.

Kumashiro, K. K. (1999). "Barbie," "big dicks," and "faggots:" Paradox, performativity, and anti-oppressive pedagogy. *Journal of Curriculum Theorizing, 15*(1), 27–42.

————. (2000). Teaching and learning through desire, crisis, and difference: Perverted reflections on anti-oppressive education. *Radical Teacher*, 58(6), 6–11.

Mio, J. S., and Awakuni, G. I. (2000). *Resistance to multiculturalism: Issues and interventions*. Philadelphia, PA: Taylor and Francis Group.

Mio, J. S., and Barker-Hackett, L. (2003). Reaction papers and journal writing as techniques for assessing resistance in multicultural courses. *Journal of Multicultural Counseling and Development*, 31, 12–19.

Mio, J. S., and Morris, D. R. (1990). Cross-cultural issues in psychology training programs: An invitation for discussion. *Professional Psychology: Theory and Practice*, 21, 434–41.

Mun Wah, L. (1994). *The Color of Fear* (videotape). Oakland, CA: StirFry Seminars and Consulting.

Parham, T. A., White, J. L., and Ajamu, A. (1999). *The psychology of blacks: An African centered perspective* (3rd ed.). Englewood Cliffs, NJ: Prentice-Hall.

Pate, W. E. (2001). Analyses of Data from Graduate Study in Psychology: 1999-2000. Retrieved July 25, 2004, from research.apa.org/grad00contents.html.

Pedersen, P. B. (2000). *A handbook for developing multicultural awareness*. Alexandria, VA: American Counseling Association.

Pence, D. J., and Fields, J. A. (1999). Teaching about race and ethnicity: Trying to uncover white privilege for a white audience. *Teaching Sociology*, 27, 150–58.

Rogers, C. R. (1980). *A way of being*. Boston: Houghton Mifflin Company.

Sue, D. W., and Sue, D. (2003). *Counseling the culturally diverse: Theory and practice* (4th ed.). New York: John Wiley & Sons.

Tatum, B. D. (1992). Talking about race, learning about racism: The application of racial identity development theory in the classroom. *Harvard Educational Review*, 62(1), 1–24.

Timpson, W., Yang, R., Borrayo, E. A., and Canetto, S. S. (Eds.). (2005). *147 tips for teaching diversity*. Madison, WI: Atwood.

U.S. Census Bureau (2004). *U.S. interim projections by age, sex, race, and Hispanic origin*. Retrieved July 24, 2004, from www.census.gov/ipc/www/usinterimproj/.

White, J. L. (2003). *Browning of America: Building a new multicultural, multiracial paradigm*. Paper presented at the 3rd Annual Diversity Challenge Conference, Boston.

Williams, M., Dunlap, M., and McCandles, T. (1999). Keepin' it real: Three black educators discuss how we deal with student resistance to multicultural inclusion in the curriculum. *Transformations*, 10 (2), 11–23.

PART IV

FORWARD MOVEMENT IN THE PSYCHOLOGY FIELD

CHAPTER TWELVE

~

The Evolution of the National Multicultural Conference and Summit

Thomas A. Parham and William D. Parham

> The wave of a movement that is built on truth and righteousness cannot be shackled by institutional policies or practices; and those of us committed to this multicultural movement are not in need of organizational or institutional permission slips to validate or approve of our efforts.
>
> —(Parham, 1999, Summit I)

The National Multicultural Conference and Summit (1999) exploded onto the professional psychology and counseling scene with an energy and enthusiasm that continues to excite our disciplines. Even after four subsequent summit conferences, there is elevated anticipation about the pending Summit 2009. What instigates such enthusiasm? With numerous regional and national conferences to choose from, professionals and students alike appear to have ample opportunity to engage the conference circuit and satisfy their search for professional development and training experiences. Yet, the energy surrounding the national summits seems qualitatively different from that of most other meetings. In this chapter we seek to provide some insight into what we believe is special and unique about the summit experiences. Furthermore, an attempt will be made to identify those variables that served as a catalyst for the conference origins and continuation. We also provide personal commentary on events surrounding the most recent 2005 and 2007 summits.

Leadership Synergy

Perhaps no single variable is more responsible for the origin of the first summit than the synergy that was created by the collaboration of several multicultural leaders. Individuals have been in leadership positions before. However, 1998 and 1999 were years when a particular group of individuals was positioned in their roles as American Psychological Association (APA) organization and division presidents to exert tremendous influence on our discipline. To begin, Dr. Richard Suinn became the first Asian American and only the second person of color to serve in the role as president of the APA. Dr. Kenneth Clark, an African American, was the first person of color to serve as the APA leader. Dr. Lisa Porche-Burke (African American) was finishing her tenure as president of Division 45, with Dr. Derald Sue (Asian American) serving as president-elect. Dr. Rosie Bingham (African American) was due to begin her tenure as president of Division 17, and Dr. Melba Vasquez (Latina American) was serving as president of Division 35.

These professionals were and continue to be significant figures in the discipline of psychology and counseling in their own right. Singularly, their contributions have been enormous in terms of publishing, teaching, and training; counseling and therapy; and social advocacy related to issues of diversity and multiculturalism. Yet they found a way to put their individual accolades and prominence aside and focus on a common mission and objective. Their synergy was the right combination at exactly the right time, focused on exactly the right project.

Their collective wisdom and expertise strategized to create a conference experience that would differ significantly from other professional meetings. Many professional conferences attended by students and professionals alike are characterized by formats heavy on individual presentations and/or symposia, with concurrent sessions, which leaves little time for discussion or interaction with the audience. Similarly, traditional conferences provide few opportunities to engage in "think tank"sessions where individual topics become the fuel for maximum critical discourse. In addition, few conferences offer opportunities for formal and informal interaction with senior scholars, who, by virtue of their status and position within the profession, are usually shielded from the masses of conference participants.

The summit organizers sought to remedy these shortcomings by creating a unique conference experience that participants would have trouble finding anywhere else. In noting that a true summit is supposed to be a conference of the highest level of discourse and presentations, the organizers formatted the meeting to maximize participant exposure to many of the "giants" in the field. This occurred through informative and inspiring keynote addresses, a special symposium on senior men of color, and opportunities to sit informally with the disciplines' most noted figures. Next, they reduced the number of concurrent sessions and focused instead on sessions that were related thematically. Third, they introduced some new features to the conference by planning "difficult dialogue" sessions, as well as sessions designed to help participants plan follow-up strategies for multicultural enhancements once they left the conference.

In highlighting the "leadership" qualities that the organizers of the summit originally demonstrated, it is important to separate the content domains from the process dynamics. While several of the content elements are mentioned above, equally significant were the process dynamics that characterized their leadership styles. First, they started with a *vision* that a multicultural summit experience could be planned and executed. Next, they *listened* to the people, in incorporating solicited and unsolicited feedback into the design of the initial 1999 summit. In addition, they held fast to their *commitment to a dedicated outcome* and exercised *patience* in both allowing the conference to take shape and navigating their way through the challenges and temporary hurdles and setbacks that inevitably come with planning such a major undertaking. Last, they held true to some important *values*, which helped to guide their planning and working relationship. These values included

- *respect* for each other as colleagues,
- a *cooperative* as opposed to a *competitive* posture in advancing ideas,
- a commitment to sustaining their *relationship* as colleagues and friends irrespective of their opinions on particular issues, and
- a goal of achieving a high degree of *congruence* between what they "preached" and what they "practiced."

Curricular Frustration

Despite the advances in diversity and multicultural education, the professions of counseling and psychology have been relatively slow in thoroughly integrating multicultural content into the curriculum. Study after study (Wyatt and Parham, 1985; Ponterotto, Alexander, and Grieger, 1995; Constantine, 1997; Constantine and Ladany, 2001) has shown that while graduate training in psychology, counseling, and counselor education has begun to address the diversity question, few programs can report optimal progress in addressing the voids in helping students and professionals alike achieve some level of proficiency, or even measure it. Hills and Strozier (1992), for example, commented on the fact that inclusion of multicultural content into graduate curriculum has been minimal. Similarly, La Frombois and Foster (1992) argued that while multicultural issues need to be considered as core components of graduate training, few programs have been successful in their inclusion. Likewise, D'Andrea and Daniels (1991) commented on the lack of consensus about the most effective types of training some ten years after the previous studies had been published. Relative to these two-decade-long observations, an important question emerges: Have graduate training programs failed to infuse multicultural content into every component of their curriculums? Or have they succeeded in moving the multicultural emphasis to the fringes of their education and training programs? Clearly, most training programs are less than adequate when it comes to diversity training.

Curricular frustration does not simply exist with graduate students, but is also reflected in the attitudes of many graduate students toward their supervisors. Ironically, the little training that does exist in graduate programs for graduate students far exceeds, in many cases, the training supervisors these students receive. Clearly, the opportunities for professional development training for psychologists, counselors, clinicians, and academicians are severely lacking. As a consequence, this is one of the first generations of graduate students who, in the context of exposure to multicultural content, may have more experience than the individuals who supervise them. The summit planning recognized this dilemma and has incorporated some specific experiences for supervisors into several of the conferences.

In Search of Competence

Those who have graduated from master and doctoral programs have fared no better in accessing curriculum that can establish and build on a multicultural base of knowledge. Continuing education workshops are now offered in thousands of locations across the country. Yet, within the context of curriculum delivered by those agencies approved to offer continuing education for credit (even that which is mandated by various state licensing boards), the number of courses that address multicultural topics pale in comparison to those that speak to issues, topics of personality disorders, substance abuse, relationship dynamics and divorce, law and ethics, psychopharmacology, managing the business aspects of private practice, domestic violence, and physical and sexual abuse. Clearly, whether the education and training one receives occurs within or outside of traditional academic walls, students and professionals have had a difficult time accessing multiculturally oriented coursework.

The desire to develop greater levels of multicultural competence and proficiency should go hand-in-hand with one's standards of professionalism. After all, academicians, researchers, clinicians, and social advocates alike are presumed to be invested in delivering the highest quality of service that they can. Hampering efforts to increase levels of competence is the difficulty in defining the standard to which students and professionals should aspire. Rarely are there forums where issues of cultural competence take center stage in the programmatic sessions being offered.

Examination of the professional conference circuit results in discovering how little substantive discussion there is on issues of diversity and multiculturalism. Even when diversity-oriented sessions are part of the conference program, they continue to be formatted in ways that minimize the importance of the topic through infrequent or concurrent scheduling, allow no opportunities for follow-up and continuity, and present very little information that allows the listener to do something different as a result of the information learned. Clearly, this not only creates a serious void for those looking for culturally specific and practical information, but it helps to fuel the demand for alternate conference programming that can better address this need. Thus, the popularity of the National Multicultural Conference and Summit should come as no surprise given the way it specifically addresses the void in multicultural didactic and experiential learning left by training programs and continuing education agencies.

Perceptions of Institutional Insincerity

Another lightning rod, which seemed to galvanize the public interest in a multicultural summit, was the perception of institutional insincerity that many students and professionals harbored. Perceptions of this sort are instigated by institutions themselves who at best have been slow and at worst have been passively or blatantly resistant to greater levels of multicultural inclusion. Included on this list of culprits are academic training programs, which talk about cultural sensitivity, yet fail to make significant strides in diversifying their curriculum, faculty, or even the student populations. Also included are community agencies, whose desire to serve diverse constituents are not matched by the organizational changes that are necessary to achieve that outcome. Similarly, state regulatory and licensing boards consider it important to talk about the need for those they certify, license, and credential to be culturally skilled. Yet few regulatory agencies have mandated that such training occur, or taken any administrative action against those who continue to be out of compliance with reasonable standards of cultural proficiency in their counseling, clinical, or consultation practices.

Historical Roots

The foregoing implies that the genesis of the National Multicultural Conference and Summit (NMCS) was born in part out of the collective frustrations of diverse communities with the ever-present professional environment whose reticence to embrace multiculturalism borders on legendary. Also implied is that the NMCS was born out of a sense that professional communities were tired of institutions that continued to be rife with disingenuous professional desire to diversify organizational culture. While these implications are not without merit, it is important to note that an excitement about embracing the proactive design and implementation of a multicultural pedagogy had already begun to emerge and it is this enthusiasm that also synergized the energies and spirit of these five leaders.

In this regard, several recent events are noteworthy. When Drs. Suinn, Porche-Burke, Sue, Bingham, and Vasquez came together to initiate the first conference and summit, the collaboration between Divisions 17 (The Society of Counseling Psychology) and 45 (The Society for the Study of Ethnic Minority Issues) on a multicultural project was nearing twenty years. These two divisions within APA were just shy of producing a seminal document, now known as the Guidelines on Multicultural Education, Training, Research, Practice and Organizational Change for Psychologists (www.apa.org/pi/multiculturalguidelines.pdf), when the seeds of "The Summit" were taking root. Division 44 (The Society for Gay, Lesbian and Bisexual Concerns) published their Guidelines for Psychotherapy with Lesbian, Gay and Bisexual Clients (apa.org/divisions/div44/guidelines.html) a few years prior. In 1999, the Surgeon General's report on mental health in the United States was published and for the first time, mental illness was recognized as a problem with definable assessment, treatment, and economic cost parameters.

The companion report on mental health in the United States relative to culture, race, and ethnicity (phs.os.dhhs.gov/library/mentalhealth/cre/specsummary-1.html) was introduced at the 2001 APA convention in San Francisco, California, by then Surgeon General David Satcher, M.D. Among its several conclusions, the report highlights that factors related to race and ethnicity need to be considered when understanding and designing interventions to respond to the mental health challenges experienced by persons of color.

History also reminds us that the need for a multicultural movement within psychology was expressed in the writings of scholars (Wrenn, 1962; White, 1972; Thomas and Sillen, 1972; Atkinson, Morten, and Sue, 1979) as early as the 1960s and 1970s. The APA's reluctance to attend to the needs of their

African American colleagues resulted in the birth of the Association of Black Psychologists (ABPsi) (1968) whose break away from mainstream APA led to the subsequent formation of the Asian American Psychological Association (AAPA) (1972), the National Latino/a Psychological Association (NLPA) (1979), and the Society for Indian Psychologists (SIP). The need to include multicultural (then, cross-cultural) awareness in the conceptualization of the counseling process was articulated at the Vail Conference (1973). The establishment within the APA of the Office of Ethnic Minority Affairs (1979); the Board of Ethnic Minority Affairs (1981); and the founding of Divisions 35 (1973), 44 (1985), and 45 (1991) provided additional historical anchors of the movement to bring multiculturalism to the forefront of professional psychology.

Outside of APA, professional psychology organizations were contributing to the chorus voicing the need for a shift from Eurocentric thinking to a mindset that valued difference across race, ethnicity, and other parameters of multiculturalism. Perhaps no organization was more in the forefront of that movement than the ABPsi (1968). Their engagement of a posture of self-determination not only allowed for the formation of what was and continues to be the only autonomous ethnic psychology association in the nation through 2006, but it also created a platform from which they could call attention to changes that needed to take place within psychology as a whole. Issues the ABPsi continued to address were related to culturally specific theories, issues of testing and assessment, the challenges of psychotherapy and counseling with African American populations, and the role of psychologists in serving as agents of change and social advocacy. The scholarship, clinical service delivery, and social advocacy of the AAPA, NLPA, and SIP added importantly and substantively to emerging perspectives and insights relative to psychology's embrace of multiculturalism.

Another less visible, but equally important, organization was the National Institute for Multicultural Competence (NIMC). Founded in 1992 by a group of psychologists committed to true multiculturalism and systemic change, the NIMC has worked behind the scenes to quietly influence the diversity/multicultural discourse, and to create organizational change within the American Counseling Association and the APA. Included among the institute's members are Drs. Patricia Arredondo, Michael D'Andrea (who also serves as executive director), Judy Daniels, Allen Ivey, Mary Bradford Ivey, Don Locke, Beverly O'Bryant, Thomas Parham, and Derald Sue. Their collective influence developed early drafts of the multicultural competencies, pushed for inclusion of more diversity-related programs at major conventions, and provided feedback and consultation on the first summit. A detailed account of the multicultural movement within psychology is beyond the scope of this presentation but can be found in several references, including D'Andrea et al. (2001) and Atkinson, Morten, and Sue, (1979).

Finally, the changing profile of America beginning in the decade of the 1970s is an important factor that influenced the emerging cross-cultural (multicultural) zeitgeist. Immigration, higher birth rates, and improved health care contributed significantly to a declining growth rate of Anglo America and a pronounced increase in the U.S. population of African American (12 percent), Latinos/as (12 percent), Asian American/Pacific Islander (33 percent), and Native American (0.9 percent) (U.S. Census Bureau, 2000). What's more, past and current projections suggest that the "ethnic minority" population of several states will exceed 50 percent by 2010 (U.S. Census Bureau, 2000). Understanding and attending to the needs of this growing constituency has never been more apparent. Suffice it to say that past and current history within psychology and shifts in the national demographics of America's citizenry provide the context for understanding the attractiveness of the NMCS venue.

Opportunities and Challenges

Excitement about constructing a new way of thinking brought with it several challenges and opportunities. One such opportunity required thinking about multiculturalism in a way that affirms the unique history and traditions of myriad disenfranchised groups and simultaneously invites mainstream America to disengage from their continued reticence to acknowledge the divisiveness of "ism" ideologies. Having each of the disenfranchised groups define themselves in a way that captures their rich within-group differences and variability is illustrative of a second opportunity. Equally formidable has been the challenge of promoting constructive dialogues across disenfranchised groups in an effort to foster unity among these disparate bodies relative to the advancement of a national multicultural agenda that represents shared input and vision. In a very real sense, then, the NMCS was born out of a need to remain current with the more broadly defined parameters of the multicultural movement. Also needed was the provision of a venue wherein continued exploration and examination would result in a proclamation around which all of professional psychology could rally as they matured in the abilities to teach, mentor, conduct research, provide direct service, consult, and advocate for an ever-changing multicultural constituency.

The evolution of the NMCS from a global examination of multiculturalism to one more specific is reflected in the themes that each of the five summits adopted. The inaugural NMCS, 1999, that convened in Newport Beach, California, embraced the theme "Creative Strategies For Inclusion" and succeeded in drawing five hundred participants. NMCS, 2001, convened in Santa Barbara, California, adopted the theme "The Psychology of Race/Ethnicity, Gender, Sexual Orientation and Disability: Divergence, Convergence and Intersections" and attracted close to seven hundred participants. NMCS, 2003, convened in at the Renaissance Hotel in Hollywood, California, adopted the theme "The Psychology of Race/Ethnicity, Gender, Sexual Orientation and Disability: Celebrating Our Children, Families, and Seniors" and attracted more than nine hundred participants. For a second time the Hollywood, California, site was selected as the location of the NMCS, 2005. The nine hundred summit attendees were invited to participate in programming that addressed "The Psychology of Race/Ethnicity, Gender, Sexual Orientation and Disability: What Works, For Whom and Under What Circumstances." The NMCS, 2007, drew close to eight hundred participants to Seattle, Washington, all of whom engaged in dialogues framed by the theme "The Psychology of Multiple Identities: Finding Empowerment in the Face of Oppression." The NMCS, 2009, will convene in New Orleans, Louisiana, and the theme is to be determined.

Author Commentary on the 2005 and 2007 Summits

In recalling the previous summit conferences, we are also mindful that the summit experiences themselves have not been without some element of tension and controversy. The following discourse reflects Thomas Parham's position, but one that was not shared by all members of the GLBT community. Thomas offered a similar version of the commentary below in an editorial written to several divisions within APA. Two divisions (45 and 17) published the piece and two refused to publish it (Divisions 44 and 35[1]).

While personally being delighted with the overall experience the summits offered, Thomas Parham was distressed at some of the process dynamics that we both witnessed, heard about, and experienced personally at a deep emotional level during the 2005 summit. One such incident involved the "Town Hall Meeting" at the conclusion of the summit, where participants are provided with an opportunity to share their perspectives on the summit as a whole and to build some momentum for the continuation of the summit in two years.

While a few of the comments were directed at thanking the summit organizing committee (including William Parham), a good 80–90 percent of the remarks addressed a situation that occurred on the preceding Thursday afternoon. There, a two-person panel of female graduate students led a one-hour session and distributed handouts on the merits of "conversion therapy" for persons identified as, using their words, homosexual, even though conversion or "reparative" therapy for people with gay, lesbian, and bisexual orientation has been denounced as unethical and harmful by the APA, American Counseling Association (ACA), and others (see www.apa.org/pi/lgbc/publications/justthefacts.html#2). This controversial presentation was submitted by Mark Yarhouse from Regents University and listed in the program under the guise of discussing "clinical implications in managing the coming out process." Any reasonable summit participant would have shown up, and many did, expecting that the presenter would be discussing strategies for helping people embrace the process and manage the anxiety, fear, apprehension, etc. that surrounds it. This was not the case, given what we describe above.

Admittedly, William and I share the frustration that our brothers and sisters in the gay, lesbian, bisexual, transgender (GLBT) community have about the specific individual and the controversial stance Yarhouse takes on issues of "coming out" and sexual orientation in general. However, where we part company with my GLBT colleagues and allies who spoke at the town hall meeting is in some of the content and the process dynamics they used at the summit town hall meeting to voice their concerns to the summit organizers and those of us in the audience.

First, Thomas reacted to the insistence by Division 44 officials and attending members of the GLBT community that the summit organizers "pull" the program once it was discovered that the person listed on the program was Mark Yarhouse. We later found out that this individual has published his views on the merits of reparative therapy in the past and has a reputation among the GLBT community as one with a track record of submitting program proposals whose content, when delivered to a conference audience, is perceived as markedly different than the title might indicate. It was unfortunate that the proposal review committee (which included William) had not been familiar with Yarhouse, his past publications, and his alleged reputation, which allowed his proposal to be selected over ones that could have contributed to advancing knowledge and support for GLBT issues. Once on the program, however, from our point of view, the issue of censure came to the forefront.

We suspect a great deal of debate and thought went into how this division should respond and what its final position should be. However, to confront the organizers with a demand to pull the program is an interesting outcome of those deliberations. In our opinion, censorship is not the answer for ideas that people disagree with, no matter how much we oppose them. The summit should be a forum where issues (even controversial ones) become topics of critical discourse and analysis. Despite how strongly people feel on both sides of an issue, there is always a larger segment in the middle who (a) is not thoroughly briefed on all of the issues and (b) could benefit from some frank intellectual exchange about the merits or fallacies of an idea or assertion. In an atmosphere where "difficult dialogues" have become a distinct feature of the summit experience, it would be a shame to see the need to be "politically correct" replace legitimate academic exchange and learning opportunities. In reality, the summit does not belong to any one group, and the NMCS organizing committee should not be yielding to the dictates of any one division or group!

In retrospect, Thomas felt so strongly about this issue because he had witnessed another situation at the 2001 summit, where one counseling psychologist with obvious strict Christian views was invited to participate on a panel discussion with another clinical psychologist with clear views on civil rights for individuals with GLBT orientation. The two panelists engaged in a productive debate in the spirit of the difficult dialogue, along with a dozen other panelists. Unfortunately the audience was less able to tolerate the conservative psychologist's views. For some, his views appeared personally threatening, and their reaction was to fight back by intellectually and emotionally maligning him—an invited panelist no less—for his views about sexual orientation. Even when emotions run hot, I am opposed to audience responses that involve name calling and insults (e.g., "homophobic" in this case). The original intent of the difficult dialogue is to create a forum where all ideas can be challenged with professionalism. In this case, the audience could have challenged the conservative panelist's views by asking him to respond to specific literature and research supporting healthy GLBT identity development. The audience could have asked him to explain how his views match up with the standards outlined by the APA Division 44's guidelines for Psychotherapy with Lesbian, Gay and Bisexual Clients (apa.org/divisions/div44/guidelines.html). These are examples of how to conduct professional discourse in a difficult dialogue. Unfortunately, nothing at that professional level occurred. In Thomas's view this particular invited panelist became a casualty of the summit experience, and to our knowledge has not been back. The tragedy there is not only was he robbed of the right to be heard and have his opinion respected, but he inadvertently served as a symbol for and warning to others who violate the unspoken rule of not expressing ones views in opposition to political correctness. In Thomas's mind, this is equally shameful and a violation of the original intent of the summit. How can we all learn

and grow if we can't even tolerate each other's different opinions and perspectives?

Beyond this point, Thomas was offended and equally bothered by the
emotional tone expressed in that 2005 town hall meeting, where the summit
was labeled as "unsafe," "unaffirming," and "unwelcoming" by GLBT-identi-
fied colleagues because of that one-hour presentation two graduate students
were sent to deliver. Additional comments were directed at a panel on "mas-
culinity for men of color" where a gay male perspective was not represented.
We do know what it is like to be left out of the discourse on race and ethnicity, given our academic training and conference participation at APA and
ACA over the past thirty years, so this was unfortunate. However, without
being gay ourselves, it is difficult to know exactly how one would feel if similarly exposed to a presentation we might find so objectionable. We are, and
Thomas was empathetic to the pain and anger one should feel at being de-
ceived by a title you believed was misleading, and being presented with ideas
you find distasteful and objectionable. However, to label the entire summit
experience as unsafe, unaffirming, and unwelcoming was, according to
Thomas, not only a gross overstatement of the facts, but a slap in the face of
the summit organizers who worked so hard and tirelessly to bring all of us a
wonderful experience, and include "gay affirmative" content within the
broader summit programming across the two and one-half days.

Thomas also argued that it seemed flagrantly disingenuous to claim such
serious injury when the messengers of the venomous words and phrases were
two undegreed, unlicensed graduate students too neophyte to seriously challenge anyone's gender identity, professional standing, sense of personhood, or
their humanity. Hurt? Sure. Angry? Justifiably so. But to critique and berate
the entire summit experience and label it as unsafe, unaffirming, and unwelcoming on the strength of a single incident raises a concern for him about
the credibility of one's claims of emotional injury.

Ironically, Thomas also felt conflicted by the posture the summit organizers (including William Parham) assumed in response to the onslaught of critical feedback from members and allies of the GLBT community during the
town hall session. On one hand, the restraint they showed in the face of some
very hostile attitudes was admirable. As such, it is not difficult to imagine
how or why they exercised that deference given that many in the audience
empathized with our GLBT sisters and brothers and their hurt and anger.

On the other hand, Thomas admitted to finding himself getting angry at
the apologetic posture the organizers took, particularly in light of the fact
that, in his opinion, they did nothing wrong and did not deserve the abuse
they decided to tolerate from one segment of the crowd. From his vantage

point, there was something strangely reminiscent about four people of color, assuming an apologetic posture, in the face of some angry white people, who berate and chastise them for not meeting their expectations. Thomas reasoned that it was the essence of a white supremacist ideology and a white privilege mentality that allowed individuals to seize the floor of intellectual exchange and then invalidate the efforts of a multicultural agenda with verbal whips simply because they find one presentation objectionable and another presentation lacking on some element of diversity someone thought should have been represented.

Respectfully, we both believe that no one presentation can ever reflect every dimension of diversity, and to denigrate a presentation or the entire summit conference because it failed to include one aspect of diversity in one presentation was unfair and unreasonable. Such a posture created needless dissention within the ranks of our cultural collaborations and helped to foster an unhealthy competition among marginalized groups around whose oppression is the greatest.

Needless to say, Thomas Parham's editorial ignited both a firestorm of critique and an outpouring of support that was talked about for months and even a year or two after that 2005 summit. In fact, it created a choice point for the 2007 summit organizers and attendees who could not ignore the tension, but who had choices in how they chose to address it. The keynote addresses were magnificent, the workshops were strategically managed, and comments from members of the GLBT community and Thomas and William Parham allowed participants to begin feeling more comfortable and validated that this summit had created more understanding, and that some healing had begun to take place.

Concrete Goals

In taking a retrospective look at the previous summits, there appears to be five goals that have framed the organization of the summits to date, irrespective of the themes that were ultimately adopted. The first goal includes a focus on theory, research, and practice relative to multicultural populations. An examination of context (e.g., race, ethnicity, gender, social class, sexual orientation, physical disability, religion) within which multiculturalism can be viewed captures the essence of the second goal. Applying open communication within and across multicultural groups using a difficult dialogue format and identifying specific and concrete strategies for increasing and maintaining solidarity among myriad multicultural groups constitute goals three and four. Strengthening across generation connections and understanding by tapping the wisdom of the elders constitutes the fifth goal. Every effort is made to achieve these identified goals using models and ways of thinking that emphasize the use of a multicultural (versus Eurocentric) ruler to measure products and outcomes.

The summits also have been organized around five areas of emphasis, namely, coalescence, content, ceremony, collaboration, and continuity.

I. Coalescence
   (a) Keynote speakers were selected who could offer penetrating insights into the multicultural movement and also excite and stimulate the masses of people to continue the conference momentum back in their places of work.
II. Content
   (a) Presentations and workshops were organized around particular themes and attempts were made to maximize audience participation and exchange.
   (b) Poster sessions were created to allow for conference attendees to display their work and be available to discuss its implications.
   (c) Difficult dialogues were conducted in order to allow for the free exchange of ideas on topics that are rarely discussed beyond private spaces.
III. Ceremony
   (a) Honoring Our Elders became a part of each summit experience (with the exception of NMCS, 2003), such that we acknowledge the legacy inherited by those pioneers who have helped to pave the way.
   (b) Remembering Those Who Have Passed Away, such that we thank them for their sacrifice for the multicultural movement and commit ourselves to walk in the paths that they laid.
IV. Collaboration
   (a) Mid-Winter Executive Committee Meetings of APA Divisions were scheduled to conduct association business while at the summit and strategize on ways to make progress within their respective divisions.
   (b) Continuation Education was offered through local psychology programs allowing participants to receive credit for attending summit sessions.
V. Continuity
   (a) The town hall meeting that signals the end of each summit provides the forum to assess the achievement of goals and generate a

follow-up agenda that attendees can then address during the twenty-four months preceding their next summit experience.

A Cautious Future

Those of us who hailed the arrival of the first National Multicultural Conference and Summit were not only impressed with its content and format, but also with the energy that surrounded its creation. The collective spirit of each of the principals mentioned earlier placed much less emphasis on personal preferences or APA divisional affiliations, and much more focus on the common good of the profession, and what they believed would be most beneficial to the people who represent the psychology and counseling communities. Personal memory reminds us that decisions to select summit and program presenters were guided by beliefs about how the rich legacy inherited by current generations of mental health professionals needed to be honored; where were the programmatic voids in other conferences that needed to be addressed in a new summit experience; in what ways was it important to help professionals grow and develop new skills; and how could participants' spirits be engaged and excited about the multicultural changes that were occurring in the present and needed to occur in the future. They (the summit architects) were looking to inspire and empower conference participants with insightful messages, stories of struggle, and affirmations of hope and optimism about the future of the multicultural movement. They achieved these goals.

The reservoir of spiritual energy was also characterized by a tone of self-determination. While there were questions raised about the potential to develop a unique summit experience, none was serious enough to cast any doubt in the minds of the summit organizers on the correctness of the concept, or the ability to transform a vision and dream into the reality that the National Multicultural Conference and Summit became. The spirit of self-determination did have to confront and manage potential obstacles which proved challenging. On the periphery of the organizing group were the skeptical naysayers who questioned whether members of the profession would support another conference, particularly one that was so close in time to the Annual Winter Roundtable Conference held at Columbia University on Cross-Cultural Counseling and Psychotherapy. This endeavor, pioneered by Samuel Johnson and more recently managed by Robert Carter and Madonna Constantine, has a tremendous following.

Beyond this, there were financial challenges to confront, as the resources to support the summit endeavor were not readily available. Not to be deterred, the first summit organizers wrote grants and were able to secure major funding from the Office of Behavioral Science Research at the National Institutes of Health and from the corporate community represented by American Express. Subsequent summit organizers were equally successful in securing funding to operate this important venue. Ultimately, obstacles became mere challenges, and those challenges resulted in successes that helped to sustain the early momentum the summit organizers enjoyed. Consequently, that initial spirit of collective good and self-determination resulted in a very successful first summit and set the stage for four subsequent meetings, each of which enjoyed success as well.

The energy that now surrounds the summit has begun to take on a different intensity. The collective spirit, which highlighted previous summits, has begun to be replaced by more competitive strivings, where different groups lobby and sometimes argue for their share of influence over the course and direction of summit programs, speakers, and formats. When viewed with a context of development, the "collective" to "competitive" shift doesn't seem unexpected. Arguably, it is a predictable by-product of an enterprise whose proven success makes affiliation safe, even wise. If this trend continues, however, the summit may have a limited future.

Undoubtedly, the need for national forums where multicultural issues take center stage will continue to be a programmatic necessity. However, a profession in need of clear directives around multicultural competencies will struggle under a system where divided loyalties present professionals and students alike with different templates, conflicting messages, and invitations to take sides and draw organizational lines in the sand. Any one summit cannot be all things to all people, and a single conference cannot be expected to reflect every dimension of diversity. Thus, those committed to sustaining the momentum created by the first five summits may need to set aside their individual and affiliation preferences in favor of a more collective vision that benefits the entire profession of psychology and counseling.

Notes

1. Dr. Martha Banks, president elect of Division 35 Society for the Psychology of Women 2007–2008, has clarified that the Division 35 decision was made in 2005 and does not necessarily reflect the sentiments of the current membership or the executive committee of that division at present.

References

Atkinson, D. F., Morten, G., and Sue, D. W. (1979). *Counseling American minorities.* Dubuque, IA: Wm. C. Brown Publishers.

Constantine, M. G. (1997). Facilitating multicultural competence in supervision: Operationalizing a practical framework. In D. Pope-Davis and H. K. Coleman (Eds.), *Multicultural counseling competencies: Assessment, education, and training, and supervision* (pp. 310–24). Thousand Oaks, CA: Sage.

Constantine, M. G., and Ladany, N. (2001). New visions for defining and assessing multicultural competence. In J. Ponterotto, J. M. Casas, L. Suzuki, and C. Alexandro (2nd ed.), *Handbook of multicultural counseling.* Thousand Oaks, CA: Sage.

D'Andrea, M., and Daniels, J. (1991). Exploring the different levels of multicultural counseling training in counselor education. *Journal of Counseling and Development,* 70, 78–85.

D'Andrea, M., Daniels, J., Arredondo, P., Ivey, M. B., Ivey, A., Locke, D. C., et al. (2001). Fostering organizational change to realize the revolutionary potential of the multicultural movement: An updated case study. In J. Ponterotto, J. Casas, L. Suzuki, and C. Alexander, *Handbook of Multicultural Counseling* (2nd ed., pp. 222–54). Thousand Oaks, CA: Sage.

Hills, H. I., and Strozier, A. L. (1992). Multicultural training in APA approved counseling psychology programs: A survey. *Professional Psychology, Research and Practice,* 23, 43–51.

LaFromboise, T. D., and Foster, S. L. (1992). Cross-cultural training: scientist-practitioner models and methods. *Counseling Psychologist, 20,* 472–89.

Parham, T. A. (1999). Beyond intolerance: Bridging the gap between imposition and acceptance. Keynote address delivered at the National Multicultural Conference and Summit, Newport Beach, CA.

Ponterotto, J., Alexander, C., and Grieger, I. (1995). A multicultural competency checklist for counselor training programs. *Journal of Multicultural Counseling and Development, 23,* 11–20.

Thomas, A., and Sillen, S. (1972). *Racism and psychiatry.* New York: Carol Publishing.

U.S. Census (2000). Projections. Retrieved on April 26, 2008 at www.census.gov/population/www/projections/popproj.html.

White, J. L. (1972). Toward a black psychology. In R. L. Jones (Ed.), *Black psychology.* New York: Harper & Row.

Wrenn, G. (1962). The culturally encapsulated counselor. *Harvard Education Review,* 32, 444–49.

Wyatt, G. E., and Parham, W. D. (1985). The inclusion of culturally sensitive course materials in graduate school and training programs. *Psychotherapy, 22,* 461–68.

~

Conclusion

Shamin Ladhani

In this book, Joseph L. White and Sheila J. Henderson have presented a number of important accomplishments: First, the explication of the multiracial/multiethnic/multicultural competency building (M³CB) model offers a "how-to" guide for individuals and groups to pursue change on four levels: (a) conceptual/theoretical/intellectual; (b) emotional through multicultural dialogue; (c) behavioral through multicultural engagement; and (d) skill building integration of the prior intellectual, emotional, and behavioral levels. As White and Henderson explain, "Both planning and action, or *planful action*, become important as one embarks upon self-study and self-initiated engagement on intellectual, emotional, and behavioral levels" (chapter 2, p. 24). Dr. White has been offering this model in presentations all over the country for many years. By presenting this M³CB model in writing, White and Henderson have provided individuals, groups, and institutions with the opportunity to pursue their multicultural competency building with a guide from which to customize plans that suit them best.

Second, they invited contributions from authors that have achieved various levels of multicultural competency themselves and then strived to take competency building to the institutional level in graduate training programs. The five examples listed in this book provide accounts of five *promising practices*[1] in different institutions. Each offers unique lessons learned for readers as they embark on bringing multicultural competency to their home departments, training programs, clinics, and/or institutions. These five programs are gold star examples among other institutions that are currently innovating in multicultural competency—but it is not an exclusive list. Someday an industrious student or early career professional might be motivated to create a website or network of programs whose demonstrated commitment to multiculturalism and cultural competence can be seen in the curriculum, faculty hires and retention, and in the policies and practices that frame the manner in which their host department or school promotes education and training. Such a network could facilitate collaboration among interested individuals who want to learn about, build upon, and study the innovations of others.[2]

Third, White and Henderson have invited discussion on important topical areas in multiculturalism, such as mentoring across cultures, mentoring academic researchers among people of color, managing resistance in the classroom and in difficult dialogue, and the interplay of aversive racism and resistance to embracing multiculturalism. These are fundamental topics to understand for any program initiating multicultural competency training.

Fourth, White and Henderson invited two leaders, Dr. Thomas A. Parham and Dr. William D. Parham of the National Multicultural Conference and Summit to provide unique insider perspectives on the evolution and challenges of one important public forum for ongoing continuing education in multicultural psychology for mental health professionals.

My training is in the area of clinical health psychology with a focus on multiculturalism in the health care setting, and I had the benefit of training in an institution where several faculty members had expertise in cultural competence assisting me in expanding my training in this area. As I moved on in my internship and postdoctoral training, I found the most urgent need for multicultural competency development in health care institutions to be in the areas of patient care and within the culture of health care workers (i.e., interdisciplinary work, physicians working with nurses working with aides, etc.). The nature of working with patients from different backgrounds and for the health care team to work together brings a myriad of multicultural contexts that need to be sensitively integrated for optimal health care delivery. The M³CB is a helpful guide precisely because it gives health care institutions concrete, practical, and flexible "how-to's" with which to approach building multicultural competency in their complex and unique settings.

In my own career, like so many others touched by the Joseph L. White Freedom Train, I have been fortunate to have had strong multicultural mentoring throughout my graduate training. In turn, I have taken on many mentees myself; they in turn mentor others. Because of the pressing need for multicultural competency in health care, I have taken leadership positions as a diversity facilitator and serve on the committee for advancement of diversity initiatives in the medical center where I work. We are in the first phase of our own hospital-wide and system-wide diversity training over three states. In these roles, the White and Henderson M³CB model will be crucial in deepening the hospital's broad diversity initiatives to actionable plans that are customized to the unique operations of each hospital, each department, and each unique system of care and tailored to the needs of the patient populations being served.

My hope is that the readers of this book, seeking to bring multicultural competency to their study groups, graduate programs, and institutions, will contact the many authors herein with intent to collaborate, share ideas, and innovate, expanding the multicultural competency in their home institutions. Certainly as learning outcomes are considered in education effectiveness (see Clay, 2008), outcomes in multicultural competence training must soon become a critical competent educational effectiveness at the high school, undergraduate, and graduate levels[3]; the same applies to outcome measurement in culturally competent health care delivery.

Whatever step readers take toward building multicultural competency— whether on an individual, group, institutional, societal, or global level—it will create a ripple effect bringing us collectively closer to the tipping point, making the full participation of all people in our global society possible. The important thing is to take a step.

Notes

1. As noted earlier, White and Henderson have credited Dr. Michael Stevenson with introducing *promising practices* in a call for manuscripts for the new journal *Journal of Diversity in Higher Education*. Dr. Stevenson wrote, "A one-size-fits-all approach to diversity and inclusion is destined to failure. An approach, strategy, program, or policy that is successful in one context (e.g. a private undergraduate-focused liberal arts college) may not be appropriate or effective in another (e.g. a large public institution). Rather than 'best practices,' the phrase 'promising practices' underscores the importance of context and the continuing need to evaluate." (See www.apa.org/journals/dhe/callforpapers.html).

2. These ideas were inspired by discussions with one of my Freedom Train mentors and esteemed colleague William D. Parham, Ph.D., ABPP, Dean of the Graduate School of Professional Psychology at John F. Kennedy University in northern California.

3. Ideas inspired by discussions with William D. Parham.

Reference

Clay, R. (2008). Are our students learning? Psychologists lead the charge to broadly define the effectiveness of college education. *APA Online Monitor on Psychology,* 39(5) 54. Retrieved on May 6, 2008 at: http://www.apa.org/monitor/2008/05/students.html

~

Afterword

A *Student's Perspective*

Camille Mottley

Where is my growing edge? One's growing edge is the point at which his/her life views and ideas, one's paradigm, are challenged in a way that produces an emotional charge and an opportunity for change. As a counseling psychology master's student in multicultural competency training, I have come to know the feel of one of my more salient edges when faced with the particular challenge of realizing that many of my American student peers (but not all) had a monocultural worldview and approach to life. By monocultural I mean belonging and relating to one single race/ethnicity and social and religious culture. Through my multicultural competency training I was able to work through this challenge toward more empathy for what they had to surmount in their multicultural training.

Monocultural is a term that describes neither my outlook nor has it been a theme in my life events. Born of mixed race and having spent my formative years living primarily in two different countries, Trinidad and the United States, it was difficult for me to comprehend and relate to to a monocultural perspective. Until the age of twelve, I grew up in Trinidad and Tobago in the Caribbean. The population of Trinidad and Tobago is made up of people of African, East Indian, French, English, Portuguese, Chinese, and Syrian descent. This stew of people descended, some by choice and others by force, on the island during the colonial period in the 1800s. Upon gaining independence, these two islands headed by one government chose as their national motto "Together we aspire, together we achieve." That is exactly as I remember the cultural climate in Trinidad when I was a child.

Trinidadians have a sense of national unity that is greater than any racial or religious difference. The Trinidadian identity includes unified celebration of various ethnic and religious rituals and historical events. For example, although all Trinidadians are not Hindi, still today many Trinidadians appreciate the Hindi celebration of Divali, the festival of lights. Children are taught about it in school, and on the evening of the celebration people of all racial and religious backgrounds participate in admiring sculptures of lights all over town. I myself have fond memories of driving with my family through the different neighborhoods to admire the lights. Over time, I was able to establish a cohesive identity despite their own history of colonization that to this day impacts Trinidadian values and lifestyle. My identity as Trinidadian is something I was aware of and had feelings of pride about.

At the age of twelve, I moved to the United States and it was not until this time that I became aware of race as a means by which to identify, define, separate, and judge myself, and others in my community. When I first arrived in the United States I attended public school where I learned to either assimilate or endure being teased. Whenever I spoke, I was mocked and misunderstood, until I began to take on the American accent. This both disturbed and challenged me.

Taught to be polite, when posed with characteristically American questions such as "Are you mixed/Hispanic?" "Do you have Asian in you?" "What's your ethnicity?" I would always answer with a polite digression on the ethnic background of my immediate family. Prior to living in America, such questions had for me never been an aspect of conversation or a means for getting to know someone better. These questions felt superficial to me. Deep down these questions evoked in me feelings of confusion, frustration, anger, and judgment. I really would have preferred to scream at the inquirer, "Why are you preoccupied with what you think you see? I am more than that!"

It was not until I had the occasion to participate in the multicultural competency training that I gained a sense of the monocultural perspective of the dominant group that for so long has defined American values and lifestyle. Here in United States, with a history of segregation based primarily on skin color, but also on ethnicity, religious preference, sexual orientation, size, class, and ability, people have learned to stick to their own. Perhaps people fear they will lose what they know, especially when they have privilege and power. But it seems that it is exactly this privilege and power that has so limited the dominant group from having the opportunity to engage with people of difference.

As part of the multicultural competency training we viewed a powerful film about slavery in America, *Sankofa* (Gerima, 1993), which presented us with the opportunity to explore slavery and its impact on individual and collective identity of European and African Americans. Also we received a guest speaker, Pamela Jenkins, who has written about the impact of slavery on African Americans today (Jenkins, 2001). This exposure to race relations in America gave me a historical context and opened my eyes to the collective psychological trauma that to this day plagues the way we relate to each other and how we deal with the differences between us in this country.

The process of working through this challenge of my own wordview versus that of some of my peers provoked in me a stronger appreciation of the diversity that colors my family and my life experiences. Also it has cultivated within me a conscious yearning to help others celebrate the richness of difference within their lives while also seeking to open them to the excitement and value of the experience that is diversity.

America the melting pot (KQED, no date)! Well, not so much. To me it seems more like a stew (Mitchell and Salsbury, 1999). with many different and unique ingredients like meat, potatoes, vegetables, and savory herbs that are simmered together to be savored within each individual bite. These elements all thrown together in a stew result in a deliciously, wholesome, unified entity, unique unto itself. The key concept for me is unified. Americans have a grand opportunity to develop a unified American identity through the recognition, appreciations, and celebration of all our differences.

I believe that White and Henderson's multiracial/multiethnic/multicultural competency building (M³CB) model is an initial force toward creating our more succinct national American identity. This American identity incorporates us all as one, as American, and includes the celebration of the many differences such as skin color, ethnicity, sexual orientation, and ability, that create intersections in our lives. Many times these are characteristics of our humanity that we are born into. It would behoove us to relinquish the fears and shame that hold us captive to judging each other based on these basic human characteristics. Ideally we must acknowledge where we are coming from, our history and name our differences, but we must also kindle the fires of curiosity about one another. In order to move forward we must acknowledge our past and make efforts to move forward differently. Multicultural competency training offers a productive platform for exploration of our fears and shame. This training serves as a guide for moving forward differently by directing our focus to the controllable dimensions of being human that we can change.

So what can we change? We can change and be in control of our feelings, and our knowledge in how we choose to interact with our community. After having successfully completed the multicultural competency training in my graduate training at John F. Kennedy University, School of Holistic Studies in Campbell, California, I was afforded the opportunity to work as a teacher's assistant in cross-cultural counseling course the next year. This opportunity proved to be invaluable to me as I was privy to witness the next generation of students' journeys toward multicultural competency.

The training challenged the group to explore concepts such as white privilege, ethnocultural identities, cultural empathy, power and oppression, and race and multicultural intersections and much more. In their exploration this group struggled to overcome deep-seated, unconscious defenses and uncover feelings of frustration, anger, indignance, and most of all shame. The students developed a deeper level of self-awareness while participating in exercises that challenged their self-perception. One such exercise required journaling about one's feelings and perceptions of African American women prior to watching the film *Sankofa* (Gerima, 1993), and then again afterwards. The journaling revealed that prior to viewing the film, many students described stereotypical ideas of African American women. After watching the film the students' journaling revealed a deeper level of feelings such as shame, repugnance, fear, admiration, and respect. The students' paradigms were shifting (Henderson et al., 2007, 2008).

Such a paradigm shift would be the ideal. The idea is that life is movement, it is colorful and comes in all shapes and textures. Our differences create meaning and purpose and breathe vibrancy into our lives. Through multicultural competency training we are exposed to a new awareness of ourselves and of our lives as rich in diversity. This is a powerful new awareness that connects us in our own diversity to that in others and that can be a force for unification through mutual respect and understanding. The M³CB model pushes us to recognize the effects of our past on our present day life.

At present, America is teeming with people of difference and is a testament to the change and diversity that contributes to the dynamism of life. In order for counseling to helpfully address the diverse needs of clients, the counselor must be open-minded and cultivate the capacity to see beyond stereotypes to the unique person sitting before her/him. Recently, in one of my classes, we were posed with the question "When do you know that you have become an expert counselor?" In response, I say expertise comes with the realization that we can never know enough or have had enough varied experiences, and in response we embrace change and difference as one of the few things we can rely on in life to be constant and meaningful.

References

Gerima, H. (1993). *Sankofa*. Mypheduh films. sankofastore.com/catalog/homepage .php.

Henderson, S. J., Karki, J., Mottley, C., Mudarri, J., Gosk, J. A., and Giffrow, H. (2007). *Identity development in African American women: Sankofa as a learning tool for non-African American graduate psychology students*. Poster Session. APAGS and Div 35, Section 1: Society for Black Women. APA Convention. San Francisco, CA.

———. (2008). Identity development in African American women: Sankofa as a learning tool for non-African American graduate psychology students. Poster Session. California Psychological Association Convention. Anaheim, CA.

Jenkins, P. (2001). African Americans "A Culture of Hope." Ph.D. Dissertation. California School of Professional Psychology, Los Angeles.

KQED. (no date). The melting pot. *The First Measured Century*. Retrieved on November 18, 2007, at www.pbs.org/fmc/timeline/emeltpot.htm.

Mitchell, B. M., and Salsbury, R. E. (1999). *Encyclopedia of multicultural education*. Westport, CT: Greenwood Press.

Index

~

About the Contributors

Joseph L. White, Ph.D., has enjoyed a distinguished career in the field of psychology and mental health as a teacher, mentor, administrator, clinical supervisor, writer, consultant, and practicing psychologist for the past forty-six years. He is currently professor emeritus of psychology and psychiatry at the University of California–Irvine. In 2007, he received an honorary degree, Doctor of Laws, which is the highest award conferred by the University of Minnesota, recognizing individuals who have achieved acknowledged eminence in cultural affairs, in public affairs, or in a field of knowledge and scholarship. In the spring of 2008, he was inducted into the San Francisco State University Hall of Fame as Alumnus of the Year. He is the author of several papers and five books; the most current book is *Black Fathers: An Invisible Presence in America* (2006). He was a pioneer in the field of black psychology and is affectionately referred to as the "godfather" of black psychology by his students, mentees, and younger colleagues. In addition to his teaching and research, Dr. White has been a practicing psychologist and consultant. He has served as a supervising psychologist and staff affiliate psychologist to five hospitals and three clinical practices in southern California. He has worked as a consultant with school districts, universities, private organizations, drug prevention programs, and government agencies. He was appointed to the California State Psychology Licensing Board by Governor Edmund G. Brown Jr. and served as chairman for three years. He is currently a member of the board of trustees of The Menninger Foundation in Houston, Texas.

Sheila J. Henderson, MBA, Ph.D., is the associate director for I-MERIT (International-Multicultural Initiatives) at Alliant International University and a Hans Sauer Research Fellow at Humboldt University in Berlin, Germany. Dr. Henderson lectures at the Pacific Graduate School of Psychology's P3 undergraduate program and John F. Kennedy University (JFKU) School of Holistic Studies' counseling psychology program, and supervises interns/trainees at JFKU Sunnyvale Community Counseling Center. She has experience in industrial organization through her consulting and process innovation that has spanned business, clinical, university, school, and healthcare system settings in the United States and Mexico. Her tenure at Hewlett Packard Company included finance management as well as internal coaching in culture transition, career development, and team dynamics. At Kaiser Hospital, she worked with multidisciplinary teams to innovate methods for improving wellness for medical inpatients. Dr. Henderson also serves on the editorial board for the *Journal of Career Development* and is a California-licensed counseling psychologist.

Evelinn A. Borrayo, Ph.D., is an associate professor in clinical health psychology at the Department of Psychology at the University of Colorado at Denver. Her area of teaching expertise is in the topics of diversity and multiculturalism and she conducts research on cultural health beliefs, medically underserved populations, and psychosocial oncology.

Anne Chan, Ph.D., is a mentoring consultant and licensed psychotherapist. Her research, publication, and practice interests include mentoring, cross-cultural issues in mentoring, diversity, and career counseling. She has worked as a psychotherapist and counselor in different educational institutions and community agencies, including Stanford University, Merritt College, The Couples Institute, and Catholic Charities of San Jose. Her dissertation research examined the practices of outstanding mentors with ethnic minority doctoral student protégés. Her forthcoming work will be a practical book on effective mentoring strategies. She can be reached at achan@midlabs.com

Ngwarsungu Chiwengo is associate professor of English at Creighton University. Her work has appeared in journals such as *South Atlantic Quarterly*, *Journal of Black Studies*, *La revue de l'université de Moncton*, *College Literature*, and *South Atlantic Quarterly*. In her book *Understanding "Cry, the Beloved Country"* (Greenwood Press, 2007), she analyzes the literary and historical background of Alan Paton's 1948 novel about racial tensions in South Africa. Her current interests are in genocide literature, the teaching of ethnic literatures, and African literature.

Kevin Cokley, Ph.D., is an associate professor of counseling psychology and faculty affiliate of the Center for African and African American Studies at the University of Texas–Austin. His research and teaching can be broadly categorized in the area of African American psychology. He has published over thirty-five articles and book chapters. His 2004 article published in the *Harvard Educational Review* challenges the notion that African American students are anti-intellectual. He is the associate editor of the *Journal of Black Psychology*, and serves on the editorial boards of several journals including *Cultural Diversity and Ethnic Minority Psychology* and the *Journal of Counseling Psychology*.

Patricia Ann Fleming, Ph.D., is vice president and dean of the faculty and professor of philosophy at Saint Mary's College, Notre Dame, Indiana. She received her Master's and Doctorate from Washington University in St. Louis, Missouri. She taught for many years at Creighton University where she led the Diversity Project, a faculty development initiative tied to the revision of a new core curriculum in which global and domestic diversity were introduced. She was also one of the designers of the Ratio Studiorum Program, a first-year program in which the diversity dialogue was successfully implemented in the freshman seminar. Now at Saint Mary's College, she has helped to establish a President's Council on Multicultural Affairs that has begun a climate audit of the campus, with the resources of National Multicultural Institute. As Saint Mary's College begins its general education revision, she looks forward to working with faculty to implement the new college outcomes of intercultural competence and global education.

Lisa Y. Flores, Ph.D., is an associate professor and codirector of the Center for Multicultural Research, Training, and Consultation in the Department of Educational, School, and Counseling Psychology at the University of Missouri. Her research focuses on the educational and career decision-making of Mexican Americans. Specifically, she has examined sociocognitive, personal, and environmental/cultural factors related to Mexican-American students' career choices and educational goals and the role of mentors in students' career development. She has coauthored thirty-seven journal articles and book chapters, and over seventy conference presentations. She serves as editor of the *Journal of Career Development*, is an editorial board member of the *Journal of Counseling Psychology* and *Journal of Multicultural Counseling and Development*, and a past editorial board member of *The Counseling Psychologist* and *Career Development Quarterly*.

G. H. Grandbois, DSW, associate professor, University of Nebraska at Omaha (11 years), Creighton University (18 years). He has also worked for several tribes in North and South Dakota along with the Bureau of Indian Affairs. His focused scholarship is on diversity, Native Americans, and critical thinking.

P. Paul Heppner, Ph.D., is a professor at the University of Missouri–Columbia, and cofounder and codirector of the Center for Multicultural Research, Training and Consultation since 1998, and the inaugural cochair of the International Section of the Society of Counseling Psychology. He has published over 130 articles and book chapters and five books. He has made hundreds of presentations at national conferences and delivered over forty invited presentations in fourteen countries. In addition, Dr. Heppner has served on several national and international editorial boards, including editor of *The Counseling Psychologist*. He is a fellow in the American Psychological Association (Divisions 17 and 52) and the American Psychological Society. In 2005–2006 he served as president of the Society of Counseling Psychology. He has been honored to receive a named professorship; he is the recipient of several awards for his leadership, research, teaching, mentoring, international work, and promoting diversity and social justice issues. He has also been the recipient of three Fulbright awards.

Erika L. Kirby, Ph.D. (University of Nebraska–Lincoln, 2000), is chair and professor of communication studies at Creighton University where she has been for eleven years. Her teaching and research interests include organizational, applied, and working/personal life communication as well as their intersections with gender. She has published articles in outlets such as *Communication Monographs*, the *Journal of Business Communication*, the *Journal of Applied Communication Research*, *Management Communication Quarterly*, and *Communication Yearbook*, and is on several editorial boards.

Shamin Ladhani, Psy.D., received her doctorate in clinical psychology from Nova Southeastern University in Fort Lauderdale, Florida, in 2005. She currently works as a clinical health psychologist in the Comprehensive Pain

Management Center of Wheaton Franciscan Healthcare in southeastern Wisconsin. Her interests are in culturally sensitive health care, and she actively participates in the diversity training of staff at the medical center, serves as a consultant to the regional team on diversity and cross-cultural competence in the medical center, and is participating in the developing committee to advance diversity initiatives in the hospital. Her clinical interests involve working with underserved medical populations, specifically adults and older adults. She has also been active in governance for the American Psychological Association.

Jeanne E. Manese, Ph.D., is director of the counseling center at the University of California–Irvine. She received her doctoral degree from the University of Maryland, College Park, with a specialization in counseling psychology. She is a fellow of the American Psychological Association (Divisions 17 and 45). Dr. Manese has published numerous articles and chapters related to training and practice with a focus on multicultural competency and social justice. She is currently conducting research and implementing programs focused on strength-based interventions for academically "at-risk" populations. Dr. Manese has practiced around the world with an education abroad program and is interested in the global application of counseling psychology.

Camille Mottley is now a counseling trainee at the John F. Kennedy University (JFKU) Sunnyvale Community Counseling Center, which is one of the final steps in completing her Master's degree in counseling psychology at the School of Holistic Studies at JFKU in Campbell, California. Born of American and Trinidadian heritage, Camille has enjoyed the experience of a multicultural upbringing, which deeply influenced her perspective as a teacher's assistant in multicultural competency trainings but also in her American Psychological Association conference participation. Before graduate school, Camille served as a flight attendant for Delta Airlines—another career that provided critical multicultural exposure around the world.

Helen A. Neville is a professor in educational psychology (Counseling Psychology Division) and African American studies at the University of Illinois at Urbana–Champaign. Her research on racial ideology and women's issues has been published in a wide range of psychology and black studies outlets. She has served on a number of editorial boards, including as associate editor of *The Counseling Psychologist* and the *Journal of Black Psychology*. She has received teaching and mentoring awards, including the Kenneth and Mamie Clark Award for Outstanding Contribution to the Professional Development of Ethnic Minority Graduate Students.

Thomas A. Parham is assistant vice chancellor for counseling and health services, as well as an adjunct faculty member at the University of California, Irvine. A proficient author and lecturer, he is a past president of the National Association of Black Psychologists. He has been elected to the title of distinguished psychologist by the Association of Black Psychologists (ABPsi's highest honor) in 1998 and more recently he received the American Psychological Association (Division 17) Society of Counseling Psychology Award for Lifetime Achievement in Mentoring in August 2007.

William D. Parham, Ph.D., ABPP, currently serves in the role of dean of the Graduate School of Professional Psychology at the John F. Kennedy University in northern California. He is immediate past president of the Society of Counseling Psychology (Division 17) of the American Psychological Association and a fellow (Divisions 17, 45, and 47). In addition, he is a member of the APA Council of Representatives, the governing body of the association. Related to this text, Dr. Parham is a two-time past coordinator of the National Multicultural Summit and Conference (2003 and 2005). Finally, he is a licensed psychologist and board certified in counseling psychology by the American Board of Professional Psychology (ABPP).

Samuel S. Park, Ph.D., is the training director at Psychological and Counseling Services at the University of California–San Diego. He received his Ph.D. in counseling psychology from the University of California–Santa Barbara. His clinical and research interests include multicultural training and supervision, Asian American mental health, men's issues, shame and loss of face, and ethnic identity development.

Carlton W. Parks, Jr., Ph.D., is a fellow-in-residence at the Rockway Institute, a National Center for Lesbian, Gay, Bisexual, Transgender Research, and Public Policy, at Alliant International University as well as a fellow of the American Psychological Association. He is a professor and director of training of the Programs in School and Educational Psychology in the Graduate School of Education at Alliant International University–Los Angeles.

Nima Patel, Ph.D., is the practicum training coordinator, a staff psychologist, and adjunct faculty at the University of Illinois, Urbana–Champaign. She received her Ph.D. in counseling psychology from Southern Illinois University at Carbondale and is a licensed clinical psychologist in California and Illinois. Her clinical and research interests include multicultural and social justice issues, Asian American mental health, identity development, retention in higher education, couples counseling, counselor training, social anxiety, and anger management.

John Pierce is the director of affirmative action and special assistant to the president for diversity and outreach at Creighton University. He earned a B.S. in education at the University of Nebraska–Omaha in 1969 and his M.S. in guidance and counseling (1972) and J.D. (1981) at Creighton University.

John E. Queener is associate professor in the Collaborative Program in Counseling Psychology at the University of Akron. He also is the lead psychologist for Minority Behavioral Health Group, a nonprofit organization that serves the mental health needs of African Americans and other minority groups.

Shannon D. Smith is an associate professor in the Department of Counselor Education at the University of Nevada–Las Vegas. He has worked as a child and family therapist in community mental health, as a director of a child-counseling clinic, and as a school counselor in the public school system. His research interests include multicultural counseling and development, issues of diversity and social advocacy, child and family therapy, school counseling, and play therapy.

Mary Ann Takemoto, Ph.D., is associate vice president for student services at California State University (CSU), Long Beach. Previously, she served as director of counseling and psychological services at CSU–Long Beach and training director at the University of California–Irvine (UCI) Counseling Center. Dr. Takemoto served as faculty member in the Department of Asian American Studies at UCI. Her interests are in the areas of Asian American psychology, multicultural counseling and training, Asian American women's issues, and leadership training.

Ashton W. Welch is associate professor of history and director of black studies at Creighton University. He was educated at Wilberforce University, the University of Wisconsin–Madison, and the University of Birmingham in the United Kingdom. His scholarly interests center on the intersection of law and society. He has written on school desegregation in Omaha, ethnicity and public policy in the United States, law and slavery in Virginia, ethnicity and jury service, emancipation in the United States, and Christian missionaries in Africa. He has lectured and presented papers across the United States and in Brazil, Britain, Canada, and South Africa.